F. Gregory Coffey
Maureen C. Kessler

W9-BIX-589

The Reflective Counselor

Daily Meditations for Lawyers

American Bar Association

Defending Liberty
Pursuing Justice

Cover design by Zaccarne Design, Inc.

09 08 07 06 05   5 4 3 2 1

Library of Congress Cataloging-in-Publication Data

F. Gregory Coffey and Maureen C. Kessler
    The Reflective Counselor. Daily Meditations for Lawyers.
    F. Gregory Coffey and Maureen C. Kessler
Library of Congress Cataloging-in-Publication Data is on file.

ISBN: 978-1-59031-956-7

Discounts are available for books ordered in bulk. Special consideration is given to state bars, CLE programs, and other bar-related organizations. Inquire at Book Publishing, ABA Publishing, American Bar Association, 321 North Clark Street, Chicago, Illinois 60654.

www.ababooks.org

"This is a remarkable book. The authors are to be commended on putting together this splendid contribution to legal education and the legal profession."

—Bob MacCrate, Past President of the American Bar Association
and Senior Drafter of the MacCrate Report

"Every lawyer could use an opportunity to pause and reflect. The Reflective Counselor provides brilliant insights on a range of issues faced by those trying to balance heavy work commitments with complicated lives."

—Theodore O. Rogers, Jr., Partner, Sullivan & Cromwell LLP

"The Reflective Counselor is a counterpoint to the non-stop, often narrowly focused days of many lawyers. It encourages lawyers to apply to their work, their work lives and their non-work lives—and the interaction among all of those—that crucially important human skill: self-reflection. The authors' backgrounds have equipped them uniquely to produce this extraordinary book. The quotation selections are terrific, and never fail to help orient and center one for the day."

—Arline Mann, Wall Street Attorney, named one
of *Human Resource Executive Magazine*'s 50 Most
Powerful Employment Attorneys in America

"The Reflective Counselor is by far one of the most uplifting and heartfelt books of its kind that I have seen. The uniquely qualified authors achieve a truly empathic understanding, and have put forth a valuable and very welcome guide for soul-searching lawyers, eager to find meaning and purpose beyond the daily grind. This book is to be highly recommended."

—James B. Snyder, M.D., Board Certified Psychiatrist
and Director and Founder, Long Island Psychiatric

"With an impressive range of non-doctrinaire selections, the authors provide nourishment for busy lawyers mindful of their own humanity."

—Christopher Morse, Dietrich Bonhoeffer Professor of
Theology and Ethics, Union Theological Seminary

"The Reflective Counselor *shares the guiding mantra of 'awareness, acceptance, and action' with those just beginning their law studies, and those already in the profession. This book helps one achieve a measure of emotional stability and spiritual well-being, putting both professional and private lives in balance.*"

—Hanita Wishnevski, Law Student

"The Reflective Counselor *will become the model for all daily meditation books! Every single page of this book overflows with wisdom that reminds you who you really are and that helps you realize who you dream of becoming. If you are a lawyer and do these daily meditations, your work will become your life practice, but no matter what you do, this book will cultivate a nobility of spirit that will transform your daily activities into a sacred art.*"

—Rabbi Irwin Kula, Author of *Yearnings: Embracing the
Sacred Messiness of Life* and President of The National
Jewish Center for Learning and Leadership

"This book is filled with wonderful quotations and wise commentaries, one for each day. Designed as 'daily meditations,' each provides a thoughtful way to begin a lawyer's often complex and challenging day. I can think of no lawyer, whether patient or friend, that I would not be happy to have this excellent book."

—Don-David Lusterman, Ph.D., Author of *Infidelity: A Survival Guide*

Introduction

This book is intended to help law students, lawyers, law professors, and others associated with the legal profession to achieve increased well-being and satisfaction in their personal and professional lives. A consistent theme of the book underscores the principle that a good lawyer is, first and foremost, a good person. The legal profession has long been positioned to change the world for good or ill, and, in fact, the profession's accomplishments are legion. In current times, however, various pressures and trends have tended to blur the vision of professionalism that has for so long characterized the noble practice of law. In fact, we are living in a time when the legal profession and too many of its individual members are experiencing great distress. Informed commentators seem to be in general agreement in suggesting that there are at least three primary maladies that are adversely affecting the legal profession today: 1) professionalism has decreased; 2) public opinion of lawyers and the profession has declined; and 3) lawyer dissatisfaction and dysfunction have increased. Despite the fact that most legal professionals competently and dutifully fulfill their daily responsibilities, the highly publicized misdeeds of some lawyers, and the well-documented professional dissatisfaction of many more lawyers, compel focused analysis and action if our chosen profession is to remain an institution of stature within American society.

In the current legal marketplace, as well as in the law school environment, extrinsic motivators (power, financial gain, prestige) too often reign as the unchallenged "crown jewels" of the profession, while the humbler, less-valued intrinsic motivators (public service, integrity, pursuit of justice, excellence) are consistently devalued, beginning in the earliest days of law school. If this unsettling trend is not recognized and rectified, on both the personal and institutional levels, legal professionals, clients, and society will experience further disintegration. Yet, while now, as perhaps never before, our ailing society and political systems need to witness a re-emerging of the "noble profession," it seems fewer "noble warriors" are likely to emerge, as research consistently documents that lawyers' overall well-being continues to decline. The legal profession far surpasses others in occurrences of depression, substance abuse, and suicide among its members. In addition, undocumented masses suffer burnout, disillusionment, loss of meaning, and anomie.

Recent studies have also shown that the path which leads to the "meaning void" experienced by so many lawyers begins during the formative law school years, and often continues unabated after entry into the profession. While the vast majority of legal initiates first appear at the law school gates brimming with energy, enthusiasm, and spirit, too many attest to being rendered greatly "dis-spirited" before the first-year grades are posted. As many lawyers have long known, and as many respected studies have now confirmed, while law schools do a very good job of teaching students to "think like a lawyer," the process too often does irreparable damage to the heart and soul of the professional in formation.

This book, structured as a series of daily meditations, is intended to re-engage the enthusiasm and the "moral imagination" of the legal professional by encouraging self-reflection, a re-identification with personal values and beliefs, and a thoughtful evaluation of certain commonly held attitudes and behaviors associated with current-day lawyering. Guidance is also provided for the development and integration of certain energizing attitudes and practices that can enhance the healing, wholeness, and growth of the individual legal professional, which, in turn, will have concomitant benefits for the legal profession and society as a whole.

Overall, the daily meditations reflect an integration of psychological, humanist, spiritual, and legal perspectives that have been interwoven to provide practical guidance for the professional who seeks greater meaning and wholeness in the practice of law.

The Reflective Counselor

Daily Meditations for Lawyers

> ## "Tell me, what is it you plan to do with your one wild and precious life?"
>
> *Mary Oliver*

Life is not a dress rehearsal. This is it, for better or for worse. And, as author Annie Dillard tells us, how we live each day is how we live our lives. "Look to this day…" advises the Sanskrit poem, "…for it is life, the very life of life. In its brief course lie all the realities and verities of existence, the bliss of growth, the splendor of action, the glory of power…. Look well, therefore, to this day."

The moments we often consider the most critical—the day we entered law school, or passed the bar exam, or got married, or became a partner—are just that—moments. Yet in each of those important days, and in every day, before and since, we have encountered all of the verities of existence—the highs, the lows, and the many in-betweens.

The daily life of the lawyer is often rushed and stressed, filled with the "news of the hour and the crisis of the moment." And whether we like to admit it or not, that stress is often intensified by near-constant preoccupation with "how we look" in any given situation. This can change, however, if we are willing to turn over the coin that reads, "What's in it for me?" to the other side, which reads, "How can I serve?"

The legal profession was, and still is, "the noble profession," notwithstanding many chinks in its armor. Even today, most first-year law students begin their training with joy and excitement, hoping to change the world for the better. Those attitudes can continue unabated in our professional lives if they are motivated by service, rather than personal gain alone.

January 1

> ## "If you are here unfaithfully with us, you're causing terrible damage."
>
> *Rumi*

The legal profession and individual legal professionals are under increasing public derision, as instances of greed, self-aggrandizement, and lawyer-involved scandals regularly bombard the public consciousness. This public derision is troubling, at best, to the legions of legal professionals who competently and professionally fulfill their daily responsibilities to their clients and our noble profession. Nonetheless, it is commonly perceived that the most salient characteristics of contemporary lawyering are power, personal wealth, and a sense of being above the law, as opposed to the traditional advocate's characteristics of pursuing justice, fighting for the underdog, service, and zealous representation. Informed commentators seem to be in general agreement in suggesting that there are three primary maladies affecting the legal profession today: 1) professionalism has decreased; 2) public opinion of lawyers and the profession has declined; and 3) lawyer dissatisfaction and dysfunction have increased.

To the extent the above maladies exist, the problem is, as lawyer-author Joseph Allegretti explains, not a problem of ethics or public relations, but a spiritual crisis, in that lawyers and the profession have lost their way. Once having examined and accepted this idea, we do not need to continue to lament the faults of our profession; rather, we may more constructively turn our focus inward, identifying and acting upon the spiritual impulses that brought us to the practice of law in the first place. Author Steven Keeva explains these spiritual impulses as follows: "To the extent that you enter [the legal profession] as a calling, the practice of law is about hunger—the hunger for resolution; for healing the lives of individuals, organizations and communities; for enabling society to function harmoniously and productively; and ultimately, for justice."

> ## "Man's main task in life is to give birth to himself, to become what he potentially is."
>
> *Erich Fromm*

We cannot become the persons and the lawyers we want to be solely by dreaming. Intentions are nothing if we do not translate them into action. Action is required, even when, or *especially* when, all we can handle are small, baby steps.

If we truly desire to transition to a form of living and lawyering that allows us to soar to the heights, to glimpse heaven on earth, we must select, adopt, and adhere to a design for living that is both practical and productive. **That is the exact purpose of this book.** It is designed to introduce, or to re-introduce, ways of thinking about our choices and our dreams that make them attainable, and then to provide a roadmap for reaching them.

We do not need dramatic actions to move toward our desired way of life; in fact, the more drama we introduce, the less clarity we will have to guide our way. Therefore, we do not need to precipitously resign from our jobs, or take extended sabbaticals, or divorce our spouses, or sign up for prolonged psychotherapy; rather, if we are serious about "following our bliss," we need only become ready to follow a courageous journey within which unfolds one day at a time if accompanied by simple, but steady, *today* actions. We shall seek to *bloom where we are planted!*

If we commit to showing up for each segment of transformation—self-knowledge, acceptance and action, each in its own season—great things will eventually come to pass. Like the coal miner who travels the mine's dark canyon, slowly and steadily, a few feet at a time, guided only by the limited illumination of his headlamp, we too need to consistently show up and step forward, letting our inner wisdom guide us to that place where our dreams reside.

January 3

> ## "You can't cross the sea merely by standing and staring at the water."
>
> *Rabindranath Tagore*

Awareness, acceptance, action—this pattern of transformation is not a mere formula, but a systematic process that requires continuous attention if we are to actually claim the lives that we say we want. While the advice of trusted companions and guides can be very helpful in our change process, the increasing trend to seek out personal coaches and motivational gurus can often leave us empty in the long run, if, by so doing, we attempt to externalize the problem, to put it "out there," for someone else to fix. If our *modus operandi* is to have another build us up through affirmance and encouragement, without our active and courageous participation in the process, we may find relief, but we will never find recovery from the conditions that ail us.

The troika of awareness, acceptance, and action, not in-depth analysis and re-analysis, produces change. People can spend thousands of hours in therapy, discussing their problems and how their lives *might* be changed for the better. Yet, if they leave the therapist's office without the committed resolve to make the necessary phone call, or to return to the gym, or to practice patience in the home, the subsequent therapy session will be yet another rehashing of the problem.

If nothing changes, nothing changes.

January 4

> "Unlike puppets, we have the possibility
> of stopping in our movements,
> looking up and perceiving the machinery
> by which we have been moved.
> In this act lies the first steps toward freedom."
>
> *Peter Berger*

Many of us came to the legal profession hoping for substantial freedom and independence in the performance of our work. We anticipated a greater range of self-management than might be found in other endeavors. We can have these hoped-for attributes only if we claim our own power to bestow them upon ourselves. We do not need others' permission to take care of ourselves in a reasonable manner throughout the workday. Stand up, put on your coat, and take your walk. *You* give you permission, no one else. While we properly take issue with bosses who make undue and overly controlling demands on our schedules, very often, we are our own worst enemy in this regard.

The next "crisis" of the hour will always be there. We will be much better equipped to respond to it if we are centered, clear-thinking, and self-nurtured. *We cannot give away what we do not have!* After appropriately attending to our needs, we are ready to face any legal question or challenge with all the clarity, creativity, and enthusiasm that is required.

January 5

"Enjoy your achievements as well as your plans."

Desiderata

A good portion of our job stress arises from our intractable insistence that we can complete an unrealistic volume of work within a given day. To aim, or even more painfully, to require, that we complete a never-ending list of phone calls and emails, letters, meetings and court appointments, is a sure recipe for burnout and failure. This approach allows no cushion for the unexpected, or for the delightful, such as a light exchange with colleagues, or a pleasant lunch. If we are *always* time-pressured, we deprive ourselves of the joy that emanates from the pleasant rhythm of naturally working our craft.

We will find little joy in our work if we continually dishonor our human needs and limitations by imposing unrealistic work demands. A more creative approach comfortably weaves fun, a short walk, a call to a friend, and other enjoyable moments into the heavy demands of our professional day. Although we may protest that we have no time for such "dalliances," in fact, these playful interludes supply the reinvigoration that fuels the more demanding aspects of our workday.

As the workday draws to a close, we can take time to reflect on what we have accomplished, and not solely on what remains undone. The sound counsel given to clients, the completion of our share of a project, the mentoring of a junior colleague—these are very important aspects of our day that require as much reflection as the phone calls that we did not have time to return.

Honesty is a prerequisite to all spiritual growth. An honest and balanced appraisal of our day's work allows us to gently and realistically chart the next day's priorities, while taking pleasure in those tasks that have been well attended to. We can then approach the evening's activities in a non-stressed and mindful manner.

> "Finally, brothers, whatever is true, whatever
> is noble, whatever is right, whatever is pure,
> whatever is lovely, whatever is admirable—
> if anything is excellent or praiseworthy—
> think about such things."
>
> *St. Paul*

In one of the most beautiful passages in all of Scripture, St. Paul encourages spiritual seekers to pursue all that is pure and noble and excellent.

The lawyer who is motivated by service is well-positioned to add purity and nobility and excellence to a sorely hurting world. Clients suffering from family break-ups, potential criminal prosecution, and overwhelming financial calamities are truly blessed to encounter a lawyer who is motivated by an ideal of service and who seeks excellence on the client's behalf.

Our clients generally present themselves in our offices when their personal, emotional, and financial security is most threatened. Their hurting and confused spirits often yearn for understanding, honest guidance, restoration, and wholeness. At such times, the greatest gift our clients can be given—whether the client is a powerful corporation seeking rightful contractual redress, or a hurting child seeking security in the home—is an advocate who seeks to attain all that is pure, all that is noble, and all that is excellent.

January 7

> ## "You cannot make yourself feel something you do not feel, but you can make yourself do right in spite of your feelings."
>
> *Pearl S. Buck*

Lawyering can be a very lonely business. Both our internal voice and the voice of the outer world seem to demand the ever-knowing, ever-strong, ever-fixing, ever-posturing lawyer-superhero. But this is a false and defeating perception. We are enough, *as is*, and we are everything we need to be for the task at hand. We have been well-trained in the law, and there is no client meeting, no court appearance, and no negotiation that is truly going to "undo" us.

When we become concerned about a particular case, appearance, meeting, or other matter, we need only bring the issue within our "transformation triangle" of *awareness*, *acceptance*, and *action*, to responsibly deal with it.

Awareness requires that we acknowledge that a certain matter needs attention, and that the time has come to place it on our priority agenda. We should also take the time to acknowledge and accept any fears that we may have regarding the matter. These are messages of fear (the acronym for "*false evidence appearing real*"), not messages of truth. If we can accept the messages for what they are, letting them run their course without harshly judging them, we can gently allow ourselves to feel the fear, knowing that we can and will accomplish our goal anyway. Feelings are not facts. We have felt this way many times before, yet we have proceeded to accomplish exactly what was needed. Our track record is more than adequate.

By accepting our fear, and placing it within an appropriate context, we then become ready to take necessary action. *Move a muscle, change a thought.* In most cases, all we need to do is make one phone call, or read one document, to move the matter ahead. We do not have to resolve everything at once.

Once we have gently entered and moved through the transformation triangle of *awareness*, *acceptance*, and *action*, we have properly positioned ourselves to competently and peacefully bring the feared matter to completion.

> "The drops of rain make a hole
> in the stone not by violence,
> but by oft falling."
>
> *Lucretius*

Once we become comfortable dwelling within our personal transformative triangles of awareness, acceptance, and action, we can begin to dream again. The "impossible" slowly becomes possible, as we are granted a daily reprieve from the most common symptoms of emotional distress: guilt, worry, fear, and anger.

The challenge for many of us lies in giving *daily* attention to our spiritual practices. The incessant demands and stresses of a busy law practice seductively lure us from the centering practices that allow us to operate serenely, even when the storms crash about us.

For many of us, the only way to overcome the "I'm too busy" syndrome is to set the clock thirty minutes earlier, and to arise anticipating engagement in our chosen transformative practices. In my life, if I do not journal, or pray, or spend some reflective time upon awakening, my entire day is often spent playing "catch-up." Without such early-morning centering, I become easy prey for the "news of the hour and the crisis of the moment." My day can thus become shaped by the competing demands of clients, family members, and others. Conversely, if I have taken the time to connect with my inner being and my higher power ("wasting time with God," as St. Augustine phrased it), I enter the day prepared to meet chaos with serenity, demands with selection, and confusion with quiet certainty.

January 9

"But think about the possible rewards [of incorporating spirituality into legal practice]: a new paradigm for success, one that takes into consideration the profession's roots in healing; a renewed respect for the beauty and mystery of what it means to practice law; a new sense of time, one that does not equate it with dollars and cents; and a new appreciation for the role of intuition, particularly as it relates to what clients seek from their lawyers. These are tools for living an authentic life...for integrating work and meaning, for bringing to the law ways of knowing and being that have for too long been dismissed as irrelevant."

Steven Keeva

"*Tools for living an authentic life, for integrating work and meaning*"—is this not what we have been craving when we wake in the middle of the night, wondering, yet again, why am I doing this? It is a common theme in the world's great wisdom literature that we have to "hit bottom" before we truly become ready and willing to find the courage to change. Perhaps we are near bottom now—perhaps we see little value in what we are doing in our law practice, in our marriages, in our lives. How many masks must we put on and replace during the course of our days in order to maintain the image we believe is required?

Is there a way to think about the practice of law that can accommodate who I am as a human being and not just as a processor of legal information? This is a very important question, since, as Law Professor Daisy Floyd explains, when we lose our sense of ourselves and our purpose, whether in our law practice or more generally, it is akin to death, since it is not merely a loss of balance, but a loss of self.

Spirituality is the way out of despair and into the light, and developing a spiritual practice that allows for the true expression of our authentic beings is our goal. Our reflections will introduce the components of many different spiritual concepts and practices, so that we can be free to choose those that enhance our spiritual growth, and leave behind those that do not. The choice is ours, as the freedom to rely upon our own inner knowing in deciding what is best for us is the essential linchpin of any true spirituality.

> "God, grant me the serenity to accept
> the things I cannot change, the courage
> to change the things I can, and the
> wisdom to know the difference."
>
> *Reinhold Niebuhr*

How often do we think that we could be, do, and accomplish so much more if it were not for the difficult people in our lives? An unhappy spouse, a boss who is never pleased, an irresponsible child—all of these people seem to interfere with the harmony and peace that is our birthright. As elusive as it may seem at first, experience teaches that radical acceptance is the answer to all such outside problems. The fact of the matter is that, although we may be able to temporarily influence another's attitudes and actions, ultimately, their choices and activities are theirs alone. Until we are able to totally accept people, places, and things exactly as they are, we will be engaged in internal, and perhaps external, conflict that will preclude all our attempts to secure inner peace.

The story is told of an old Sufi who, when asked how he could bear living next to a group of whirling dervishes, replied simply, "I just let them whirl." If we truly seek inner peace, we too must learn "to let them (our spouse, our boss, our child) whirl" in whatever way they choose, for we will find no serenity until we do. While we are responsible for speaking our truth and working to change unpleasant conditions that are within our sphere of influence, we must learn to adjust to conditions that are not changeable by us if we are to know peace.

January 11

> "Through wisdom a house is built and through understanding it is established."
>
> *Proverbs 24:3*

Beauty, truth, deep love, divine presence—these are some of the very few things that do not intrinsically change in this world, although our understanding of them may evolve over time. Everything else—our bodies, our minds, our relationships, our concerns, our possessions, our status—is subject to the ebb and flow of change. Change does not necessarily mean total replacement by the new—it may, especially in the life of the spirit, be more akin to recycling, reformulating, or re-membering. The "old," supplemented by new experience, pain, wisdom, compassion, and acceptance, becomes the "new" guiding values or principles by which we can successfully navigate each evolving chapter of our lives.

Some of us gathered the necessary tools for living early in our childhoods as we experienced significant nurturing. Others of us have had to overcome painful and dysfunctional beginnings in order to find our own place on the road to wholeness. Yet, whatever the nature of our initial learning, we can now uncover within ourselves the unique wisdom that can guide us to experience the full and meaningful lives that we were meant to live.

January 12

> "Life is a process of becoming, a combination of states we have to go through. Where people fail is that they wish to elect a state and remain in it. This is a kind of death."
>
> *Anais Nin*

After a number of years in practice, many of us may experience a lessening of enthusiasm and compassion in dealing with our clients. The routine assault case, the lease question, the termination of government benefits—once we have handled these things many times over, we may be tempted to go on "automatic pilot" in dealing with the client and the legal issues.

When this happens, we need to remind ourselves that there is great danger in following the path of least resistance. Steven Keeva, author of *Transforming Practices, Finding Joy and Meaning in the Practice of Law*, describes the devastating consequences that can occur when we cease to honor the spiritual impulses that drew us to the practice of law in the first place. When caring, compassion, and a sense of transcending purpose begin to slip away from our lawyering, Keeva describes the forms of alienation that may be experienced, including: 1) *separation from self*, when an emptiness replaces our sensing, caring nature; 2) *separation from our clients*, when we begin to view ourselves and our clients solely by role, rather than as human beings, as "problem presenters" and "problem fixers"; 3) *separation from colleagues, friends, and family*, when cohesiveness and integration are replaced by stress and concerns about balancing our priorities; 4) *separation from life*, when we begin to identify ourselves by reference to the public's often skewed image of the legal profession; and 5) *separation from the law and the legal profession itself*, when we begin to perceive the imperfections inherent therein as the cause of our personal dissatisfaction and lack of meaning.

While these forms of separation are serious, *change is possible*. As we travel the path of change through spiritual practice, we can reclaim the reintegration of our inner and outer selves. At such juncture, we make a choice to stop leading "divided lives," as author Parker Palmer describes it, where we *feel* one sort of internal imperative for our lives, yet we outwardly *respond* to another. "This is the human condition, of course; our inner and outer worlds will never be in perfect harmony. But there are extremes of dividedness that become intolerable, and when the tension snaps inside of this person, then that person, and then another, a movement may be underway."

> "Therefore be at peace with God, whatever you conceive Him to be. And whatever your labors and aspirations, in the noisy confusion of life, keep peace with your soul."
>
> *Desiderata*

In Rabbi Jeffrey K. Salkin's book, *Being God's Partner, How to Find the Hidden Link Between Spirituality and Your Work*, he advises eight steps to consider if we are truly serious about restoring balance to our work lives:

1. Live a life beyond our profession and the material possessions it provides. Volunteer in a literacy program, feed the hungry, do anything that helps to make the world more whole.

2. Rediscover the Sabbath in a manner that evokes a sense of cosmic rest, replenishment and re-souling. Salkin advises that we observe the Sabbath in accordance with its original purpose: a 24-hour protest against materialism, careerism, and competition.

3. Pray daily, not in accordance with some alien ritual, but with our heartfelt gratitude, supplication, and a desire to reconnect with divine guidance in meeting the tasks of our day.

4. Don't define ourselves by our careers, but by reference to a higher calling. As Deuteronomy 29:9-10 says: "You stand this day, all of you, before the Eternal your God…from woodchopper to waterdrawer—to enter into the covenant of the Eternal your God."

5. Accept failure on the path to success. As Mother Theresa explained, "We are not here to be successful, we are here to be faithful."

6. Stop trying to be perfect, recognize the margin of error we and the world can tolerate, and remember that only God is God.

7. Accept limits and boundaries of time, of effort, of aspiration. "Learn which aspect of work requires a 'yes,' and which requires a 'no,' or 'not yet…'"

8. Make room for God as a partner in our success and accept that we are not the sole progenitors of all that we do. Know, as Moses taught, that it is God who gives us power and sustenance to perform our work and to acquire the benefits thereof.

> "Truly, I say to you, unless you turn
> and become like children, you will never
> enter the kingdom of heaven."
>
> *Matthew 18:3*

What is it about children that can pierce the heart of even the most committed misanthrope? Is it the child's trust in others, the innocence, the lack of critical judgments, the candid reactions and truth-telling, or, is it the awe and appreciation for life, and the inability to wear a mask or pretend to be someone else?

And just when did we lose these qualities of trust, faith, wonder, hope, and candidness? Only the adult human being is able to be one thing and pretend to be another. Yet, if only we would listen to our inner voice, we would come to understand that, in so many ways, our souls yearn for the innocence of childhood. In our rush to "be somebody," to become successful, powerful, and famous, to compete with, and surpass others, we have lost touch with what most refreshes us: to sit and be simply and totally ourselves, as open and innocent as a child.

The opportunities for such refreshment do exist, but only for the seeking and the vigilant. Can we view a star-hewn sky, an elderly couple walking hand-in-hand, the reflection of the moon on a Vermont lake, and allow its full impact to take hold? Can we revisit our high school friend, and let ourselves laugh, till the tears run, as we did when returning from our Saturday football games? Can we sit on the floor and play with our small children, relishing the chance of winning a game of *Candyland* as enthusiastically as when we were six?

Our innocence and playfulness still reside within, and, if invited, will joyously come to the fore, providing a most remarkable lightness of being. If even for a few moments each day, visit life anew, with unmasked eyes of wonder, and know joy!

January 15

> ## "Avoid loud and aggressive people
> ## for they are vexatious to the spirit."
>
> *Desiderata*

The less drama we allow into our lives, the more peace we will know. The amount of drama present is very often proportional to our failure to establish and maintain personal and professional boundaries. While service is the most salient characteristic of the legal profession, a balanced approach to our responsibilities requires that we establish the appropriate parameters in which we can properly function.

It is not uncommon to find that a few clients or a few colleagues require an inordinate amount of our time. Author Julia Cameron refers to these people as "crazy makers," explaining that, although they are often charming and persuasive, they create storm centers in our lives that can be enormously destructive. If we hear ourselves frequently saying "so-and-so is driving me crazy," *pay attention.* The bullying boss who regularly demands a memo on his desk by the next morning, the client who persistently leaves "urgent" messages and demands that we be interrupted while attending other matters, the colleague who daily harangues us with an unending list of personal crises (most of which resulted from the colleague's own acts of commission or omission)— these are the crazy makers in our lives. They love drama, and cast everyone around them in supporting roles to support their dysfunction.

Once we become aware of the existence of a crazy maker in our lives, it becomes our responsibility to take the action necessary to correct the imbalances. As with any difficult professional situation, our choices broadly include accepting, changing, or leaving the problematic situation. Reflection and discernment of the appropriate course are necessary if we are to maintain healthy balance and productivity.

January 16

> "We must let go of the life we have
> planned so as to accept the life
> that is waiting for us."
>
> *Joseph Campbell*

Despite the popular images of the strong-willed, independent, hard-hitting, know-it-all lawyer, we should not attempt to travel the road of spiritual growth on an isolated basis. It is very difficult for lawyers, perhaps more than others, to lay aside the "public facade" and ask for help, especially in the most intimate sphere of personal growth and change.

But "difficult" is what lawyers do, what we are trained for, and what we excel at. Just as no self-respecting trial lawyer would decline a case because it would be difficult to try, we cannot decline the most important assignment of our lives, that of claiming our best possible selves, just because of the difficulty involved.

Besides, "difficult" is often more perception than fact. More pre-wedding jitters than actual commitment avoidance. "Just do it," says the Nike ad, and, when properly armed with a growing awareness of ourselves, our strengths, our weaknesses, our joys, our fears, and our dreams, we become ready to face the "difficult" task of asking for help and guidance. Whether we choose to communicate with a therapist, a friend, a spouse, or some other person, the most critical transformations in our lives begin with the humblest of entreaties: *"I'd like to discuss something with you."*

January 17

> "Why not let people differ about their answers to the great mysteries of the Universe? Let each seek one's own way to the highest, to one's own sense of supreme loyalty in life, one's ideal of life."
>
> *Algernon Black*

We may have heard it said that faith is the opposite of fear, and that fear and faith cannot exist at the same time. While these are intriguing thoughts, they are not necessarily consonant with our experience, at least until we define what we mean by faith.

Many spiritual seekers have come to understand that acknowledging the existence of God, or other higher power, is a very different matter from *having a relationship* with God or a higher power. The latter requires that we devote time and attention to our relationship partner, and that trust, honesty, and connectedness characterize our encounters.

Frederick Buechner, a brilliant author, is one of the few individuals of very deep faith who can provide good-humored guidance and comfort to the questioning seeker. In *Whistling in the Dark, A Dictionary for Doubters*, Buechner explains that he thinks of faith as a kind of whistling in the dark, because, in much the same way as whistling, faith helps us to have courage and keep the shadows at bay. "To whistle in the dark isn't to pretend that the dark doesn't sometimes scare the living daylights out of us. Instead, I think it demonstrates, if only to ourselves, that not even the dark can quite overcome our trust in the ultimate triumph of the Living Light."

It matters little whether we label the "Living Light" as God, or Truth, or otherwise. What does matter is that we acknowledge that a benevolent force exists that is greater than ourselves that will effect results in our lives that we cannot produce by our unaided will.

January 18

> *"...and what does the Lord require of you*
> *but to do justice, and to love kindness,*
> *and to walk humbly with your God."*
>
> Micah 6:8

Justice, kindness, and humility—the formula presented in Micah's words is simple, but it is not easy. The allures and pressures of a fast-paced, materialistic culture make the business of right living an anomaly at best and an impossibility at worst. Seductive short-cuts and easy fixes can appear more appropriate than old-fashioned hard work. Seemingly endless calendar calls, overly protracted and often purposeless meetings, urgent emails, uncooperative adversaries, unsympathetic or bullying superiors—all of these severely threaten even our most valiant attempts to adhere to Micah's mandate.

The pressures of our daily rounds can, and sometimes will, overwhelm us if we do not rigorously set aside undisturbed time for ourselves. If we act as if we cannot afford self-caring and reflective time, our lives will be endless cycles of playing "catch-up," and we will move anxiously from one crisis to the next in both our professional and personal lives.

Psychotherapist Wayne Dyer, in his book, *Being in Balance*, advises that the most critical tool for gaining balance is knowing that we alone are responsible for the unbalance that exists between what we dream of in living our best lives, and the daily habits that we engage in that drain life from those dreams. If we develop the habit of centering ourselves through self-reflection and assessment, our dreams will be revitalized and realized.

January 19

> ## "There are as many universes as there are people."
>
> *Carl Rogers*

Each individual is like no other. We each are created with our own signature and handprint. In the assembly line of gene distribution, we come into the world with a unique package of gifts and strengths, and it is our job to identify and fully realize these potentialities.

Sometimes life's experiences interfere with our seeing ourselves as we truly are. These blind spots need to be overcome in order for self-actualization to occur. Blind spots often take the form of unmet basic needs. Attend to your need to love and be loved. Make sure your confidence, self-esteem, and sense of connection to those in your circle of love (family, mate, children, friends) remain intact. Keep your mood even by remembering to eat properly, sleep enough, exercise regularly, stay tuned-in socially, and maintain a healthy love relationship.

Self-actualization is the last step of the ladder that bridges the span from life being a tolerable existence, to leading a life that is personally satisfying and worth living.

January 20

> "The continued existence of a free and democratic society depends upon recognition…that justice is based upon the rule of law grounded in respect for the dignity of the individual and the capacity through reason for enlightened self-government…."
>
> *Preamble to the Rules of Professional Conduct*

At their best, lawyers help to establish and protect the safeguards that affect every aspect of an individual's life, assuring the protections of a free society. It is truly noble work to participate in creating a society characterized by security, unity, order, and peace.

At its best, the rule of law is majestic to behold. In its purest form, the rule of law evolves from a proper combination of reason, knowledge, ideals, values, experience, and legal precedent. The majestic rule, applied fairly and tempered with compassion, is as beautiful an art form as can be imagined this side of Paradise.

Quite appropriately, one of the majestic titles ascribed to the Divine in Handel's *Messiah* is "Mighty Counselor." A compassionate counselor-at-law, who ably practices the legal craft for the well-being of others, co-creates justice and excellence in the shadow of the Mighty Counselor.

January 21

> "New frameworks are like climbing a mountain—
> the larger view encompasses rather than
> rejects the more restricted view."
>
> *Albert Einstein*

Each generation is called upon to broaden the achievements of its predecessors. The American dream, the ever-expanding rainbow of life's possibilities, has as its cornerstone the sustained and persistent progress of each generation.

As lawyers, we are asked to improve upon the poetry and artistry that has been fashioned by previous generations of legal scholars and enthusiasts. Today, just as 200 years ago, lawyers are called upon to rightly define, and equitably apply, the elemental principles that produce an enhanced quality of life for the collective citizenry. While these principles must be judiciously adapted for modern application, our job is to continuously safeguard and keep vital the cherished concepts of fundamental fairness and justice that are definitional for our collective existence.

Whether we look backward or forward, or survey our current landscape, we see lawyers struggling to define, secure, and defend individual rights, right relationships between citizens, and right relationships between the government and the governed.

These fundamental aspects of the lawyer's pursuit will last, we presume, in perpetuity. May perpetual light shine upon them.

January 22

> "The divided life is a wounded life, and the soul keeps calling us to heal the wound. Ignore that call, and we find ourselves trying to numb our pain with an anesthetic of choice, be it substance abuse, overwork, consumerism, or mindless media noise."
>
> *Parker Palmer*

Parker Palmer's classic, *A Hidden Wholeness, The Journey Toward an Undivided Life*, sets forth a guide for imagining new visions of the shape of the integrated life, the meaning of community, education as transformation, and the effecting of paradigm shifts in societal consciousness.

Palmer's discussion of the deleterious effects of living a "divided life" constitutes a clarion call to each of us to begin shedding the many masks we wear to satisfy the strong professional and societal pulls toward conformity. Most of us unthinkingly respond to the immediate payoffs associated with such conventionality, never realizing the cost to our souls as we do so.

Palmer explains that we stifle possibilities for our lives because, in the process of imagining, we are reminded of the painful gap between the roles we play in the world, and who we truly are and want to become. We thus "…lose touch with our souls and disappear into our roles." The negative consequences are incalculable as we: "…sense that something is missing…we feel fraudulent, even invisible…we project our inner darkness on others…real relationships [become] impossible…[and] our contributions to the world—especially through the work we do—are tainted by duplicity and deprived of the life-giving energies of true self."

The solution to living a divided life, Palmer says, involves setting aside our fear, and going deeply within to seek the inner wisdom that will allow us to live fully integrated and authentic lives.

January 23

"Work is love made visible."

Kahlil Gibran

What an odd equation: work is love. Love is probably one of the last things we envision when we think of our office lives. Yet, how else can we characterize the faithful assistant who has worked with us so patiently and kindly all these years, or the mail delivery person who always has a smile and a cheerful word, or the law librarian who absolutely delights in finding just the right legal jewel that we seek? How about the very senior partner who never lost his enthusiasm for the firm and its clients, or the younger attorney who, without fanfare, regularly provides *pro bono* assistance to indigent tenants? If this is not love made visible, then what is?

In his best-selling book, *The Road Less Traveled*, Scott Peck gives a very workable definition of love: "The will to extend one's self for the purpose of nurturing one's own or another's spiritual growth." In the most basic terms, all of our life's work is about spiritual growth, about transcending our comfort zones, about moving from fear to love. Self-love and love of others become demonstrable only through our exertion. Love is not effortless, in fact, it is effortful, and yes, work is love made visible.

January 24

> "I know of no more encouraging fact
> than the unquestioned ability of a man to
> elevate his life by conscious endeavor."
>
> *Henry David Thoreau*

By now, we may have begun to embrace the idea that we can achieve personal transformation through living the troika of awareness, acceptance, and action. However, just as every good trial lawyer anticipates the weaknesses of the case to be presented, we also do well to understand the most common impediments to our personal growth that will arise, no matter how sincere our commitment to change. As we rightfully begin to try to make the changes that will transport us to happy, joyous, and free living, we may find obstacles at every turn. Do not be discouraged. Time, persistence, and *daily* attention to spiritual practices will yield the changes we seek. We must acknowledge and be content with patient improvement rather than perfection. A lifetime of faulty attitudes and behaviors cannot be undone in a day.

The primary obstacle to growth encountered on the spiritual path is fear—mainly fear that we won't get what we want, or that we will lose what we have. Since the lawyer's task often involves handling difficult people and challenges with seeming bravado, it seems anomalous and difficult to confront the fact that fear so deeply corrodes the very infrastructure of our lives. While denial, justification, and the donning of masks may cover up this fear, this corrosive thread will continue to undermine our growth until it is squarely confronted and accepted for what it is.

The wisdom of the ages confirms that few things yield more positive results in transforming our characters than an honest exploration and analysis of the fears that bind us. When we become willing to discuss these fears with a trusted therapist or friend, their hold over us is immediately lessened. Stay the course, and untold changes will occur.

January 25

> ## "Beyond a healthy discipline,
> ## be gentle with yourself."
>
> *Desiderata*

The word "discipline" normally connotes harshness and enforced obedience, evoking such disturbing images as a crying child, a punitive drill sergeant, or a never-ending list of ethical requirements. Yet, the word "discipline" actually derives from the same root as that of the word "disciple," and refers to the more gentle and positive activities of teaching and learning, in the manner of a pupil following the teachings of an esteemed master. The dictionary definition of the word references "training that corrects, molds, or perfects mental faculties or moral character."

As we evolve into the people we were meant to be, we begin to understand and appreciate the use for, and eventually, the pleasure of, a life that reflects a healthy and gentle self-discipline. The patterned daily activities that bring order and gentility to our days should be mindfully and gently chosen. We can "try on" different healthy behaviors to ascertain the specific activities that most readily contribute to the peace and tranquility that we seek. Once we begin to incorporate certain simple, but generally non-negotiable, practices into our daily lives, whether they be journaling, physical exercise, meditation, spiritual reading, or other such activities, our lives will reflect a healthy and pleasurable rhythm that does not require continuous mental checking to keep us on track.

A simple, but regularly observed, set of self-nurturing tasks, chosen by and for us, results in greater simplicity, harmony, and satisfaction in life.

January 26

> "Anytime I am looking to somebody else
> as my source, I am coming from scarcity.
> I am no longer trusting God or
> the Universe for my harvest."
>
> *Jan Denise*

Some of our deepest hurts and feelings of abandonment can derive from a sense that our intimates are "not there" for us when we need them. In times of extreme turmoil, we might cry out resentfully: "If not now, when? What kind of spouse/lover/friend is this, who doesn't understand how much I hurt, and how much I need them at this moment?"

Henri Nouwen, theologian and author, frequently addresses the issue of profound loneliness in his writings. Nouwen explains that the primary source of this pain derives from a confusion of "first love" and "second love." The first love, an unconditional love that knows no limitation of depth, breadth, understanding, or availability, can be found only in the realm of the Sacred. The second love, which contains many elements derived from the first love, is what we can receive, if we are truly blessed, from our loved ones. However, since our loved ones carry their own personal baggage of hurts, alienation, character defects, and pain, they are not actually capable of consistently manifesting a sanctified "first love," which is truly without limit.

When we are able to distinguish who and what can actually satisfy our different longings and needs in any given situation, we become open and available to receive the healing nutrients that are supplied by both first love and second love.

Go where it's warm!

January 27

> "A bone to the dog is not charity.
> Charity is the bone shared with the dog,
> when you are just as hungry as the dog."
>
> *Jack London*

The use of money as a means to exchange love and service is a joy to behold. While acclaimed philanthropy certainly fulfills many important societal needs, our individual use of money, in our less notorious lives, is also critically important.

No matter how much or how little we have, nothing "jump-starts" a calming sense of abundance and prosperity more efficiently than generously sharing a portion of our material goods. Who has not been moved by the poignant Depression-era stories, or those involving concentration camp victims, where the desperately lacking shared their meager food and supplies with others who were even more vulnerable? These incredible acts of generosity not only immensely benefited the recipient, they also produced a heightened sense of personhood and meaning amid otherwise brutish and desperate circumstances. Even within such sordidness, the beauty and majesty of the self-giving human spirit shone through brightly, elevating the humanity of both the giver and the receiver.

By beginning to live from an inner place of generosity and abundance, we too, in our very ordinary circumstances, can experience the most abundant flow of life's riches.

January 28

> "Just make up your mind at the very outset
> that your work is going to stand for quality…
> that you are going to stamp a superior
> quality upon everything that goes out of
> your hands, that whatever you do
> shall bear the hallmark of excellence."
>
> *Orison Swett Marden*

What events in our lives, personal, familial, ancestral, professional, mythological, or otherwise, converge to create and shape the essence of who we are as people, and our own capacity to impact history?

While not all of us are the geniuses, or artists, or leaders whose contributions will indelibly impact humanity for untold years to come, our job is to contribute all that we can to this "big now" moment.

Our work as lawyers requires a form of double vision. Not only are we responsible for tending to the details of lawyering, we are simultaneously responsible for keeping watch over the ever-changing larger context of a situation or project. We must consistently self-motivate in order to elevate our game beyond the ordinary. We must honor our natural internal striving for excellence, pushing far beyond the "first draft is good enough" policy.

Good lawyering, like the retelling of a good joke, improves incrementally with each iteration, until it assumes its final polished form. As lawyers of excellence, we push forward, stretching beyond our set-point comfort zones, until the quality of our labor, and its attendant thoughtfulness and care, shine through.

January 29

> ## "Satisfaction lies in the effort, not in the attainment, full effort is full victory."
>
> *Mahatma Gandhi*

Happy endings are something we strive to achieve in all our human endeavors. Yet, mature legal professionals know that happy endings are never foregone conclusions in the practice of law. As every seasoned practitioner can attest, few things are as disheartening as the downward tilt of the client's face, the questioning eyes, or the dropping off of the voice, as we near the conclusion of our work with a client.

As lawyers, we are called upon to sometimes defend the ruthless, to reason with the unreasonable, to support the vulnerable, to engage in ego-bruising confrontations, to engage in negotiations conducted in other than good faith, to deliver hard truths, and to accept the severe limits, and sometimes, the actual injustices, of the law and the judicial system.

How do we *not* assimilate the ill effects of these difficult circumstances into our very beings? How can we maintain our professional stance of neutrality and protect ourselves from the anxiety associated with a never-ending stream of "unsolvable" problems and unjust situations?

Well, we can at least begin this formidable task by remembering that we are responsible for the footwork, and not for the outcome. It is not our responsibility to totally solve our clients' problems; rather, our job is to seek the best legal resolution possible through appropriate counseling and zealous representation.

Having fulfilled our rightful tasks, we can move on, without regret, to do the next right thing before us.

January 30

> "For to be human is, after all, to be other than 'God.'
> And so it is only in the embracing of our torn self, only in
> the acceptance that there is nothing 'wrong' with feeling
> 'torn,' that one can hope for whatever healing is available
> and can thus become as 'whole' as possible."
>
> *Ernest Kurtz and Katherine Ketcham*

The story is told of the devout Desert Father who spent countless years in the desert, praying, meditating, fasting, and seeking spiritual enlightenment concerning the real meaning and purpose of life. When he finally emerged from his many years of self-imposed isolation, his followers eagerly awaited news of the great truths that had been revealed to the Desert Father. "Abba, Father," they begged, "tell us of your great wisdom, what are the true fruits of your enlightenment?" The esteemed spiritual leader responded with a mere two words. "PAY ATTENTION," he said.

And just what is it that we are supposed to pay attention to? Almost all spiritual and philosophical traditions agree that *honesty with self* is the sustaining nutrient of spiritual growth. When the Desert Mothers and Fathers separated themselves from all distractions and dwelled within the desert, they were left to ponder the truth of who they *actually* were, warts and all. In so doing, they were also able to cultivate the exquisitely beautiful virtue of compassion, through which they were able to see that others' weaknesses, like their own, were all part of the finite human condition.

Almost any list of the qualities that a good lawyer should possess contains the word "compassion." Few are the teachers, however, who can guide us in developing this rare quality. The desert saints, instructing us through their own actions, teach: *pay attention to yourselves, your foibles and your halting successes, and before long, you will be able to embrace your own torn self, as well as the other "torn selves" that surround you.*

To be human is to be at once perfect *and* imperfect, not perfect *or* imperfect.

> "Every moment and every event
> of every man's life on earth
> plants something in his soul."
>
> *Thomas Merton*

In law, there are days when we feel we are treading water, accomplishing very little that is significant. But as we continue upon our journey, the consistent body of work we have accomplished will at points brush up against greatness, and sometimes will constitute groundbreaking work. When we look through the telescope and see what appears to be an as-of-yet unnamed star, we should take center stage and proclaim in a loud and clear voice our name and the name of that new heavenly body. Just as in golf, it is that one great shot that keeps us coming back, time and time again, to recreate that elusive moment of brilliance.

February 1

> "We are one, after all, you and I,
> together we suffer, together exist and
> forever will recreate each other."
>
> *Pierre Teilhard de Chardin*

It has been said that different people enter our lives for a lesson, a season, or a lifetime. There are, in reality, very few people who remain lifetime intimates; however, each one of them is precious beyond imagination.

One's spouse or committed life partner is the jewel in the crown of all relationships, yet this "jewel" is the one most likely to become tarnished by neglect or lack of appreciation. While in some ways we pay our partner the ultimate compliment in "letting it all hang out" by being our true, unadorned selves in their presence, this intimate privilege can sometimes be distorted into disrespect or lack of valuing if we do not remain mindful of the incredible blessing inherent in the unique relationship.

It does us well to frequently recall that it is a privilege and an honor to bear the title of "husband" or "wife" or "life partner." These privileged titles carry within them, however, the corresponding covenant that, no matter how much tumult exists, and how much the rafters might be shaken, neither of us is leaving. Not for good, anyway. The unspoken commitment is that after all the anger recedes, and the shouting ends, and the last door is slammed, both parties will re-engage in the necessary clean-up; thus resolving and working to eventually return to their sacred arena of love and commitment.

February 2

> "Abundance is not something we acquire.
> It is something we tune into."
>
> *Wayne Dyer*

Abundance is a state of mind, not a number on a bank statement. Abundance is a deep knowing that we are and have enough, no matter what our material circumstances. When we enter into the deep flowing waters of giving and receiving, where labels marked "yours" and "mine" are superfluous, and material attributes flow in and out of our lives like water flows through our hands, then we know true abundance. It is when we try to hold tightly to things such as money, power, attention, and prestige that these gifts are transmuted into the barriers to an abundant life. Fear that we won't get what we want or that we will lose what we have turns out to be the corrosive thread that unravels all that is good and peaceful and abundant in our lives.

When money and material possessions are seen as a means of exchanging love and service, we will know wealth beyond measure. The bumper sticker got it right: the best things in life are not things.

February 3

> ## "Joy in looking and comprehending
> ## is nature's most beautiful gift."
>
> *Albert Einstein*

Practicing law, like practicing life, can lead to unexpected delights if we are but open to them. By sincerely committing to a path of spiritual growth, we can also anticipate being surprised and shocked by joy. Joy is often experienced as an elated response to feelings of happiness, pleasure, and satisfaction. This type of joy is rooted in a deep connectivity with our inner selves, the Sacred, nature, and all of creation. Now and again, even amid turmoil, we are privileged to experience the joyful dimension of simple delight in being alive.

When we are at peace with ourselves, we have the eyes to see those delights that previously were hidden from us. The normally harsh judge who unexpectedly responds with tenderness, the ever-posturing adversary who uncharacteristically acquiesces in a just settlement offer, the previously resentful spouse who testifies truthfully in the divorce proceedings concerning his own defalcations—these rare slices of humanity's beauty can be glimpsed only by those who "have the eyes to see."

When we have devoted the time and attention to our spiritual nurturance, the resulting clarity reveals many such delights and joys. Shades of mercy, justice, fairness, and truth, where before there were none, are some of the first fruits of right and joyful living.

February 4

> "Keep interested in your own career, however humble;
> it is a real possession in the changing fortunes of time.
> Exercise caution in your business affairs, for the world
> is full of trickery. But let this not blind you to what
> virtue there is; many persons strive for high ideals,
> and everywhere life is full of heroism."
>
> *Desiderata*

The noble profession of law provides one of the most effective vehicles of change in today's society. I always told my law students that they were becoming credentialed to change the world. No profession holds as much power, individually and collectively, to change the course of human events as does the legal profession.

The story is told of the young man who dreamed of changing the world, but found that was not easily attained, so he dreamed of changing his country. As he became a little older and wiser, he focused his sights on changing his local community, and as he grew even more in wisdom, he focused on changing himself. By changing ourselves we do change the world. By working collaboratively, that change evolves more readily. As Margaret Mead said so many years ago, "Never doubt that a small group of thoughtful, committed citizens can change the world; indeed, it's the only thing that ever has."

Each time a lawyer deals with an adversary in a manner that combines zealous representation with integrity, intelligence, and compassion, the lawyer, the adversary, the client, the legal profession, and the whole of society are changed for the better. Each time a lawyer's motivation evolves from "What's in it for me?" to "How can I serve?" the world is transformed in the way that a pebble dropped in water creates ever-widening circles of movement and change. Be the change you seek.

"Don't die with your music still in you."

Wayne Dyer

Our lives often parallel the movements of a great symphony. As with any great musical work, there may be occasional instrumental solos or duets, but it is often the full orchestra crescendo that moves the listener to the greatest heights.

Each meaningful aspect of our lives—our lawyering, our family, our friends, our personal interests—each plays its unique role in the symphony that is our life. The threads of each intertwined motif create the great symphony of a deeply meaningful life. When, however, one or more aspects of our life begin to claim an overly large space, as happens, for example, when our work is claiming the largest part of our physical, mental, and emotional energy, we lose the balance and symmetry that, as in the symphony, render great power and poignancy.

In his book, *Being in Balance*, psychotherapist Wayne Dyer writes that it is critically important for each of us to acknowledge that we alone are responsible for any imbalance that exists between what we dream for in living our best lives, and the daily habits that drain life from those dreams. We alone can create the balance between what we truly desire and how we conduct our lives on a daily basis.

As we will read so often in our reflections, honestly acknowledging the true conditions of our lives is the absolute first step toward claiming the transformed lives that we seek.

The good news and the bad news here are identical: *We are responsible*. We are responsible for restoring balance by reducing the width of the chasm that exists between our dreams and our actions. This restoration will begin when, working with the reflections in this book, we take up residence within the heart-space that encompasses our willingness to embrace awareness, acceptance, and action—our own transformation triangle.

February 6

> "But this: that one can contain death…
> can hold it to one's heart gently, and not
> refuse to go on living, this is inexpressible."
>
> *Rainer Maria Rilke*

I have always been fascinated with the title of C.S. Lewis' book, *A Grief Observed*, wherein the author chronicles the course of his wife's final illness and death. While the heartbreak of such separation was the particular grief Lewis related, the title itself provokes consideration of a very important professional and personal question: are we able to summon the courage needed to observe and abide grief—our own, our clients', and that of others?

While the work of lawyering is often about "fixing" different situations, spiritual maturity requires that we come to accept that not all things can be "fixed," and, just as importantly, that "fixing something" does not necessarily mean transforming it. Can we allow ourselves to recognize moments of utter powerlessness, either in our own lives or the lives of others? Can we stand silently in the threshold places, where the voices of both spiraling despair and hopeful transformation desperately compete for attention and sole allegiance? Or must we fill the pregnant, silent space with lawyerly and wordy theories, lest we come face-to-face with unspeakable grief?

Sometimes, no matter how diligently and skillfully we have worked on a client's behalf, the client still goes to jail, the faultless parent still loses custody of a much beloved child, and the wrongfully dismissed employee still stands powerless in the face of the mighty and arrogant employer. When these events occur, despite our most arduous and noble effort, we do well to recall that we do not have to run away from the grief, or weave elaborate theories on how it can become undone, or deny that it exists. In the face of extreme grief, sometimes the only appropriate response is respectful silence.

Having done our best work, we can stand confidently in observing what is, ascertaining any lessons to be learned from the experience. Then, when we are ready, we can move out into the sunlight.

> "Gratitude is not only the greatest of virtues,
> but the parent of all others."
>
> *Cicero*

How often do we recognize how lucky we are to have received all the gifts, blessings, and advantages that make us who we are today? Acknowledgment is the first step in living a grateful life. Recognition of who we are and where we came from helps frame our present lives from the proper perspective.

The journey has many twists and turns, ups and downs, bumps in the road, and opportunities for derailment. Sometimes it helps to stop, look, listen, and reflect upon where we have been before stepping forward in bold adventure. The vision ahead is properly framed by the road we have traveled.

February 8

> # "The best things in life
> are not things."
>
> *Author Unknown*

Our lives become more difficult to navigate when they are cluttered—mentally, physically, and emotionally. Generally, we already have enough of what we need, and, with few exceptions, we do not need "more" of any*thing* to comfort our aching souls.

Rather, we would benefit from an appreciation of what we already have, instead of rushing out to buy one more thing, and attempting to satisfy our insatiable list of material demands.

It's an inside job, yet again!

A very practical and symbolic life task involves cleaning out a cluttered closet or desk. Separating the "wheat from the chaff" is always a satisfying enterprise, no matter what domain we labor in. This self-caring exercise allows us to set aside the unnecessary, the unwanted, and the things that no longer serve us. The remaining "treasures" then have a rightful chance to shine, to be employed, to be appreciated. We are left with an increased sense of order, abundance, and harmony, which is very soothing to our souls.

Both the material and the spiritual realms offer many unclaimed treasures that are there for the looking, the sorting, and the claiming.

February 9

> "The human race now stands on the brink
> of a historic transformation, with new eyes,
> new ears, new minds, and new hearts emerging
> from the cosmic drama of human evolution.
> As an embryo becomes a baby, we are becoming
> a new more spiritualized version of ourselves."
>
> *Marianne Williamson*

Everywhere in the world people are grappling with the dilemma of finding meaning, purpose, and a higher sense of order in the experience of living. Some predict that we may stand at the dawn of a new understanding, and an imminent resolution, of the spiritual crisis that has been brought about, in part, by our separation from ourselves, our tribe, our traditions, our institutions, our previously honored values and beliefs, and the lands that we once held sacred.

Many others are more pessimistic in their assessment of our collective future. They predict that, as we remain ensconced in our individual and collective angst, shallowly clinging to the materialistic trophies of a consumerist society, our spiritual desolation will only deepen.

Yet, as we discuss throughout our reflections, we who mindfully attend to our own personal and spiritual growth do not need to await the development of universal solutions to age-old problems. At this very moment, we have everything we need to stop living "divided lives," and to start living the lives of wholeness for which we were created.

We must separate, yet again, from the maddening crowd, seek our solitude, and *be still and know*. In so doing, we can craft our individual inner solutions to the "meaning void" that plagues so many.

February 10

> # "That's what it's all about.
> You need 25 guys to contribute."
>
> *Joe Torre*

The team approach to lawyering is becoming more prevalent as individual specialists within a firm are called upon to solve their clients' complex legal problems. Although many lawyers tend to be loners in their work style, team collaboration can inspire us to move past our normal comfort zones to the area of "collective consciousness," where the whole can be much greater than the sum of its parts.

From a psychological perspective, teams are intriguing structures that operate with a unique motivation and production system. Law, in some ways, is not dissimilar from professional sports. Both have their superstars, but even the superstars need good teams to back them up. And good teams are built on players treating each other with respect, and overcoming idiosyncratic tendencies to achieve a common goal.

Social scientists have long known that social skills are directly and positively impacted through participation in team activities. Teams teach us the values of hard work, dedication, selflessness, sacrifice, responsibility, and risk-taking, and promote the development of the individual team member's confidence and self-esteem.

In what ways do we participate as members of a winning team? What is our role on that team, and how could our individual and collective performance be improved? The better the team we are on, the better the players we become.

> "He has told you, O mortal, what is good;
> and what does the Lord require of you,
> but to do justice, and to love kindness,
> and to walk humbly with your God?"
>
> *Micah 6:8*

The above words were spoken during a recent eulogy for a lawyer-friend. The minister, a long-time pal, described how the lawyer had lovingly attended to each aspect of his life—the person, husband, father, family member, soldier, law student, long-term legal practitioner, friend, child of God, and Sunday duffer—with an innocence, purity, and humility that were a delight to behold.

While the crowded church dwelt amid an observed grief, it was clear that the celebration and joy of the lawyer's lived existence far surpassed any temporary sorrow. This was certainly a person who knew who he was, and who had *tried* to live his beliefs and his values (not perfectly, as some humorously pointed out), in an ordinary way, without fanfare, but with daily attention to that which was important to him—his own character, his family, his God, his friends, and his work. The lawyer was laid to rest with the eloquence and elegance that only a life well-lived can command: "*Well done, good and faithful servant.*"

A lawyer who loves justice and kindness, and who walks humbly with the divine, however conceived, is a power of example and an example of power for all to behold. When the glitter fizzles, when the spotlight dims, when the accolades are no longer forthcoming, and, certainly, when death approaches, if we have been diligent about our earthly work, we, and those around us, will continue to experience the deep-running peace that has always nourished our souls.

February 12

> ## "Courage consists in the power of self-recovery."
>
> *Ralph Waldo Emerson*

There is a riveting scene in the movie "City Slickers" where Billy Crystal recounts the magical childhood power of unilaterally stopping time and erasing history, merely by authoritatively shouting, "Do Over!" In uncontested solidarity, everyone and everything stopped, and past results were undone, whether it was the last race to the corner, or the strikeout at bat. After a properly asserted "Do Over," prior defeats were, as we lawyers like to say, *void ab initio*.

While we may not claim such distinctly magical powers today, life is forgiving and generous in that, whenever we are truly "sick and tired of being sick and tired," we can commence a new beginning by quietly claiming a "Do Over" in our adult lives. While we cannot, as in childhood, erase the past, we can decide that, going forward, we will pick up the simple kit of spiritual tools offered in this book and elsewhere, and begin a slow and steady period of reconstruction within our own lives.

We do not need to see another therapist, or attend another conference, or read another book, to begin the reconstruction. What we do need is honest self-reflection, a sincere desire to change those inner qualities that appear to be holding us back, and the commencement of daily activities needed to accomplish desired changes. The formula is simple, but not always easy. Yet, whenever we become discouraged, we need only consider the experience of others, who, like us, began their transformative journeys with a firm decision and a single step.

February 13

> ## "Don't quit five minutes
> before the miracle."
>
> *Author Unknown*

Everything can change in an instant. We trudge through vast portions of our life with an unexamined theory of who we are and how we operate and then, zim, bam, boom, change occurs to us. All of a sudden an axial shift occurs internally and we no longer view the world the same way. Coping with the little things becomes easier. Time now seems on our side. The questioning doubts and feelings of being overwhelmed that are the hallmarks of the desert experience give way to the relaxation and leisure attitudes of life's oasis. We breathe more fully and deeply. The step returns to our stride and laughter re-emerges as a defining marker of who we are. How does this shift occur? Often the breakthrough is forced by an accumulative buildup of stress that muscles us into re-examining the underlying assumptions of who we are and how we choose to go about doing life. Reflection is the first step in the transformation process.

February 14

> "...the moment one definitely commits oneself, then Providence moves too. A whole stream of events issues from the decision, raising in one's favor all manner of unforeseen incidents and meetings and material assistance, which no one could have dreamed would have come his way."
>
> *Goethe*

How do we commit ourselves to change so that all that we are seeking comes within our grasp? Well, to begin with, we must accept that we do not think ourselves into new ways of living, we live ourselves into new ways of thinking. Awareness, acceptance, and action, in that order, can set us on the path to lasting transformation. Living mindfully within this transformational triangle, our lives can unaccountably transform. However, daily and persistent attention to the task is required if we are to reap all of the joyous rewards of living a mindful existence

Before beginning, it is important to appreciate that our commitment to such mindful living runs counter to cultural norms, most especially the prevailing norms of our professional world. Almost every societal stimulus charges: "be more," "have more," "do more." Yet our counter-cultural attempt to live within the "transformation triangle" equates to crossing over a bridge into a land in which a different tune is softly chanted: "we are enough," "we have enough," "we do enough."

Our inner-directed approach to our lives may not be understood by many, however, in committing to operate within the realm of transformation, we are longer living our lives by reference to "the good opinion of others."

February 15

> "As far as it can be discerned, the sole purpose of
> human existence is to kindle a light of meaning
> in the darkness of mere being."
>
> *Carl Jung*

At some point in our professional lives, we may find we have crossed a line where, no matter what rehabilitative actions we may take, the practice of law, as we experience it, has no meaning. Even worse, we may perceive that, because of our responsibilities, our bills, or our limited horizons, there is no way out of this deepening abyss.

At times like this, we may have to pull ourselves up short, and seek to construct an appropriate context for our situation. While it is true that we must honestly and courageously face what Julia Cameron labels "the profoundly disturbing impact of heart-wounding work," we can stop our precipitous spiraling down by first remembering that we will not only survive this dark time, but we may well uncover new sources of strength in dealing with it, emerging from the crisis stronger than before.

We have an excellent track record. Remember all those times we thought we would never make it through certain life passages—succeeding in law school, passing the bar, finding a job, arguing our first motion, creating a healthy family life, dealing with health issues, and even the death of loved ones? While we certainly did not enjoy all these challenges, we survived them, and in so doing, we carved more of the sculpture of our authentic selves. "Circumstances do not make a man," says James Allen, "they reveal him."

Finding meaning in our lives, including our work lives, is a crucial aspect of our existence. Human beings, *qua* human beings, seek to make meaning in every situation. Our life challenges function akin to the foyer of a home—they are the entrance ways into the true meaning of our existence.

February 16

> "Let me be clear. At its core the legal profession faces not so much a crisis of ethics, or commercialization, or public relations, but a spiritual crisis. Lawyers and the profession have lost their way."
>
> *Joseph G. Allegretti*

When we entered law school, many of us believed that we could help others, that we could make changes, and that we could alleviate the pain of a hurting world. Recent studies report that most current law students begin with the same ideals; however, by the end of the first year, these ideals have too often been replaced by anxiety, alienation, and grueling competition for grades, class rankings, and journal positions.

Longitudinal studies conducted by Law Professor Larry Krieger and psychologist Ken Sheldon confirm that after the critical first year of law school, most students reorient themselves away from personal values (service, justice, etc.) and towards more extrinsic values (power, possessions, and prestige), leading to a loss of self-esteem, life satisfaction, and well-being. This pattern carries over into the practice of law.

The negative symptoms of this faulty value ordering are everywhere. Studies and samplings show abnormal levels of psychological distress and dysfunction among legal professionals. Additionally, above-average rates of substance abuse, divorce, and even suicide, are salient characteristics of the legal profession.

As our personal growth continues, we come to understand that self-defeating learned behaviors can be unlearned. Just as the law student and lawyer learned to replace internal values with external prizes, so this approach can be unlearned. The need is great, since, as we have seen, outward measures of success prove to be no substitute for the loss of inner meaning.

February 17

> ## "For many men that stumble at the threshold are well foretold that danger lurks within."
>
> *William Shakespeare*

I was recently involved in rescuing a young family who attempted to forge a narrow strip of water that separated two bodies of land. Unbeknownst to them, serious rip tides often passed through this area. Early training as a lifeguard, a little luck, and a nearby canoe, saved five lives. The family's trouble arose from the failure to assess the territory they were travelling before setting out.

How many of us actually understood the legal terrain before claiming it as our own?

All lawyers have obviously made a major investment in becoming legal professionals, beginning with the law school entry process, the investment of many thousands of dollars in tuition, three grueling years of study, the bar exam, finding a legal position or positions, and then beginning the arduous work of legal practice. Yet, many of the "darker forces" of legal practice—the hours, the stress, the loneliness—generally remain unacknowledged and unexplored during law school, and encounters with these unexpected challenges often ambush unsuspecting neophyte lawyers upon entering practice.

Law school reform advocates strongly support the full disclosure and discussion of the challenges faced by the profession, and the individual practitioner, during the training process. They rightfully maintain that if authentic discourse concerning these challenges, and the potential responses to them, are integrated into the curriculum, young lawyers will be better equipped to avoid lurking rip tides, and find more balance and meaning in the practice of law.

Whether or not we actually understood the legal terrain as we began our individual legal journeys, we can certainly assess it today. Just as our golf game improves with greater course knowledge, so too, in planning the future contours of our legal careers, we should become sophisticated in scoping out the anticipated terrain.

February 18

> "Climb the mountains and get their good tidings.
> Nature's peace will flow into you as sunshine flows into trees.
> The winds will blow their own freshness into you...
> while cares will drop off like autumn leaves."
>
> *John Muir*

When a wave of anxiety or irrational guilt crashes over us for no apparent reason, we can seek solace in quiet, contemplative places. Being in nature, amid its enormity and splendor, can lift our spirits and elevate our moods in subtle, yet tangible, ways. The brief moments of reprieve from the worries of the day can inspire us to a new level of creativity and productivity. The brilliance of the sun's warming rays, irresistibly splashing color on our dark brooding, can restore purpose and perspective to our battered souls.

Corrective and self-caring action is required when our mind seems unreasonable, and our emotional responses are disproportionate to the events at hand. Feelings and states of mind are deeply affected by a change in setting. While this solution may seem elementary or even childish, seemingly complex problems often have simple solutions. *Move a muscle, change a thought.* Move yourself from the habitat of chaos and disorder to nature's peaceful and serene setting, where well-being, mindfulness, and balance can be restored.

February 19

> "Not only is every call unique, but the hearing of every call is unique also. One sign…is a certain restlessness, a certain dissatisfaction with things as they are… [or] a sense of longing, yearning, or wondering…"
>
> *Suzanne Farnham, Joseph Gill, Taylor McLean, and Susan Ward*

We should do the job in front of us, and, if necessary, also do the job to the left or right of us, if we are the person for the job. Some jobs can be done by anyone, and some jobs can only be done only by us. It is our calling to do the job that only we can do.

Sometimes, though, a calling speaks in a language all its own, and we seem beckoned in unusual and unintended directions. Sometimes we are the only ones who can manage the frequently changing status of aging parents, or wayward children. Sometimes siblings call on us at odd moments in life, at the same time that the competing loyalties of family, spouse, and profession pull us in opposite directions. Sometimes the calling is toward a mid-life professional change, that perhaps confuses our partners, our children, and ourselves.

Whatever the particulars of the job that only we can do, we should allow the unique language of the calling to speak to our hearts, and to surely guide us.

Be not afraid.

February 20

> "Our duty, as men and women, is to proceed
> as if limits to our ability did not exist.
> We are collaborators in creation."
>
> *Pierre Teilhard de Chardin*

What factors, intrinsic and extrinsic, create the upsurge of psychic energy necessary to maintain our motivation and momentum as we journey through a busy day of lawyering?

As we face the new challenges of each day, we can alternately consider the application of our "tried and true" solutions, as well as more novel, creative, and experimental approaches. Approaching familiar problems with a new creativity and enthusiasm adds that *joie de vivre* to our day, and an air of confidence and playfulness to our demeanor.

Why not enrich our daily reality by adding a touch of the truly innovative, thereby bringing our unique "good stuff" to each challenge?

February 21

> "Laughter is one of the very privileges of reason,
> being confined to the human species."
>
> *Thomas Carlyle*

The practice of law is most often perceived as a sobering and serious affair, and, in many ways, this is true. However, when anyone, anywhere, deals with the human condition, as attorneys most certainly do, there is always room for irony and humor. Laughter seems to be the body's natural response to the gaps between our aspired perfection and our experienced imperfection, of which there are many in the practice of law!

It has been said that God created human beings because God loves stories. Few truly entertaining stories lack a sheepish acknowledgment of the always aspiring, yet "always missing the mark" (the original meaning of the word "sin") human creature.

During my many years of practicing law, I was often surprised and dismayed to find that so many lawyers were unable to "wear life like a loose garment" and appreciate the comedy inherent within the human condition. Yet, I was often fortunate to find a similarly oriented soul mate in the workplace, someone who could also appreciate the ironies and absurdities of the many obtuse situations presented during the course of the lawyer's day.

Laughter, the natural tranquilizer, can serve as a delightful elixir in lightening the burden of doing very serious work in a hurting world.

February 22

> "To laugh often and much; to win the respect of intelligent people and the affection of children...to leave the world a better place...to know even one life has breathed easier because you have lived....This is to have succeeded."
>
> *Ralph Waldo Emerson*

Do we ever stop to think about what characteristics of young children, peaceful animals, and serene adults make them so incredibly attractive? The disarming lack of guile in these enticing creatures often stirs something deep within us, first to attraction, and then to a form of pensive respect, if not reverence. We stand in the presence of the "real," and, whether or not we consciously give voice to this awareness, our souls fully recognize the full import of this truth.

In the presence of these rare beings, as in the presence of the holy, appearance is reality. There is no glitter, buzz, or self-promotion in their existence. Their presence attests to the ultimate meaning of our oft-used lawyerly term, *res ipsa loquitur*, in that their humble, non-adorned being, does, in fact, speak for itself. These creatures present unself-consciously, in the complete fullness of being. There are no masks, no pretensions, no efforts to be anything other than themselves.

We might ask ourselves what, if any, environments allow us the unself-conscious freedom to just be, to come and to stay, just as we are? Is it when we are thoroughly engaged in reading a well-chosen book, or when we are hiking or running, or when we are just sitting quietly in a peaceful space? Is it when we listen to certain music that our hearts seem literally uplifted to heavenly spheres? Is it just before we go to sleep, when we contemplate that our partner is beside us, and our children are safely asleep in their loving home? Is it when we compassionately journey with another who has earnestly sought our help? Or, is it just sitting in the presence of a compassionate and loving person, one who seeks nothing more than to be his or her authentic self?

If we seek these environments of freedom with ardor, we will find them, for as *Desiderata* tells us, "...for all its sham, drudgery, and broken dreams, it is still a wonderful world."

"God comes to us disguised as our life."

Paula D'Arcy

While it does our soul good to acknowledge the hurts and slights encountered in our daily rounds, it is a far more energizing and refreshing task to reflect on the joys, mini-or-otherwise, that we so often come upon. The gentle words of a friend. An exciting project. A case settled amicably. A child's acceptance into college. A baseball game in the spring. Progress in controlling our tempers. A fascinating book. The beauty of our home. Sunset on a hot August evening. A delicious meal. Unexpected laughter. The cat's reassuring presence. A peaceful resolution of a wrenching custody case. A client's grateful recognition of our work.

As we allow ourselves time to survey the full landscape of our lives, we will be amazed before we are halfway through. The blessings, the grace, the luck, the skill, the excellence, the compassion, the help—call it what you will, the gifted goodness is ubiquitous and extraordinary.

Gratitude, a state of mind and a way of life, can also be the foundation of our most creative living and lawyering, but not if we rush past, driven to the next drama, or wanting more, or envying another for what we do not currently have. We cannot be grateful when we are compulsively driven, competing, comparing, and coveting. However, when we seek the good life and the good of others, in a spirit of gratitude and service, our souls will revel in indescribable joy.

February 24

> "We know truth, not only by reason,
> but also by the heart."
>
> *Blaise Pascal*

The renowned psychologist and philosopher, Carl Jung, had a wooden plaque over his office door that announced, "Bidden or unbidden, God is present." This declaration is as true today as it has ever has been. We do not bring God into our law office, the courtroom, or our client's place of business, since the Ultimate One either exists or not, without reference to our consciousness thereof.

Whether we understand "God" to be the Majestic Lord of all the Universe, the Great Spirit, the g-o-d of "good orderly direction," or the positive energy that causes the planets to revolve on their axes, all we really need to know is that this god is *for us*, as Albert Einstein observed, and this god is present, whether or not, at any given moment, we are aware of that presence.

Thus, without regard to our consciousness or approval, a dynamic force is at work, surrounding the universe with untold goodness, functionality, abundance, and beneficence. Just as the sun supplies over 700 million tons of energy *per second*, and the process of photosynthesis daily converts billions of tons of carbon dioxide to life-sustaining oxygen, so this ultimate force emits immeasurable levels of energy, love, and sustenance to all of creation on a continuous basis.

While we rightly continue to keep the focus on our selves, our profession, and our spiritual development, we can comfortably rest in the assurance that a power greater than ourselves is properly attending to those matters and functions which are not, and need not be, within our sphere of concern or influence.

Life is good.

February 25

> "Peace is not merely a distant goal that we seek,
> but a means by which we arrive at that goal."
>
> *Martin Luther King, Jr.*

We have "enough" when we experience and appreciate physical, mental, and spiritual peace. Some of the most powerful words ever uttered are: "I am enough, I have enough, I do enough." These words can be honestly professed only by those willing to join the path of courageous seekers who insist on defining their own destiny. The "peace that passes all understanding" is the peace derived from right living. This peace cannot be purchased, found, extracted, created, sculpted, or owned. While pleasure can be temporarily found in the enjoyment of people, places, and things, true peace and happiness, of the enduring sort, derive only from good living, from the daily and unspectacular "suiting up, showing up, and doing the next right thing."

This eternal truth has been discovered and rediscovered by every generation, under every circumstance. Prisoners in concentration camps, people living in extreme poverty, inmates serving life sentences, together with people living in ordinary circumstances, continually rediscover the truth that has been an integral part of every spiritual tradition: happiness is an inside job. Always was, and always will be.

We will attain our own bliss when we have taken the time to define and select those values and beliefs which are most meaningful to us, and then attempt, as best we can, to live in accordance with them.

February 26

> "The function of education is to teach one to think intensively and to think critically…intelligence plus character—that is the goal of true education."
>
> *Martin Luther King, Jr.*

There are several emerging and energetic movements within legal academia that attempt to engage students in activities that preview the realities of legal practice and its challenges. For example, Professor Patrick Longan, an ethics professor and recent recipient of the ABA Award for Innovation and Excellence in Teaching, has developed a course entitled "*Living in the Law.*" Distinguished guest speakers are invited to class to discuss issues such as the challenges of finding meaning in the practice of law, how lawyers can find a higher calling to service within their profession, and how lawyers can integrate their professional and spiritual lives.

One class assignment requires that each student participate in an "oral history" interview of a prominent local attorney. In these interviews, the students hear the reflections of senior members of the bar regarding the challenges and joys of life in the law, and write a paper relating the interview to concepts they have studied in class. The students must also choose a biography or autobiography of a famous lawyer, and facilitate a class discussion of the book.

According to Longan, the course introduces students to the idea that professionalism, and the special kind of life that lawyers live, are part of a long tradition from which they can draw sustenance. Longan posits that there is great comfort in knowing that others have fulfilled the expectations of professionalism and lived that life with success and deep joy.

We are all well-advised to seek out such lawyers of stature, since, as Longan says: "…students who are gaining an understanding of the importance and magnitude of what they have undertaken need heroes whose example will sustain them in times of doubt or temptation."

> "Creativity is an experience—to my eye,
> a spiritual experience. It does not matter which
> way you think of it: creativity leading into spirituality
> or spirituality leading to creativity. In fact, I do
> not make a distinction between the two."
>
> *Julia Cameron*

Creativity is the gentle art of allowing our playful spirit to permeate our life's work. When our creativity flows, unencumbered by fear, distraction, or other negativity, we show up for our lawyering fully empowered to give our all to the day's journey. At such spirited times, we bring to the fore every learning, every knowing, and every intuitive impulse within; and, as C.S. Lewis phrases it, *this* moment contains all moments.

The act of creation requires that we broadly branch out from our initial staging area to experiment with many different strands of thinking. To do this, we need to temporarily suspend our "inside-the-box" thinking. While logic, probability, reasoning, and judgment are the good and faithful friends of the successful lawyer, they should sometimes take a back seat to the playful musings of the non-judgmental child within, whose mental sand castles may contain the exact solution we need.

February 28

> "...when you make time for what you love—
> when you nurture your nature—it overflows.
> It causes an energy to overflow into the rest
> of your day or the rest of your life and
> it affects everything else you do."
>
> *Jim Cathcart*

If we aim to live a life that is happy, joyous, and free, we will need at least two things. We need to commit to a path of increasing spiritual growth; and we need to identify those particular people, places, and things that delight us, and partake of these enjoyments as often as possible.

We *do* deserve the comfort and joy that minor, and occasionally, major, treats afford us. The busy and pressured life of lawyering, combined with the ever-increasing demands of our personal lives, require that we allow time for a healthy dose of delight and indulgence, to provide a necessary balance in living our lives.

For some, freshly brewed coffee, sipped quietly in a small café before the work-day begins, or a short afternoon walk on a late fall afternoon, can be the right tonics for increased vigor. For others, choosing a favored wine or dessert for the anticipated evening repast, or browsing through a favorite bookstore, or stopping by a colleague's office for a refreshing break, can mean the difference between an "okay" day and a delightful day. A midday laugh with friends can brighten even the most grueling of workdays.

These small but precious delights stir an inner response of "Oh yes, life is good, just as it is." While the news of the hour and the crisis of the moment will eventually pass, as surely as the sun will set each evening, the enriched experience of living each day, with sufficient "creature comforts," will bring us to a deeper and more satisfying way of being in the world.

> ## "The voyage of discovery lies not in finding new landscapes but in having new eyes."
>
> *Marcel Proust*

Many people properly assert that it is their absolute right to determine for themselves whether or not a deity exists. Yet, the adage that there are no atheists in foxholes holds true for the many of us who, despite our ideology or lack thereof, have urgently whispered our own "foxhole prayers," which usually run along the lines of: "If you get me out of this one, I'll do anything."

Historians and anthropologists tell us that throughout the millennia, in most every time and place, a majority of people have believed in the existence of a power greater than themselves. A Gallup poll (May 2007), reveals that roughly nine in ten Americans believe in God or a higher power (78 percent and 14 percent, respectively).

While so many Americans believe in the existence of a transcendent being, both research and experience reveal that many fewer enjoy an enriching, meaningful, and personal relationship with a superior being. Many explain this lack of connection as resulting from their understanding of a punitive deity presented by parents, teachers, religious leaders, and others.

I certainly can appreciate this "disconnect," since, even though I have been an ordained minister for several years, during my young adulthood, I refused to participate in anything "religious," as I half-heartedly pondered the relevance of the questionable God of my *misunderstanding*. Fortunately, the God I have since come to know had patience, welcomed the formerly cynical, and was in no way dependent for existence upon my lack of understanding.

As practicing lawyers, and as educated people, we are, of course, free to explore these matters for ourselves. If we seek such a relationship, however, we should accept that we alone are responsible for sculpting the contours and dynamics of that relationship, in that the "hand-me-down" religion of prior ages may not be suitable or satisfying.

If the experience of so many others means anything, it may be wise to consider developing a more meaningful I/Thou relationship with our Creator. Assessment of our current theological status, coupled with a look at where we might proceed, followed by initial action steps, is all we need to begin shaping the relationship and meaning we seek.

March 2

> "Friendship is born at that moment when
> one person says to another, 'What! You too?
> I thought I was the only one.'"
>
> *C.S. Lewis*

Fewer activities yield more "bang for the buck" than speaking honestly with a trusted friend or advisor. One colleague speaks of the fearless intimacy involved in "taking off his inner clothes," when engaged in deep and honest discussion with his close friend. Many others speak of the huge weight that dropped from their shoulders as they were finally able to speak with candor about long-buried fears and guilt. *We are as sick as our secrets.* When these secrets are finally revealed through honest discussion with another, they lose their powers to usurp our vital life energy. Letting go of our secrets can release a flow of energy that has been dammed up for a very long time and can reenergize us to the very core. Life is fun again, as we are able to look the world in the eye and go forward with a new confidence.

An amazing by-product of the revelatory process is discovering just how "boring" our worst secrets are, when conveyed to a person who "listens with the heart." The truly compassionate listener accepts that each one of us, given the proper circumstances, is capable of any act of humanity, no matter how distasteful. The caring listener often recounts portions of his or her own personal history, which makes the speaker even more comfortable. Before long, the recounting of repressed fears and past actions that we swore we would "carry to the grave," is no longer viewed as a pointless exercise, but instead is experienced, on a very deep level, like throwing open the windows on the first warm day of spring.

How long will we carry the wounds that bind us? How much longer will we deprive ourselves of the opportunity to be happy, joyous, and free? Do we, or do we not, want to be emotionally free and healthy? If not now, when?

> ## "We are so obsessed with doing that we have no time and no imagination left for being."
> *Thomas Merton*

Awareness is the most effective defense against absorbing and unconsciously living the "negative norms" of the outside world. As we become more self-reflective, we can begin to discern those people, places, and things that leave us feeling light, harmonious, whole, and fulfilled, and those that that have the opposite, dissipating effect. We can then choose to "live in the light," by increasing our association with positive people, places, and things.

With all the busyness in our lives—the rushing from one court appearance or client meeting to the next, and then scurrying from work to home to assume a whole other set of responsibilities—we often assume that there is no time, and probably no need, to look back and evaluate the interactions of the day. We often feel that our time is so limited that only a forward view will fortify us to meet the next upcoming challenge. "What's done is done…can't change it now…must move on," seems the guiding principle.

This is exactly the point where we begin to identify ourselves as "human doings" rather than "human beings." If we treat ourselves as mere legal mechanics, fixing one broken valve and routinely moving on to the next, we deprive ourselves of the experience and expression of our full humanity. There is a wholeness that results from experiencing the full human range of involvement in our lawyering, allowing for each of our body, mind, and spirit to participate.

We are much more than good intellects. Whether we choose to acknowledge it or not, instincts, emotions, reactions, remembrances, emotional intelligence—all of these contribute to our human experience. While as professionals, we often appropriately limit the full expression of these responses when dealing with clients and colleagues, we act at our peril if we hide them from ourselves.

March 4

> "…the moment one definitely commits oneself, then Providence moves too. A whole stream of events issues from the decision, raising in one's favor all manner of unforeseen incidents and meetings and material assistance, which no one could have dreamed would have come his way."
>
> *Goethe*

"*I made a decision…*" These are perhaps the most powerful words a human being can utter, and, in their utterance, human beings become their most powerful and God-like.

When we finally arrive at the critical juncture, where we move from "I really want to stop smoking," or "I have to find a legal position that is more satisfying," to "I have decided to stop smoking," and "I have decided to undertake the necessary steps to find meaningful work," our full personhood comes to the fore as we transition from a sphere of vague desire and wanting to a sphere of cognitive commitment and change.

In fact, the power of the declaration, "*I have decided to…*," situates us within a realm of potentiality that contains the most energetic source of creation and recreation known to humanity.

We often marvel at the most dramatic iterations of this power—the drug addict who completely turns his life around, the tragically injured athlete who walks again, the impoverished single mother who, against all odds, successfully raises her children. Yet, amazingly, we too draw from this very same well of courage and potentiality, when, through our own transformative decisions and ensuing actions, we announce to ourselves and the universe: "*This I must do if I am ever to live the life that I choose.*"

Whether the moment of decision and action is backed by minutes, years, or a lifetime of desire, the instant we commit to move from "I want" to "I will," the world as we have known it changes, as the ultimate exercise of our human powers reverberates throughout the universe.

> "It is the highest form of self-respect to admit our errors and mistakes and make amends for them. To make a mistake is only an error in judgment, but to adhere to it when it is discovered shows infirmity of character."
>
> *Dale E. Turner*

When we are wrong, we should promptly admit it, first to ourselves, and then to others, if it will be helpful. When this is done, we can go forward unencumbered, toward the exciting business of living life.

Acknowledging our errors, without unnecessary angst and drama, constitutes a realistic and honest acceptance of our imperfect humanity. Amends should reflect an honest desire to make right those situations that we have negatively influenced by our attitudes and behavior. By having the courage to honestly assess and speak about our part in a situation, we are relieved of the paralyzing effects of our own judgments, blaming, negativity, fear, rationalization, and self-justification. Making amends sets the matter behind us, once and for all, setting us free to live our best lives.

Since we are the actors who are looking to regain our balance and integrity, we do not need to be concerned if our amends are countered with anger or resentment. Our job is to speak our truth, quietly but firmly, and then to move on. We can walk away from the encounter with our heads held high, for we know that we have courageously completed "the next right thing."

March 6

"I cannot name them by name or hold the image of their faces in my mind, because I do not know their names and I have not seen their faces. I do carry each of them in my grateful heart for each morning that I wake again.

The research renegades and rebels of convention, the pioneers… exploring unmapped microscopic territories, and the altruistic money movers and policy makers. Most of all, I am indebted…to the women who volunteered for…experimental treatments that may or may not have helped them live longer, but led to the current treatments that help me live longer."

Dalene Entenmann

Our initial reflections on the people and things that make life possible, and so worthwhile, typically reveal only the first layer of the abundance of life. Our family, profession, health, homes, friends, meaningful activities—these are the gifts that come to mind when we begin a survey of life's gifts. As we go deeper however, we begin to appreciate, like the cancer survivor quoted above, that there are incredible numbers of people whose very passion for life and their life's calling, have made our lives possible and incredibly richer.

Shortly after 9/11, a friend and I tried desperately to come to terms with what had just happened. I will never forget the tears in his eyes as he passionately proclaimed that every person who had viewed the incredible bravery of the 9/11 heroes should do no less than drop to the ground, and kiss the boots of every firefighter and emergency worker they met.

And what of our ancestors, who unflinchingly braved overwhelming challenges to emigrate to an unknown country, driven by a passion to create a better life for their children? And what of the family doctors who came to our homes, the comforting bus driver who added color to a rainy Monday, and the one teacher who really "got us"?

All of these circles of love, seen and unseen, have given us innumerable reasons for gratitude.

Author and minister Frederick Buechner writes: "The life I touch for good will touch another life, and that in turn another, until who knows where the trembling stops or in what far place my touch will be felt."

Considering that we have been the recipients of such untold goodness, bestowed by so many, including those whose names we do not know and whose tales we have not heard, we too are called to give the world the best we've got, letting our gentle goodness come to rest wherever it is needed.

> "It doesn't interest me to know how old you are.
> I want to know if you will risk looking like a fool,
> for love,
> for your dream
> for the adventure of being alive."
>
> *Oriah*

There are definite pay-offs in staying stuck, in convincing ourselves that there is no way we could change jobs, or do anything other than practice law in just the way we have done it all these many years. We can stay within our own self-constructed comfort zones, and, in so doing, we will never have to face the fear of change, of challenge, and possible failure.

Lawyer-educator George W. Kaufman observes that there are many reasons why lawyers live with career patterns that don't serve their long-term needs, including: 1) a "herd mentality," where lawyers mistake what the legal community labels as success for their personal happiness; 2) the allure of the seductive aspects of success—the power, prestige, and possessions that society values; and, 3) the fear of "losing the investment" associated with our legal education and training. As Kaufman so astutely phrases it, "The more we climb the ladder of success, the more reluctant we are to admit we placed the ladder on the wrong wall."

The long and short of it usually is that we believe that if we stay with the tried-and-true, no matter how soul-crushing, we will feel safer than if we follow the longings of our heart, which include no sure-fire way to define ourselves, or to pay private-school tuitions.

Few lawyers need to be reminded of the value of prudence in considering career changes. In fact, social scientists' studies confirm that one of the outstanding characteristics of practicing lawyers is "prudence," also described in the literature as pessimism and risk-avoidance. Whether we consider ourselves prudent or risk-aversive is not material. The true issue is whether we will continue to devote our precious time and energy to matters that no longer matter to us.

As poet David Whyte writes: "There comes a time when you find that you've promised yourself to things that are just too small."

March 8

"How do you manage your work and your life? Do you live to work or work to live? Does it matter? What does matter? What are your relationships like within your family? At work? Do you spend enough time with the people you love? How healthy is your lifestyle?...Does money buy happiness? How much 'stuff' do you really need to be happy? What about spirituality and service to others; do they have any meaning for you?"

Don Hutcheson

Admonitions about living in accordance with our personal values and beliefs mean little if we have not taken a *recent* inventory to assess what those values and beliefs are. What mattered to us in the early days of our careers may no longer be relevant. With the children grown, have we decided what priorities, along with our work, will replace our childcare responsibilities, or have we merely defaulted mindlessly into spending more time at the office?

Lawyers have little training in goal-setting and career design to guide them throughout the distinct stages of their careers. Yet, we alone are responsible for mindfully choosing what we cherish, and what would cause us to suffer the most if lost, and then, living in accordance with those choices. While family members, mentors, religious leaders, and others may have provided a historical context for our character formation and development, today, we alone are responsible for selecting the current, relevant guiding principles of our lives.

The questions posed in the above quotation must be answered if we are to live a life filled with meaning and satisfaction. If we do not properly reflect on these essential properties of our lives, we will never appreciate who we are at the core, and what things we must undertake in order to be in alignment with our very being. We may also find that, lacking enumerated values and beliefs, we will lack the security of an anchoring frame of reference when difficult challenges are encountered.

Determining who we are, why we are here, and the primary purpose of our lives, are the most sacred aspects of our life's work.

> "In the middle of the road of my life
> I awoke in the dark wood
> Where the straight road was lost."
>
> *Dante*

Through a uniquely styled analysis, Old Testament scholar and theologian, Walter Brueggemann, charts the flow of the sacred Psalms, and of our lives, as frequently moving from being securely oriented, to being painfully disoriented, and finally, to being surprisingly reoriented. Brueggemann loosely categorizes each of the Psalms under the three themes of "orientation," "disorientation," and "new orientation," seeking to demonstrate how such groupings correspond to the actual flow of human life throughout different seasons.

The "orientation" Psalms are typically the familiar poetry of praise and gratitude, uttered from a place of relative safety and security. In discussing the Psalms of "disorientation," Brueggemann specifically identifies and embraces the tradition of protest found in the Psalms, the "how could you do this to me, a faithful follower?" genre. Brueggemann strongly encourages particular attention to the "disorientation" Psalms when we are seeking to find our own way through loss, longing, and depression, finally moving toward the "new orientation" and phases of wholeness and health.

There may be a select few individuals who primarily live in the "orientation" phase of life. Many more of us, it seems, try to keep our heads above water as we struggle to reach the distant shores of the joyful "new orientation" that Brueggemann describes. Yet, like the cozy home and warm meal that await after a particularly stormy day, the hoped-for passage onto new shores will eventually materialize, and will restore our tired bodies and sagging spirits, if we faithfully continue to suit up, show up, and do the next right thing.

March 10

> "It's only when we truly know and understand that we have a limited time on earth—and that we have no way of knowing when our time is up, we will then begin to live each day to the fullest, as if it was the only one we had."
>
> *Elisabeth Kubler-Ross*

Do we ever celebrate the "ordinary" events that occur in our everyday lives? Waiting for an extraordinary celebratory moment can place undue emphasis upon the event itself, rather than our human enjoyment and need for celebration itself.

We all benefit from the enhanced perspective that derives when we incorporate positive and playful events into our lives. For maximum effect, the nature of the event or celebration should be uniquely satisfying to our sense of enjoyment. Variety and diversity in our celebratory days or evenings will result in heightened refreshment.

A major purpose of these "everyday celebrations" is to add levity to a life that is chock-full of lawyerly responsibility. If we seek maximum vitality, we need to change the pace, the rhythm, the scheduling, and the venues of an otherwise overly controlled and predictable existence, lest, as Joseph Campbell warns, we begin sleepwalking through our lives. Time for romance, whimsy, nature, laughter, and play are the daily celebratory activities that can stave off the profound alienation that can result from too many nights and weekends at the office.

We should often look within, find our bliss, and plan just the right events to satisfy the playful, creative, and joy-seeking soul within.

March 11

> ## "Imitation is a necessity
> ## of human nature."
>
> *Oliver Wendell Holmes*

As children, we all initially seek to please our fathers and our mothers. This is a primary and universal motivational source. As we go further through life, our parents begin to fade into our motivational background, while our spouses and newly created family claim center stage. In the middle of our lives, a healthy person begins to parent himself or herself; however, the principle of achieving and modeling the behavior of a parent figure continues throughout our later years. We should seek to find a mentor figure within our professional sphere who can serve the role of guide, model, and supportive person to nurture our successful journey through the stormy seas of law and life.

March 12

> "If you were going to die soon and
> had only one phone call you could make,
> who would you call and what would you say?
> And why are you waiting?"
>
> *Stephen Levine*

We are here for a short time on the earth. It is easy to get lost in the trappings of the good life and the fast lane. But time waits for no man. Develop a wise head on a young body. See the short span of time you have to achieve your good work. Realize that you are but a grain of sand in the vast desert of time. Realize your overall insignificance in your place of work. In your life, what mark will you leave? Whose lives will you touch positively? What is your positive spread of effect? Are you responsible for achieving something that will outlast you? When you approach your work from this vantage point, it allows you to bring your higher self to the task at hand.

March 13

> "Man was made for joy and woe,
> and when this we surely know,
> through the world we safely go.
> Joy and woe are woven fine,
> a clothing for the soul divine."
>
> *William Blake*

The blessings received in life, starting with the gift of life itself, are truly incalculable for those who have eyes to see and ears to hear. Making a daily gratitude list can jumpstart a day that is graced by a flowing abundance, rather than one in which we trudge every reluctant step, clawing away for what we think we need. Profound gratitude consists of not only realizing what blessings we currently have, but also remembering when we did not have them. Thus, today we can not only appreciate the joys of a loving family and a meaningful work life, but we can also recall when these blessings seemed totally beyond our grasp, reserved for others, perhaps, but not for us.

My early-morning journaling begins with a recognition of my four major gratitude categories: gratitude to my God for never-ending, undeserved grace; gratitude for the circumstances of my current life; gratitude for the specific people who so enrich my life; and gratitude for the things that enhance my daily living—good work, good health, and so many others. Though the categories remain static, the particular entries vary in accordance with the ebb and flow of the particular day.

Having so reviewed our daily blessings, it becomes difficult, if not impossible, to ask "why me?" when minor difficult circumstances are encountered. These petty annoyances can be more readily absorbed when viewed within the larger landscape of our innumerable blessings.

March 14

> "It is not the strongest of the species that survives, nor the most intelligent that survives. It is the one that is most adaptable to change."
>
> *Charles Darwin*

It sometimes takes a psychic-shattering experience to displace old hardened ways of thinking before we will allow in the porous gray matter of new thought. Yet, as we pursue our personal growth, we also have the preferred option of prospectively interrogating our long- standing beliefs, some of which may no longer serve us. Unexamined, these beliefs may go unchallenged during our entire life-cycle, from childhood through adolescence, and fully into adulthood.

The world is a vastly changing place, where adaptation, resilience, flexibility, and an open approach toward all possibilities are the desired coins of the realm. Today, our lives and our world are changing so rapidly that it is not at all unthinkable that the evolution of a new, "modern-day brain" may be in the offing. Thus, we might spend some time imagining that much of the significant information we have learned about the world might turn out to be limited, superseded, or just plain wrong, possibly overturning many of our foundational beliefs.

Flexibility and openness position us for adaptation in a modern-day world that is caught in the currents of very rapid and radical change.

March 15

> "The idea of twenty-four hour living applies primarily to the emotional life of the individual. Emotionally speaking, we must not live in yesterday, nor tomorrow."
>
> *Bill Wilson*

Living one day at a time allows us to be immediately present to the innumerable happenings that occur during the course of a single day. If we are still ruminating on yesterday's court appearance, or fearful about tomorrow's meeting with our boss, we do not do justice to the "very life of life" contained within the present day. As the Sanskrit poem tells us, within these mere twenty-four hours "…lie all the realities and verities of existence."

Throughout the ages, we have been sagely advised to study the birds of the air, and the lilies of the field, for "…while they neither toil nor spin, not even the splendors of Solomon could be more splendid." While human beings, including those who live in the most affluent country in the world, seek to "warehouse" an excessive amount of material possessions, the birds of the air are content to seek and use what they need for the moment.

Although we live in one of the wealthiest countries in the world, and labor within one of the highest-paying professions, many of us harbor an innate fear that the future holds within it the calamity that will lead to our ultimate financial and emotional unraveling.

While we have all witnessed or experienced financial struggles along the way, the truth seems to be that few who have committed to a life of continuous personal development have found these obstacles to be insurmountable. The spiritually mature have always known that freedom from fear is much more important than freedom from want, and, by keeping the focus on their inner spiritual condition, they have generally been able to deal with, or overcome, these difficulties.

Serenity, one of the first fruits of spiritual development, does not guarantee freedom from the normal storms of life, however, it steadfastly delivers the shelter and solace that keeps us afloat during such times.

March 16

> "In ordinary life we hardly realize that we receive
> a great deal more than we give, and that it is
> only with gratitude that life becomes rich."
>
> *Dietrich Bonhoeffer*

Psychological studies now confirm what the wise have always known: the mindful cultivation of gratitude can measurably change a person's attitude and a person's life.

Psychology professor and author, Dr. Robert Emmons, comprehensively presents the current scientific research on gratitude in his very readable book, appropriately entitled, "*Thanks*." The research confirms that those who undertake simple practices, such as keeping a daily gratitude journal, often experience better feelings about their life as a whole. In particular, they are more likely to attain their personal goals, have higher levels of positive emotions, and have lower levels of stress. Such persons place less emphasis on material possessions, and often engage in giving service to others.

In short, scientists, now joining philosophers, theologians, and sages throughout the centuries, concur that if we choose to live our lives in an intentionally grateful manner, we can live longer and more meaningful lives.

All lawyers can begin to catalogue their gratitude particulars by reference to their professional standing, whether or not they also enjoy the blessings of health, family, friends, and earthly delights. As lawyers, we are educated, trained, employable, respected, and capable of attaining an unlimited number of professional goals through the practice of our noble profession. The word lawyer is, in a practical manner, synonymous with choice, and that, in itself, is a matter for great rejoicing and gratitude.

March 17

> "Hope begins in the dark, the stubborn hope that if you just show up and try to do the right thing, the dawn will come. You wait and watch and work: You don't give up."
>
> *Anne Lamott*

Accounts of the intractable human desire to find "quick fixes" for characters and other matters in need of repair are legion. Since at least the recorded beginnings of civilization, human beings have sought to address their perceived or actual deficiencies through the "easier, softer way" of the quick fix. Yet, if it has taken us years of dereliction to "get into the woods" with a particular behavior pattern, we cannot realistically expect to reverse the consequences thereof overnight.

Yet, rather than face the discomfort associated with the recognition that something about us is not working and needs fixing, the human penchant to seek and fashion fast-acting, *faux* cures seems nearly universal. The wisdom of the ages requires, however, that if we truly seek transformative recovery, rather than temporary relief, we must undertake the work required in tearing out the faulty foundation underlying our behavior and building a new one.

Quick fixes—whether in the form of alcohol, drugs, over-spending, overwork, continuous web-surfing, gambling, or other mood-altering occurrences, or perhaps, the media's daily offering of "magical" diet pills, 10-day body-building plans, or 15-minute management techniques—may be quick, but they are seldom long-lasting or healthy.

Although a more realistic plan will take time and intentional action, we need only approach the needed undertaking on a one-day-at-a-time basis. Olympic medals have been won, great literature and art have been produced, bar exams have been passed, and dissertations and theses have been completed, following this simple model.

One day at a time, one right action at a time, we can let tomorrow take care of itself.

March 18

> ## "I have discovered that all human evil comes from this, man's being unable to sit still in a room."
>
> *Blaise Pascal*

The less chaos we allow into our lives, the more serenity we will know. If we can keep our focus on our chosen tasks and attitudes, we will be better equipped to sidestep the drama created by others.

It is often the case that the people who most ignore their own personal growth will seek to impose their disorder on others. We all have encountered people who seem to harangue everyone they meet, describing in inordinate detail their ever-increasing list of trials, tribulations, and daily crises. It is in our best interest to learn to politely but firmly set boundaries with such people, or they will continuously distract us from meeting our own responsibilities for the day.

While thoughtful listening to others is an important part of the lawyer's daily rounds, we should identify those persons who continuously "live in the problem," and not in the solution. Excessive discussion about past and projected difficulties is unhealthy for both the speaker and the listener. As much as is practicable in any given situation, we should attempt to gently but firmly distance ourselves from such discussions, so that we can preserve the peace and orderly completion of tasks that we are working so hard to attain.

March 19

> ## "This is one of the sacred duties of imagination: Honorably to imagine your self."
>
> *John O'Donohue*

The manner in which we look at things determines what we see. When we view the world with grateful eyes, the world reveals more of its unlimited graciousness. When we view the world with fear, the world becomes even more threatening, and we perceive our inability to meet its ceaseless challenges. Perception creates our truth and determines whether we will live "hell on earth" or "heaven on earth."

Joshua Ferris begins his first novel, *Then We Came to the End*, a humorous take on the "rat-race" dynamics of the work world, with these intriguing words: "We were fractious and over-paid. Our mornings lacked promise. At least those of us who smoked had something to look forward to at ten-fifteen."

"Our mornings lacked promise!" We, the citizens of the greatest country in the world, with every convenience and opportunity at our fingertips, and *our mornings lack promise!!!* Shamelessly paraphrasing Paul Newman's infamous words in *Cool Hand Luke*, what we have here is a failure of imagination!

So many of us perceive a flattened world because our looking has become dulled and lacking promise. "*Another day, another dollar, same old, same old,*" we cynically repeat to ourselves and others. We have tragically lost touch with the sacred and mysterious aspects of encounter with each thought process, each creature, each happening. We can no longer appreciate the stories, the hope, the delight, the ironies, the kindness, and the solutions, that the current day, and the immediate moment, hold.

If ever we have stood, listening, outside a child's playroom, we may have been given temporary access to the paradise of imagination, where battles are enacted, heroes emerge, victory speeches are uttered, nobility reigns, and the great warrior sets off again for the next challenge. Smiling poignantly, we may wonder, at what point in time did our world cease to hold such magic, such purity and righteousness? Where and when did we lose our sense of romance, our ideals, our clear sense of right and wrong, our noble and heroic impulses? When and why did we cross those lines from "being adventurous," to "being practical," to "being bored and boring"?

And, most importantly, is there any chance we can find these things again?

> ## "Pride makes us artificial and humility makes us real."
>
> *Thomas Merton*

We as lawyers have enjoyed the hospitality and encouragement of a privileged place in society, and as leaders, we are at times, deservedly or not, exalted, and placed on societal pedestals. This rise to stardom can be destabilizing and uncomfortable, particularly if we do not have the esteem to acknowledge and appropriately appreciate our accomplishments.

Striking a healthy balance between knowing who we are, and what we are capable of, while at the same time remaining humbly grounded in our humanity, is the daunting task of this high-wire act. While following a path graced with intellectual and economic privilege, it is often easy to mindlessly wander toward grandiosity, arrogance, self-indulgence, and conceit.

Attention to our chosen spiritual practices can and will provide sturdy barriers to guard against such meanderings.

March 21

> "There is no greater gift than awareness...as a lawyer you can make a great difference—greater than you might imagine—in your own life and in the lives of others, by reclaiming your right to a balanced awareness of both the inner and outer dimensions of life."
>
> *Steven Keeva*

There is a spiritual axiom that holds that we cannot attain the spiritual goals that we seek because we are already have them. What is missing is awareness, and, despite our many academic accomplishments, we actually have to be taught to see, to attain the oft-discussed "beginner's mind" of the wisdom literature. The spiritual greats, whether Buddha, Jesus, or other masters, uniformly spoke of being awake, of having the eyes to see, and of clearing the lens of our biased perspectives. As William Blake wrote: "If the doors of perception were cleansed, everything would be seen as it is."

Painful as it is to admit, we usually see everything through the lens of our own self-centered agendas. "How will this affect me?" or "How will this make me feel?" are usually the first reactions to new stimuli. If we are to attain desired spiritual growth and wholeness, we need a new lens through which to view life, one that is wiped clean of our fears, fears that we won't get what we want or that we will lose what we have.

In the world of cleansed awareness, we move toward seeing things as they really are, and not as we would have them be. With practiced mindfulness and awareness, we begin to move away from fear and into the realm of love that "casts out all fear." As we come to regularly practice mindfulness, we can observe our mental and emotional inner journeying over a period of time, seeing that we largely create our own experiences through our perceptions of them.

As a man thinketh, so shall he be, said Jesus.

March 22

> "There is not one big cosmic meaning for all,
> there is only the meaning we each give to our life,
> an individual meaning, an individual plot, like an
> individual novel, a book for each person."
>
> *Anais Nin*

What percentage of a professional's life should be devoted to work? As lawyers, we take pride in our work ethic, and recognize the need for a quality process if we are to produce a product which is satisfying to all concerned. However, we must guard against the compulsive tendencies whereby we become a human doing, as opposed to a human being. Is the process of how we live our lives as valued as the outcomes we have produced in our lives? Do we measure our process and progress one day at a time, one year at a time, or do we measure it at all?

We all attempt to sift meaning from the sometimes unpredictable events and patterns of our lives. We need to take the time to survey our personal landscape, evaluating who we are, where we are, and how far we've come, in order to both claim the growth attained, and to cast a forward eye upon the unexplored terrain that awaits us.

March 23

> ## "There is more wisdom in your body
> ## than in your deepest philosophy."
>
> *Friedrich Nietzsche*

Somewhere within deep recesses, our body holds, on a feeling level, our primitive, instinctive reactions toward different situations, contexts, and sets of circumstances. It is uncanny and mysterious that we record and know intuitively where potential danger lurks, and where solutions to problems dwell. Our body leans instinctively toward health and homeostasis, and is exceedingly competent in sensing impending peril, and identifying all types of hazardous substances and scenarios.

Our lived experiences have a form all their own, and negative ones have a distinctive pattern that resonate inner discord, known as body memories. The body knows when someone, something, or someplace is not good for us. We need only to tune into the faint echoes within for direction.

This internal GPS system was primitively hard-wired into our biological makeup to meet survival and procreation needs in our ancestral past. In our modern times, we have forgotten to listen, and the signals appear to have grown faint. Yet, we can rest assured that the purpose and nature of the body's guidance system continues to emit telling signals for those who have the ears to hear. *Be still and know.*

March 24

> *"Tradition means giving votes to that obscurest of classes, our ancestors. It is the democracy of the dead."*
>
> *W.H. Auden*

Kind thoughts travel encased in deeds, gestures, notes, and flowers. When we allow the time for sentiment and thoughtfulness to take on a form, we breathe life and vibrancy into the rich tapestry of life.

We are symbolic creatures with a penchant for romance, harmony, order, and delight. We like to occasionally dress up, and celebrate life's sweeter moments with some pomp and circumstance. We hail each new season with the excitement of new themes, colors, clothes, and festive celebrations. Our lives are like the movement of a grand old ballroom waltz, which has a set form and order, a curtsy and a bow, where the prescribed form is followed even in merriment. Culture, manners, protocol, and tradition refine and elevate our lives, providing order and harmony, and easing the discomfort of often-chaotic environs.

Despite the countless "lawyers' jokes," we are generally admired by our fellows as examples of the professional life worth leading. If we ever wish to reinvigorate the noble profession, it is our responsibility, and our privilege, to reflect upon the habits, protocols, characters, and statesperson-like qualities demonstrated by our legal predecessors of excellence, who so ably shaped the learned society of which we are now esteemed members.

After glancing backward, the next step focuses on the future, which will be shaped, for good or for ill, by each current legal practitioner. Two questions seem in order: How does my daily practice as a lawyer reflect, or not reflect, the highest ideals of the profession? And, what will be my contribution to the legal heritage bequeathed to those who are just beginning their journey in the law?

> ## "Jump, and you will find out how to unfold your wings as you fall."
>
> *Ray Bradbury*

Is there relief in sight? Can we see our way out of the forest of disillusionment, rancor, and unholy misery? Sometimes our way is blocked by fear. We are afraid to rock the boat, to change paths, to set out on uncharted waters, and to go where no person that we know has successfully gone. So we stand by and abide in our discontent, accepting second-best, rather than risk the loss of social position, professional status, and other compensating factors. And, we timidly query, what if we dare to change course, and arrive at a place that is no better, and, potentially far worse, than where we stand today? *Then what?*

In this state of psychic paralysis, we metaphorically attempt to hold court over our lives. Like an ailing king, we are reluctant to spend all of our energy and attention on the matters of our kingdom, for the kingdom is divided. There are parts of our current dwelling place that we value, cherish, and desire, and there are parts, like a septic limb, that we would sever. The psychic energy needed to deal with our conflicted situation is ever-depleting.

There comes a time, says poet Anais Nin, when the risk of remaining tight in the bud becomes more painful than the risk it takes to blossom. Life itself, like a push me/pull me toy, ultimately paves the way for an axial shift toward the new or the old, or even the unexpected, but, as always, mindful awareness and courageous action are required. Our charge is to deal with the fear that overhangs the uncharted waters of our lives through continued attention to the spiritual practices contained in our reflections.

March 26

> ## "A man may fulfill the object of his existence by asking a question he cannot answer, and attempting a task he cannot achieve."
>
> *Oliver Wendell Holmes*

What does a self-actualized lawyer look like?

Many of us may recall Abraham Maslow's psychological theory that, in its basic form, holds that as humans' basic needs are met, they are able to increasingly satisfy higher needs within a set hierarchy. This hierarchy is often depicted as a five-level pyramid, beginning with physiological needs at the bottom, followed by safety and social needs, followed by esteem, cognitive and esthetic needs, finally culminating in the highest levels of self-actualization and self-transcendence.

Maslow describes self-actualizing people as those able to "…embrace the realities of the world (including themselves) rather than denying or avoiding them; they are spontaneous in their ideas and actions; they are creative; they are interested in solving their own and others' problems; they feel a closeness to other people; they have a system of morality that is fully internalized and independent of external authority; and, they employ methods of discernment in navigating life's journey."

Today's legal profession is in great need of self-actualized lawyers. It is hoped that the practices suggested in our reflections might lead us, one small step at a time, to the highest levels of self-transcendence.

March 27

> "Many of us spend our whole lives running from feelings with the mistaken belief that you cannot bear the pain. But you have already borne the pain. What you have not done is feel all you are beyond that pain."
>
> *Kahlil Gibran*

It is sometimes very difficult to meet the day with courage when we feel increasingly worn down by situations not of our own making, and, therefore, not of our own correcting. When struggling, yet again, with an ailing parent, an emotionally hurting child, a spouse in the throes of depression, we may find ourselves asking the new day: "What's the use? Yesterday, and many yesterdays before that, I showed up for the situation, with a positive and energetic attitude, and what happened? Just the same old negativity, the same old descent into hell. Why even try again today?"

Why? Because we have been given one precious life and one precious day to experience that amazing gift, with all of its unique mystery, joy, confusion, beauty, messiness, pain, and awe. And, as Mother Theresa taught, it was never between us and them anyway, it was always just between us and God.

We have choices. We can approach the day with yesterday's leftover negativity and worry, or we can spend some quiet time seeking new courage, new direction, new gratitude, and new energy to recharge our sagging spirits. We can sit humbly in the presence of that which is sacred to us, and ask for the courage to simply "suit up, show up, and do the next right thing" for this day *only*.

During times of despondency, we often become increasingly aware that lack of power is our ultimate dilemma. Thus, it is only when we seek assistance and direction from a power greater than ourselves, however defined, that our problems begin to diminish.

While the image of the powerful and ever-competent lawyer may predominate our consciousness, our vulnerable humanity can revisit frequently, like an unwelcome cousin at our doorstep, dressed up in emotional turmoil that we can neither conquer nor wish away. True courage requires that, at such times, we neither run nor recriminate. True courage requires that we enter the place of pain, accept its disturbing and frustrating manifestations, and remember that we are much more than the problem at hand.

Having so equipped ourselves, we are ready to take that one small and extremely courageous step toward living in the light, whether that involves calling an advisor, helping another who is in crisis, or setting off to do a productive day's work.

Now, my friend, you have not only borne the pain, you have gone beyond it.

March 28

"Sometime in your life, hope that you might see one starved man, the look on his face when the bread finally arrives. Hope that you might have baked it or bought it or even kneaded it yourself. For that look on his face, for your meeting his eyes across a piece of bread, you might be willing to lose a lot, or suffer a lot, or die a little, even."

Daniel Berrigan

A fierce and vital energy lies at the heart of our legal craft.

Aggressively and zealously, we labor to safeguard our clients' rights. We defend those who are weak, and we come to the aid of the accused, attempting to protect not only the individual involved, but also our treasured concepts of justice and order. As advocates, we strenuously work on behalf of those in need, whose pain is genuine, and whose loss, anticipated or realized, runs deep. The plight of the vulnerable requires the assistance of able counsel, and, for this, we were called.

We do not hesitate to fight the good fight to redress wrongs done, nor do we recoil from combating injustice of any kind. These are the impulses that originally stirred our imaginations toward the practice of law, and, through awareness and reflection, they are the impulses that continue to move us toward all that is excellent and noble.

March 29

> ## "We dance around the ring and suppose,
> ## but the secret sits in the middle and knows."
>
> *Robert Frost*

I remember the joy of discovering, well into my adulthood, that I could actually straighten a single drawer in my kitchen without cleaning the entire house.

Life and lawyering are not "all-or-nothing" propositions. We can research a single point in our upcoming argument, even if we do not have the time to deliver up the fully composed brief, bluebook citations and all. In fact, there can be a great sense of accomplishment derived from the completion of small, but essential, elements of a larger task, and then moving on with fluidity to the next matter that deserves our attention. Like an artful dancer, even on busy days, we can move in and out of diverse projects, client meetings, administrative functions, and other responsibilities, one graceful move at a time.

"All-or-nothing" thinking, a first cousin to the ultimate saboteur, perfectionism, is an always destructive tool that sets us up for failure from the very start. This type of attitude demands that we either complete an undertaking, fully and finally, or we have failed completely. A single imperfection or lack of completeness equates to total failure.

We can challenge this thinking by recognizing that few things, most particularly, complex legal matters, are so black or white, or can be completed in a totally linear fashion. Few legal questions and issues can be readily marked "yes" or "no," and put in our outbox with deliberate speed. The lawyer's craft is comprised of evolving analysis, judgment, and deliberation, and the frequent reworking of previously perceived solutions. Periods of rest, coupled with attention to unrelated matters, provide the creative space in which answers to problems are allowed to gracefully emerge, sometimes fully formed. This explains why so many solutions "magically" appear when we are in the shower, or attending our child's soccer game. The creative process cannot be forced in accordance with our time demands. Like the maturing of a fine wine, our best answers often emerge during the unattended fermenting process, as the natural rhythm of creative problem-solving gives way to the resolution.

March 30

> ## "Wear life like a loose garment, and don't take yourself too darn seriously."
>
> *Michael A. Murphy*

Gregory Pierce, author of *Spirituality at Work, Ten Ways to Balance Your Life on the Job*, lightheartedly explains the components of a spirituality of work for those who consider themselves "piety impaired." Pierce sees the need for developing such a spirituality since, he believes, there is a creative energy in our work that is somehow tied to divine energy, and if we can come to truly appreciate that connection, remarkable results may occur.

In Pierce's view, a spirituality of work is not pious, or serious, or accompanied by grand displays of religiosity. It is something quite different, in that the spirituality essentially derives from the work itself, and becomes activated when we become aware of the intrinsically spiritual nature of the work we are doing. If we can maintain conscious contact with God or our other sense of ultimate reality during the busyness of our workdays, we will perform our work in accordance with our deepest sense of meaning.

Pierce suggests ten ways of incorporating such a spirituality into our work lives, which include: surrounding our workplace with objects that are sacred to us (family pictures or travel mementoes, for example), learning to live with our own and others' imperfections, assuring quality in the work we do, showing appreciation for our co-workers, cooperatively building community in the workplace, employing the Golden Rule in all our dealings, balancing and rebalancing our life priorities, and engaging in ongoing personal and professional development.

By employing these and the other practices discussed in this book, we can come to discharge our professional responsibilities in a manner that is better aligned with our personal values and beliefs, and, thus, more intrinsically satisfying.

> "It is not enough to be busy;
> so are the ants.
> The question is:
> What are we busy about?"
>
> *Henry David Thoreau*

Becoming still and centered allows us to identify "what's in our boat," that is, what are the things we are responsible for, on any given day.

If we take care of our lives, our needs, and the specific responsibilities of the current moment, we are much better positioned to have a peaceful and fulfilling day. However, only quiet discernment will reveal what we should take responsibility for within any given context. Although innumerable situations and people within our sphere of influence may require assistance of some sort, we are finite individuals, with limited physical, mental, and emotional resources. If we attempt to become the "healer" of all, we will lose our grounding, our centeredness, and our effectiveness.

Each new day requires a new appraisal of where our energies should be directed. Morning quiet time yields a sharper focus for the day's assessment of "what's in my boat."

April 1

> ## "Is there some principle of nature which states that we never know the quality of what we have until it is gone?"
>
> *Herman Melville*

Many years ago I heard a minister preach a sermon entitled *"Things We Have Not Lost."* The minister related the story of a woman who had just received word that her son, a captured POW, was about to be released. Local and national media carried the uplifting story of the mother's joy, including her repeated exclamations of how this was "the happiest day of her life."

The audience had no problem relating to the deep gratitude and joy associated with this "lost and found" story. It is the rare individual who has not experienced a health scare, or an endangered child, or some other potential critical loss, where they would have traded *everything* in order to be relieved of the crisis. Yet, the minister's message and accompanying challenge ran much deeper. "Why," he asked, "do we not daily exclaim with euphoric joy over those people and things which *do* exist in our lives, those people and things that we have *not* lost?"

Well, we may cavalierly ascribe our lack of expressed gratitude to the normal human tendency to become complacent, to take things for granted. Yet, as we become more self-aware and soulfully conscious, we might remember that what is "normal" in today's over-stressed and often joyless world may be neither healthy nor appropriate for us. Even a cursory review of the major facts of our lives—that we live in the greatest country in the world, that we are educated and employed, that we have people who we love and who love us in return, and that we are sufficiently healthy to read this book—these factors are stunning in their magnificence, if only we have the "eyes to see and the ears to hear."

As people who live in untold abundance in a world where most people go to bed hungry each night, it is not "good enough" for us to await a potential tragedy before cultivating and living our gratitude. Soulful awareness requires, at a minimum, that we take stock of our blessings, at least as much as we bemoan the potential loss of those things that we cherish.

> "Whatever your life's work is, do it well.
> A man should do his job so well that the living,
> the dead, and the unborn could do it no better."
>
> *Martin Luther King, Jr.*

In many ways, time is truly an illusion. At birth, we are not just given future time; rather, we are given the potentiality of creating and living a purposeful and meaningful life and legacy. We can live that life with unbounded energy and abundance, or we can hoard our vitality, parsimoniously doling it out, as if allocating ten-minute intervals to a client's billable hours.

The oft-heard complaint "I have no time" can be disingenuous. Einstein, Picasso, and Beethoven had the same twenty-four hours in a day that we have. And, is it not true, that when we firmly decide to do something that our heart desires, we accomplish it, no matter how busy the day? The question is not whether we have enough time to do a satisfying day's work, or balance our professional and personal lives, or integrate true passion into our workdays. The real question is whether we will undergo the spiritual conditioning that is necessary if we are ever to know our true desires, and then act in a manner that assures that they will come to fruition.

If we allow these desires to continually "default" to the bottom of our "to do" lists, we can be assured that our dreams will never see the light of day.

April 3

> ## "If you can spend a perfectly useless afternoon in a perfectly useless manner, you have learned how to live."
>
> *Lin Yutang*

Few things in life are as precious, refreshing, and absolutely required as "unproductive time." If we are not permitting ourselves our required amount of downtime, creating good work will become more and more difficult, as we are giving out from an unstocked pond. If we are not reinvigorating ourselves with what sounds like an oxymoron, "scheduled downtime," we will soon arrive at the point of exhaustion, frustration, and depression. It is important to actually calendar our free time as carefully as we would schedule a client meeting, in that experience shows that downtime is the first thing to get downsized when the demands on our time exceed the supply. The downtime allowance is as essential to a lawyer's functioning as a well-Shephardized brief.

As we learned early in our law school days, the law *is* a demanding mistress. Nonetheless, an essential part of any spiritual journey to wholeness requires that we pay attention to body, mind, and spirit. With proper attention to each dimension, we can resume our work with a heightened sense of creativity and enthusiasm, better equipped to attend to the task at hand.

April 4

> ## "He who is not every day conquering some fear has not learned the secret of life."
>
> *Ralph Waldo Emerson*

The wise have always known that a daily review of character paves the way to self-knowledge and living a better life. A frequent review of our relationships and interactions with family, friends, work, community, and life in general, can pinpoint those situations that bring joy, and those that are vexatious, and in need of alteration or acceptance. While we often use the exterior circumstances of our lives as the starting point for our review, the "eye of our eye" should ultimately center on our inner selves, and how our attitudes and behaviors have influenced the events of our lives.

When I journal in the morning, I quickly sketch the activities and encounters of the previous day, allowing any and all reactions thereto, no matter how petty, to appear on the page. In doing so, I get to "live life twice," the first, in "actual" time, during the frenetic give-and-take of a busy life; the second, in "reflective" time, when the deeper shape and meaning of each encounter is revealed. Allowing the time to nurture a greater awareness of everyday events, I come to a better appreciation of what is right in my life, what needs correction, and, most importantly, what is transpiring in the "now" of my life.

How many times does a day, a week, or a season go by, when we have no idea of the rhythm, tenor, and pattern of the many events that have transpired? Without reflection time, our attention remains focused on the news of the hour and the crisis of the moment. With reflection time, we are able to grasp a clearer understanding of who we are, who we wish to be, and our progress in "becoming ourselves," as the poet May Sarton phrases it.

April 5

> "Somewhere there are people to whom
> we can speak without having the words
> catch in our throats.... A circle of friends.
> Someplace where we can be free."
>
> *Starhawk*

Love and belonging are basic human needs. The business of law can be cold, cruel, and bruising at times. The law can be unfair, and people can amplify the unfairness. When we are downtrodden and in need of support, we need to go where it is warm and where our spirits will be lifted up. Go where the love flows freely. Each of us must be able to locate the "warmth" within our respective circumstances. We should not isolate with our misery. Darkness broods in the inner sanctum of our psyche. We can consciously release our negativity to the universe and join in the warmth and harmony of the good people and circumstances around us.

April 6

> ## "No one is as capable of gratitude as one who has emerged from the Kingdom of night."
>
> *Elie Wiesel*

When life gets tough, as it sometimes does, time spent in grateful reflection provides needed understanding, perspective, and balance. Inner reflection, viewed through the lens of gratitude, is a very effective tonic for restoring sagging spirits and restoring equilibrium.

True gratitude reflects thankfulness for our blessings, and can also include a remembrance of what life was like before those blessings entered our lives. We are twice blessed when, for example, we experience gratitude for our loving family, and also remember prior days, when the comfort of loved ones was not to be found.

Viewing any situation through the lens of gratitude both illumines our current gifts and reveals the contours of a purposeful plan, much greater than our own, that has brought us to exactly the spot where we stand today. This beneficent plan has played well in every major area of our lives, yet its goodness is most often recognized only retrospectively. Thus we see that whenever we *needed* (not just *wanted*) particular events to come to pass, they eventually did, albeit not in our time frame, or in accordance with our specific "delivery demands." Reviewing the path we have travelled, we see that we always received what was necessary to allow us to move to our next level of learning, meaning, and growth.

Today, our gratitude can include both a sincere thankfulness for the current blessings of our lives, as well as a profound thanksgiving for the beneficence that has brought us to this day, and that will continue to maintain us as we move forward.

April 7

"There is a central will to create that is part of our human heritage and potential. Because creation is always an act of faith, and faith is a spiritual issue, so is creativity. As we strive for our highest selves, our spiritual selves, we cannot help but be more aware, more proactive, and more creative."

Julia Cameron

Our busy days as practicing lawyers, coupled with our multi-layered personal lives, often allow little time for purposeful reflection. At nightfall, even if we do take the time to mentally tally up the day's events, we often find ourselves creating yet another "to-do" list for tomorrow. It seems that our untamed busyness presents two exhausting alternatives: either we are actually running from one crisis to the next, or, during our so-called "free time," we are, in fact, planning how to respond to *upcoming* crises!

There is a middle ground, however, and this can be found in journaling. With the proper mindset, we can let our mind, emotions, and spirit "speak" their truth, unfiltered, on the written page. In so doing, we can let our inner, creative self fling joys, concerns, discoveries, unformed fears, and every free-floating fragment of our consciousness across the page. Journaling relieves much of the burden of carrying our questions, concerns, fears, and projections throughout the day, thereby unblocking a great spiritual force of creativity.

Julia Cameron, author of *The Artist's Way*, the seminal book on creativity, provides a simple yet effective method of journaling that she describes as the "morning pages":

"The morning pages are three pages of stream-of-consciousness longhand morning writing. You should think of them not as art, but as an active form of meditation.... In the morning pages, we declare to the world—and ourselves—what we like, what we dislike, what we wish, what we hope, what we regret, and what we plan."

I have utilized the morning pages approach for over twelve years. Increased clarity, self-understanding, and the adoption of a proper respect for my own uniqueness have been consistent and ever-evolving gifts derived from this spiritual practice.

Why not try journaling for thirty days? The book and web site for *The Artist's Way* give further guidance for developing the discipline, and few who sincerely attend to the practice will want to give it up after the trial period.

> ## "A long habit of not thinking a thing wrong gives it a superficial appearance of being right."
>
> *Thomas Paine*

Resentment is a potent obstacle to spiritual progress. As long as we continue to hold on to the negative energy associated with recalling and recounting the wrongs of others, real or imagined, we cannot be free. The simple question, "Do you want to be right or do you want to be happy?" underscores the intractable nature of resentment. While the attitudes and actions of others may, in fact, be inappropriate, wrong, or even reprehensible, we will never find peace and serenity if we continue to harbor resentments toward those who have harmed us.

Resentments can be overt or covert. Some resentments can be immediately recalled—the irrational judge, the non-paying client, the child who "just won't listen." Other resentments are more covert—they seem to lie dormant, below the surface, until some stressful or painful event triggers their full-blown resurrection.

An inventory of our resentments—old and new, deep and slight, silly and profound—can be an effective method of "naming our demons," thereby identifying the hurts that bind us to our "smaller" selves. Once aware of our resentments, we can begin to move toward a healing acceptance. Over time, sustained awareness of the spiritual illnesses suffered by so many, including those who have harmed us, may move us toward greater compassion for all concerned.

In the interim, we should continue to keep our side of the street clean, making a conscious decision to set aside the thoughts of others' wrongs, so that we can live our day happy, joyous, and free.

April 9

> "But in the last analysis it is the desire for the respect and confidence of the members of the legal profession and the society which the lawyer serves that should provide to a lawyer the incentive for the highest possible degree of ethical conduct.... So long as its practitioners are guided by these principles, the law will continue to be a noble profession."
>
> *Preamble to the Rules of Professional Conduct*

A diverse weaving of many strands of our heritage encompasses each of us where we stand today. Our family heritage is layered with its unique assembly of heroes, characters, and rogues. Our spiritual heritage embraces its unique weavings of the wisdom and the experience of the ages. Our democratic heritage is founded upon a rule of law grounded in respect for the individual and enlightened self-government. Our legal heritage has encoded within it the hopes, dreams, and ideals of equal justice for all.

As legal professionals, we can proudly take our rightful place in line with those who have come before us, those here today, and those who will follow. We are called to add integrity to the strong chain of worthy characters who have so ably contributed to our noble profession. We also stand positioned, as no other group is able, to further the ideals, and correct the flaws, of our esteemed but sometimes beleaguered profession. No person is perfect. No system is perfect. No profession is perfect. These facts, however, do nothing to mitigate our calling and responsibility to work to achieve all that is noble, all that is pure, and all that is excellent. In so doing, each of us will have changed the world for the better.

April 10

> ## "Be the change you want to see in the world."
> *Mahatma Gandhi*

Casting blame upon others is an effective barrier to personal, spiritual, and professional growth. Whenever we falter in our professional responsibilities, a supposed easy "out" can lie in blaming others. The boss whose ego got in the way, the adversary who employs underhanded tactics, the client who will not cooperate—the list of possible "blamants" is endless. Similarly, personal defalcations may be attributed to childhood issues, dysfunctional families, philandering partners, and bad breaks. Yet, as ever, *to thine own self be true*.

Having made it to the point where we proudly bear the title of "Esquire," few can seriously debate the fact that, at least relatively speaking, life has shined favorably upon us along the way. Only 370 of every 100,000 Americans bear the coveted "attorney at law" title, and are therefore entitled to the rewards, benefits, and prestige normally attendant thereto. Contrast this to the cruel and offensive fact that, according to World Bank statistics, of the 6 billion-plus people on our planet, over 3 billion live in conditions that lack adequate food, shelter, health, and education.

While there is certainly a time and place to honestly critique the manner in which certain people and situations have affected our lives, for better or worse, a proper sense of perspective is required if we are to attain an honest assessment thereof. Today, we alone are the captains of the ships that are our lives. Honest evaluation of others' conduct, rather than childish blame, allows us to retain our power and dignity as discerning adults. Helpless children we are no more!

April 11

> "Finish each day and be done with it. You have done what you could. Some blunders and absurdities no doubt crept in, forget them as soon as you can. Tomorrow is a new day, you shall begin it well and serenely."
>
> *Ralph Waldo Emerson*

Guilt is also a formidable obstacle to personal growth that has rightfully earned its status as a primary contributor to "transformation arrest." So, for example, we say to ourselves, "How can I ever expect peace and happiness if I have done such heinous things in my past, and have hurt so many people?" Yet, guilt so often operates as an unarticulated excuse for staying stuck—by wallowing in the guilt of yesterday, we can decline to say "yes" to positive attitudes and behavior today.

The fact of the matter is that we have all done dishonorable acts in our past—that is part of the fallible human condition. However, the question is not whether we have done such things, for that is a given, but whether we can learn from them, and resolve to move forward in a more excellent and noble manner.

No person who walks this earth, no matter how rich, or powerful, or celebrated, can change the course of yesterday. Our power and our nobility lie in the present, in the decision to go forward faithfully, with courage and honor. If we insist on carrying the baggage of disappointment with ourselves, of thwarted expectations, and "failed" relationships, the "*shoulda, coulda, woulda*" of yesterday, today cannot be well-lived. Guilt can thus be used as an effective smokescreen to "shield" us from the serious business of spiritual growing up.

See this distraction and impediment to growth for what it is, and go forward in the power and energy of this day.

April 12

> "A hero ventures forth from the world of common day into a region of supernatural wonder, fabulous forces are there encountered and a decisive victory is won. The hero comes back from this mysterious adventure with the power to bestow boons on his fellow man."
>
> *Joseph Campbell*

What precedes reality but a vision? A dream of what might be possible inspires a quest toward our goal. Yet, as achieving dreamers have always known, without the magical, mystical, and mythological, there is no inspired reality.

A myth often includes a hero's effort and quest. The quest must be worthy of the mighty hero, for there are dragons to slay, maidens to rescue, and ultimately, a name to etch and render eternal in the annals of time.

If we were to reflect upon the impulses that brought us to the practice of law, using the format and style of a mythological tale, would the following rendering suffice? If not, how would our tale differ?

"As we began our legal journey, we envisioned not just wealth and power, we envisioned a profession in which we would become learned, and, following in the footsteps of our noble predecessors, we would assume the mantle of the great defenders, journeying on toward desired vistas. On our way, we would engage "fight to the finish" battles against oppressors of the defrauded, the violated, the innocent and the vulnerable, from which battles we might emerge bloody and bruised, but never bowed. The downtrodden would be restored to wholeness, and we would ride on, amidst celebrity, to do battle against the next injustice. We would take pride in our prowess, but we would never become arrogant, as we were possessed of knowledge of higher forces which figured greatly in the success of our quest. We would be welcome and revered amongst our peers, who were equally skilled, righteous, and perseverant in their tasks. At the time of our twilight, we would be lovingly honored, revered, and ultimately missed, by those whom we had served, and those who knew our legacy."

While it is doubtful that any of us have ever engaged in such a sketching of our anticipated epic quest, most of us entered the practice of law with a named or unnamed desire to engage our higher faculties and abilities, to help others, to be honored among peers, to obtain the righteous rewards of our good work, and to leave the world just a little better than we found it. *This, my friend, is none other than a noble quest.* If our vision has become dulled, or if our enthusiasm has waned, *now* is the time to start our quest afresh.

April 13

> "We spend precious hours fearing the inevitable.
> It would be wise to use the time adoring our families,
> cherishing our friends, and living our lives."
>
> *Maya Angelou*

A malady that is closely related to fear is worry. The story is told of the dying man who was asked what he would change in his life if he had it to live over. "*I just wish I hadn't worried so much*," was the doleful reply.

A good friend is often able to arouse me from my worries by asking: What is the worst thing that could happen, and what is the *real* probability of that happening? For good measure she asserts: "And remember, if it can be solved with money, it's not really a problem."

The fact is that the vast majority of our worries never see the light of day. A few do, but, strengthened by the spiritual practices we have been discussing, we will find the grace and fortitude to withstand them. While we might wish it were otherwise, we are not given a lifetime supply of grace and fortitude to handle our difficulties. Rather, we receive such nutrients one day at a time, and always in the appropriate measure to meet that day's challenges.

We can worry if we wish, but an honest appraisal reveals that we are wasting precious energy by so doing. I once reported to a friend that *I could not possibly fall asleep* until my three teenage sons returned home safely after their evening's activities. She wisely advised that I should do my best to go to sleep, since I would surely be notified if there were a problem, and, not being sleep-deprived, I would be better able to respond to any such news. That advice has saved me many sleepless nights.

If we focus on meeting today's *actual* challenges, with today's energy, we can live to good purpose in a joyful fashion. An incredible lightness of being results from living without the spirit-depleting "what-ifs," and by living life the way it was designed to be lived— one day at a time.

> "Be yourself. Especially do not feign affection.
> Neither be cynical about love; for in the face of all aridity
> and disenchantment, it is as perennial as the grass.
> Take kindly the counsel of the years, gracefully
> surrendering the things of youth."
>
> *Desiderata*

It is no secret that many, many people spend untold amounts of time and energy in attempting to present a perfect exterior, lest others detect the fear, self-doubt and other personal misgivings that lie just below the surface. The appearance factor is especially valued in the legal community where, it is perceived, "only the strong survive."

The truth is that every human being, lawyer or not, carries the imperfections and scars that result from being finite human beings. We all have our unique set of fears, doubts, resentments, angers, and other such attributes that appear and reappear during the ups and downs of our individual life-cycles.

While we might properly be working to correct one or more of our particularly troubling character defects, we need not, and should not, go to extremes in hiding or denying the essence of our humanity from others. We are, as the saying goes, as sick as our secrets, and a prideful refusal to accept these imperfections as an inherent part of the human condition can be a block to our spiritual growth. As Emerson so succinctly explained: "There is a crack in everything that God has made."

April 15

> "When you were born,
> you cried and the world rejoiced.
> Live your life so that when you die,
> the world cries and you rejoice."
>
> *Cherokee Saying*

How do you define success? Are you a person you would want to meet? Do you make the world a better place? If you had never been born would anyone notice? Have you left your positive mark on your family? Your life-partner? Your co-workers? The law? If someone were describing you, would they say, "This is someone I wish I were more like?"

What are the hallmarks of a winner? In the end, true winners give it away. They are selfless people who see the larger picture. Life contains many layers. We succeed or fail to a greater or lesser degree in each of these layered tiers (school, marriage, family life, professional life, community). Ultimately, we are known for what type of person we were, what values we stood for, and what good we did for others. Give it away as you go through each day.

April 16

> "Think not forever of yourselves, O Chiefs, nor of your own generation. Think of continuing generations of our families, think of our grandchildren and of those yet unborn…"
>
> *Peacemaker*

When I was ten years old, with the passing of the melancholy of childhood, I wished for time to stand still, to forever hold close my secure family structure and my amazingly wondrous life.

In the middle of my earthly tenure, with hair receding, I experience life another way. With growing children, a busy spouse, siblings scattered, a mother enfeebled, a father 20 years gone, I experience my personal golden age of creativity and productivity. Yet, as all things do, this too shall pass, so that one day, well-settled in the second half of my life, I will see through the eyes of one whose dreams have flourished, grown wings of their own, and have taken flight.

I foresee a day when time will seem unmoving, when I live in the fullness of each day as if it were the first and only. I will smile there, in the presence of my middle-aged children, rearing young ones of their own.

My life today must be mindfully lived so this future image will be gratifying, peacefully reposed among elegant choices. In that place, I hope to supply a deserving presence, so that my grandchildren, in the fullness of their innocence, might wish to make time stand still.

April 17

> "Principles are deep fundamental truths...
> lightly interwoven threads running with
> exactness, consistency, beauty and strength
> through the fabric of life."
>
> *Author Unknown*

The process of growth in our professional competencies is circular and spiral, like a vine circling a tree in its upward climb. Maturity, wisdom, and creativity in our selected domain of legal expertise usually ferment and develop at a measured pace.

Unlike certain artists who arrive early to greatness, stellar legal achievements tend to be more closely correlated with knowledge, experience, motivation, and talent. A lawyer of true excellence evolves when these attributes are developed in tandem with a character sustained by lived values, and chosen motivating principles.

April 18

> ## "In general, pride is at the bottom of all great mistakes."
>
> *John Ruskin*

Pride is certainly no stranger to the legal community. While inner and outer expectations often drive us to maintain an aura of bravado in our daily professional lives, we will not attain the balance and peace we seek if we are unable to distinguish the authentic and the non-authentic aspects of our demeanor. The "egomaniac with an inferiority complex" is a readily recognized legal persona found at negotiation tables, in courtrooms, and in law offices around the country. When self-centeredness, grandiosity, and egotism falsely masquerade as self-esteem and righteousness, we may fool others; however, we will experience an alienation from self, and, eventually, a loss of self, if we do not truly take stock of ourselves. As the gap between our insecure insides and our grandiose outsides widens, the more confused and disheartened we become.

As with other impediments to personal growth, unhealthy pride begins to diminish immediately upon exposure to the light of intentional examination and discussion. Once so reviewed, we can begin to separate the wheat from the chaff, claiming ownership of those attributes that enhance our personal and professional lives, and, one day at a time, relinquishing those that cause us to lead "divided lives."

April 19

> ## "Experience shows that if a person thinks that they may have a problem with alcohol or drugs, they usually do."
>
> *Author Unknown*

While it is estimated that 10 percent of American workers have an alcohol or drug problem, the percentage of substance-abusing lawyers is nearer 20 percent. ABA statistics reveal that more than 45 percent of attorney disciplinary proceedings involve *documented* evidence of substance abuse, while some studies estimate that such abuse is a contributing factor in up to 75 percent of such proceedings. Ironically, the positive attributes that are often associated with skilled advocacy often make lawyers slower to recognize, accept, and surrender to the addiction.

Help is readily available for the impaired lawyer. For over 30 years, the ABA has worked diligently to advance the legal community's knowledge of attorney impairment and the appropriate and compassionate responses to this issue. Today, every state has some form of legal assistance program that provides confidential assistance with alcohol and drug problems. These programs employ the use of intervention, peer counseling and referral to Twelve Step Programs to assist in the lawyer's recovery process. Groups of recovering lawyers helping other lawyers are numerous.

Addiction is a disease, not a disgrace, and the American Medical Association has recognized it as such for more than 50 years. Any legal professional who is having a problem with drugs or alcohol need only pick up the phone to obtain confidential advice and assistance. There is a solution, but we must pursue it.

April 20

> "So you say to people who you think you may have injured, 'I'm sorry.' If we all hold on to the mistake, we can't see our own glory...we can't see what we're capable of being. You can ask forgiveness of others, but in the end the real forgiveness is in one's own self."
>
> *Maya Angelou*

Once we have reviewed our personal impediments to growth, both past and present, and have discussed them with a trusted friend or advisor, we are ready to leave the past behind and move steadily forward. But before doing so, it will be wise to take the time to amend any festering harms we have caused others, so that we will not be pulled back into emotional pain and discomfort as we attempt to journey forward. If, for example, we have unfinished business with a former spouse or law partner, we should consider the best possible ways to "close out" these situations, so that we can travel forward unencumbered by painful memories and continuing conflict.

In so doing, we are not committing to re-establishing those relationships or assuming responsibility for the other person's actions. Rather, we are courageously owning up to the harm we have done in the situation, proffering whatever restoration is appropriate and practicable.

Thereafter, we are free to move on or to stay, knowing that we have undertaken the measures necessary to fully restore our personal integrity, always cognizant that we are responsible for the footwork, and not the outcome.

April 21

> "To exist is to change, to change is to mature,
> to mature is to go on creating oneself endlessly."
>
> *Henri Bergson*

When we have reviewed a few of the more common barriers to our personal and professional development, including fear, worry, pride, blame, resentment, and guilt, then have undertaken the needed reparations, we become ready to channel our revitalized energy into the exciting business of living our best lives. Each ensuing day can present as a welcome guest, offering a unique assembly of people, places, and things that invite our positive and rewarding engagement.

Life is not meant to be hard, it is meant to be creative, fun, challenging, and rewarding. In fact, it is meant to be joyous! A wise friend advises that there are several levels that we can select in determining how to live our lives: We can choose the "survival" mode; the "good enough" mode; or, as unbelievable as it sounds, the "heaven on earth" mode. Our existence in any one of these levels is a matter of choice, notwithstanding some difficult life circumstances that we may encounter along the way.

"We see life not as it is, but as we are," states the Talmud. If our interior life is in order, we will not be swayed by every ill wind that blows. A deep-seated peace and tranquility will guide us through even the most tempestuous storms.

April 22

"I dwell in possibility."

Emily Dickinson

Today could possibly be the best day of our lives.

In fact, there are many bright clouds on the horizon already.

We have already traversed some very rough patches. Sometimes, when we thought we could not go another step, we always did, and those particularly painful days are now behind us. We have learned new wisdom about ourselves, and we have learned that we can ask for help. We have grown stronger, and are none the worse for wear. We have learned who and what we can trust, what we value, and what impassions and drives us. We have shed many masks, and, as the poet May Sarton states, *now, we become ourselves*. We can intuit who and what to let into our lives, which practices move us toward wholeness, and which have an opposite, demoralizing effect.

Our professional lives can now be viewed as an integrally satisfying component of our whole lives. We can find or create meaning in our lawyering, no longer permitting the extrinsic glitter of power, possessions, and prestige to divert us from the more meaningful aspects of our profession. We can view our lawyering through the lens of love and service, hoping to provide some comfort to a sorely hurting world. Money can hold its appropriate place in our lives, serving as a tangible way to exchange love and service. The opinions of others need no longer concern us, if to our own selves we are true. We can see that few relationships are beyond repair, if we are willing to humbly attempt to amend them. We no longer need to stand above the crowd, or hide beneath it; we are content to be one among many, doing what we alone were created to do. We are grateful for the innumerable gifts that we have not earned, yet we enjoy. Solitude no longer frightens us, as we have come to trust God, *as we understand God*, or alternatively, we have put our trust in *"good orderly direction,"* believing that some higher organizing principle is working for our best interests and is on our side. We seek progress not perfection, looking merely to suit up, show up, and do the next right thing.

Yes, with these attitudes, behaviors, and accomplishments, today could just be the best day of our lives, *so far.*

April 23

> ## "Nobody has a more sacred obligation to obey the law than those who make the law."
>
> *Sophocles*

What persons and occurrences, great and noble, do we find in our personal heritage to hearken back to for support and guidance? Most of us stand in a long line of accomplished people, whose good work has been generously handed down to us.

Within the legal tradition, we also find beacons of leadership and accomplishment, whose example can buoy us in times of darkness and disillusionment. We are the current players in an ever-elongating chain of practitioners who have strived to achieve a just and fair world through the practice of law. We attempt, individually and collectively, to protect a reasonable and hospitable societal structure, so that individual members can choose how to live the good life.

Ours is a noble craft and a critical cause to be expertly carried out by people of highly developed character, for, in the last analysis, it is only our contact with our own humanity that serves as the necessary compass to guide our journey.

April 24

"Your days are short here; this is the last of your springs.
And now in the serenity and quiet of this lovely place,
touch the depths of truth, feel the hem of Heaven.
You will go away with old, good friends. And don't
forget when you leave why you came."

Adlai E. Stevenson

It is not a commonplace occurrence to personally witness acts of heroism. Recently, I was blessed to witness a man overcoming pain and fear, as he struggled to breathe on his deathbed. A man of great faith, he looked past me in a reverent, fervent gaze, as if deep in meditative prayer, and as if looking directly into the eyes of God. I held his hand and prayed silently that his suffering might be eased. I felt privileged to so proximately bear witness to such love, courage, and faith.

Faith is deeper and more abiding than belief. Faith is like the engine and steering wheel of a car, powering and directing the actions of our lives. While the ultimate mystery of life remains veiled and unknown, living a life of faith allows us to surrender to the deep force that flows through us, and in whose currents we are swept along.

Having chosen to live our lives in accordance with spiritual principles, we are also called, particularly at critical life junctures, to choose whether or not to live our lives in communion with a cohesive force much larger and greater than our singular, insular selves.

April 25

"No one to fool but myself."

Parker Palmer

Have you ever watched a movie during which you suddenly saw ungainly specifics of your own life splayed across the screen, for the entire world to see? It is uncanny how a well-crafted movie can ignite such strong identification that we find ourselves squirming in our seats, looking sheepishly from side to side, trying to ascertain if the surrounding members of the audience have identified us as the true protagonist of the tale.

And just how is it that we should authentically be known? Does the courteous, hail-fellow-well-met persona of the business day dissolve into that of the snarling curmudgeon upon our arrival home? Do all our office socialization filters fall away within the confines of our living rooms, such that we feel free to judge, criticize, demand, micro-manage, complain, and rant?

We *sometimes* fool some others, but we *seldom* fool our intimates, and we *never* fool ourselves as to what is going on here. Self-centered behavior that makes us hard to live with, whether resulting from fear, pride, arrogance, or otherwise, must be squarely faced and dealt with, if we are ever to become the people we aspire to be.

April 26

> **"I am always doing that which I cannot do,
> in order that I may learn how to do it."**
>
> *Pablo Picasso*

We are too often overly harsh critics of our professional undertakings. If we have put in the required preparation, we have done our job *well enough*, no matter what the result. The time has come for us to accept that *we are responsible only for the footwork, not the outcome.*

It is also appropriate to realize that the concept of "doing our best" is not a realistic standard for *every* situation. As the Olympic contender appreciates, our personal best—the expenditure of ultimate physical, mental, emotional, and spiritual energy—must be reserved for those situations that truly warrant our utmost concentration and abilities. In the more ordinary daily rounds, we can be guided by the reasonable lawyer standard, a clearly recognized concept in our jurisprudence.

Yet, it is only the mindful individual who can be the arbiter of those situations that require the "personal best" standard, and the many more situations that more properly warrant the "reasonable person" or "reasonable lawyer" standard. *Be still and know*, thereby becoming a good and thoughtful steward of our life's vital energy and resources.

April 27

> ## "Life loves to be taken by the lapel and told, 'I'm with you, kid. Let's go.'"
>
> *Maya Angelou*

Today, the word enthusiasm normally implies interest or excitement, while in ancient times, it referenced inspiration or divine possession. So, for example, Socrates spoke of the divine inspiration of the poets as a form of "enthusiasm." However we currently define the term, most lawyers will agree that sustained enthusiasm in lawyering is a rare phenomenon today.

In today's business environment, even the most successful lawyers are besieged by challenges on every side—increased competition, working longer hours, rushing from crisis to crisis, the pervasive use of alienating technology that invades our personal and family time—these factors, and many more, seem to mitigate against the enthusiastic practice of law.

Yet, law, like life, was meant to be lived with enthusiasm. Passionate lawyers, like passionate people generally, have always found reasons and methods for approaching challenges with zest and fervor. A former legal colleague and I would frequently have lunch together, and, upon returning to the office, my friend would nearly sizzle with enthusiasm, anticipating the latest challenges presented by her clients during our short absence. Yearning to possess a similar passion, I began to seek out those professional endeavors that would similarly integrate my values, skills, and level of excitement.

As spiritual writer Parker Palmer deftly informs us: "Our deepest calling is to grow into our authentic selfhood, whether or not it conforms to some image of who we ought to be. As we do so, we will not only find the joy that every human being seeks—we will also find our path of authentic service in the world. True vocation joins self and service, as Frederick Buechner asserts when he defines vocation as 'the place where your deep gladness meets the world's greatest need.'"

> "Interruptions can be viewed as sources of irritation or opportunities for service, as moments lost or experience gained, as time wasted or horizons widened. They can annoy us or enrich us… depending on our attitude toward them."
>
> *William Arthur Ward*

When we have thoughtfully planned our day, it is sometimes difficult to deal with unexpected interruptions. Yet, the needs of others do not necessarily present only when it is convenient for us. It is very possible that the interruption carries a message, a thought, or an opportunity to gain perspective that is necessary to appreciate the evolving moments of our day. Perhaps we need to be reminded of our interconnectedness. Maybe the urgent phone call presents an opportunity to help someone who is suffering or confused, or who just needs a few words of encouragement to start an overdue project.

The unexpected does not need to be a source of frustration if we are able to unselfishly step back from our immediate concerns and attend to others. Our tasks can usually be postponed for a colleague or client who is in need, and we will often return to our own work bolstered and refreshed by the opportunity to be of service.

As we continue to take care of ourselves and grow stronger, we are able to help others through their rough patches without losing our own center. Balance and self-care are the keys to this new freedom.

April 29

> ## "In the name of God, stop a moment, cease your work, look around you."
>
> *Paul Tillich*

Beauty comes in so many shades and hues that we may miss untold manifestations if we are not vigilant. The beauty of a child's trusting eyes, the beauty of a perfectly crafted legal argument, the beauty of a family united around a bountiful Thanksgiving table—these beauties seem to manifest in two "flavors": extraordinary and super-extraordinary.

Beauty can be regularly encountered in our daily work rounds, if we but have the eyes to see. The loyal and helpful legal assistant who, against all odds, always manages to pull it all together. The never-tiring copy person who willingly stays until the last brief has been bound. The humble superior who stands beside the most junior associate when there is a "rush" job to be completed for a client. The embrace of a cozy home and a warm meal at the end of our workday.

These "ordinary" manifestations of beauty are ours for the taking, if we but take notice, and allow their natural nourishment, warmth, and comfort to fill our weary souls.

April 30

> "To find your mission in life is to discover the intersection between your heart's deepest gladness and the world's deepest hunger."
>
> *Frederick Buechner*

How many of us went into the law because we were attracted by the attributes of the "noble profession"? How many of us still privately harbor dreams of the "just world theory," where justice and mercy are meted out properly, and law and order abide? There is a romantic part in all of us that is driven by the ideals of love, truth, goodness, beauty, courage, and integrity. These ideals move us toward the best that is possible in human nature. Our current system of jurisprudence is considered by many to be the best and most humane justice system in the world; however, our system also requires substantial improvement. As we proceed through the professional stages of law student, young lawyer, seasoned professional, and senior counselor, we have an obligation to leave our own mark of excellence on the profession, and to improve upon an already good system.

"The success of any great moral enterprise does not depend on numbers."

William Lloyd Garrison

Can the legal profession be restored to its former glory? Does our environment permit the space and the shaping of a profession that bespeaks integrity, nobility, reverence, and true justice?

The legal profession, of yesterday *and* today, more than any other profession, shapes the very manner in which individual citizens navigate their world. Our charge, like no other, contains the potential to lift up downtrodden spirits, to elevate and model the qualities of a value-driven life, to inspire the creation of work that is noble and excellent, to further justice, freedom, fairness, and compassion, and to restore confidence to cynical spirits and fearful eyes.

Our world is a deeply hurting one. Beyond one's intimates, trust is nearly extinct. Lack of trust in our "institutions"—political, governmental, media, religious, professional, commercial, medical, and otherwise—has reached monumental proportions. The resulting cynicism, fear and alienation experienced by so many make reform efforts at any level seem doomed before they begin.

And yet, the truth of Margaret Mead's teaching remains as true today as when originally uttered: *"Never doubt that a small group of thoughtful, committed citizens can change the world. Indeed, it is the only thing that ever has."*

In most instances, the lawyer deals in an autonomous manner, and each client matter is considered singly. Even in large law firms, the lawyer sequentially focuses on each client's matter, even if for only a few minutes. The fact is that there is *nothing*—no law, no billable-hour policy, no management directive, no opinion of colleagues—*nothing,* other than the chosen attitudes, values, and beliefs of the individual lawyer, that determines whether the matter will be handled in a manner that is worthy, noble, and excellent, or in a manner that is merely expedient.

From this day forward, each lawyer, working on each client matter, in each city of the United States, will mold the future state of the legal profession, depending on whether, in opening each client's file, the lawyer's mental state can be characterized by: *"How can I serve?"* or *"What's in it for me?"*

> ## "You may say that I'm a dreamer,
> ## but I'm not the only one..."
>
> *John Lennon*

What would the world look like if, on a daily basis, each of us sought to be instruments of peace, to bring love, compassion, and joy to a sorely hurting world? What would happen if each lawyer truly "loved justice and walked humbly"? What if our concern for other people at least equaled our concern for ourselves and our immediate families? What would the courtroom or the meeting room look like if we substituted healing, reconciliation, and restitution for unprincipled challenge, hostility, and the desire to win at any cost? What if we were able to reduce our own cynicism and fear, thereby allowing expression of our true inner essence, and helping others, by our example and encouragement, to do the same thing?

And what might the legal profession look like if we sought to reclaim the ideal of the "lawyer-statesman" described in exquisite detail by Anthony Kronman, in his groundbreaking book, *The Lost Lawyer, the Failing Ideals of the Legal Profession.* According to Kronman, the ideal of the "lawyer-statesman" embodies several discernible elements, including, most importantly, an excellence of judgment that derives from a well-developed character, and an enthusiastic participation in the development of the public good.

We who have witnessed incredible events in our lives, both public and personal, from the fall of the Berlin Wall to the healing of a loved one's "terminal" illness, can appreciate the potential fulfillment of dreams that may currently be considered totally beyond the pale.

You may say that I'm a dreamer, but I'm not the only one.

May 3

> "Living is a form of not being sure, not knowing what is next or how. The moment you know how, you die a little. The artist never entirely knows. We guess. We may be entirely wrong, but we take leap after leap, in the dark."
>
> *Agnes De Mille*

Letting go is one of the hardest of life's lessons. So much time and energy is wasted in un-resolvable conflict. Decide what can and cannot be changed in others and yourself. Live your expectations according to these parameters. Expect only what another is capable of giving. See life as it is, and not as you would have it be. Realize that what locks us into an angry position is a faulty set of assumptions about life, and a limited capacity to problem-solve and reinterpret an ever-changing experience called reality. Letting go of past transgressions, real or imagined, frees up space and energy for productivity, creativity, and interpersonal connection that can exponentially enhance the meaningful framework of one's life.

Keep apace with the ever-changing patchwork quilt that is your life. Be mindful of the spirit of the times by adopting an open, flexible attitude that can shift gears in stride with the ebb and flow of life's seasons. Life is a series of transitions, stages, phases, and adaptations to the demands of our evolving environment. Change is a constant. Sameness, a psychologically secure construct, is in fact, constantly in a state of flux. Other than temperament, which one is born with, most psychological processes undergo fluctuations, if not radical changes, during one's lifetime. Be at peace with the way things really are. When your assumptions about reality are grounded in truth, it is easier to navigate life's winding path.

May 4

> "If we refuse to think of anything except what we are doing or the person that we are with, we develop the habit of being present to the present moment. In a way, the present moment becomes as sacred as being in church."
>
> *Thomas Keating*

What traditions, if any, do we hold sacred? Sacred is an odd word in a secular world. Sacred implies the deepest level of reverence and personal significance. When we have traditions that we revere and hold sacred, some part of who we are, and what we stand for, transcends our current being, as well as our current time and space. Sacred implies beyond self. What part of our collective heritage stirs an inner calling, a sense of energizing desire to merge into something bigger than ourselves?

Is there any room for sacred traditions in a society where self-interest reigns supreme, and our next purchase, our next meal, and our next vacation so often take center stage?

The good news is that our everyday experiences hold potentially sublime, transcendent moments within them. Whether working, commuting, speaking with a colleague, or laughing out loud, the positive reception of the "sacrament of the present moment" allows us to reverentially appreciate the energy, power, love, and mystery of every task, every encounter, every thought process. *"To see the world in a grain of sand, and heaven in a wild flower,"* as William Blake so eloquently expressed it. Like a vibrant rainbow of colors, fully experienced and appreciated moments can underlie sacramental happenings, given the proper time, care, attention, and framing of the experience.

Many independent studies on spirituality confirm that we humans are most inspired, productive, creative, and satisfied, when the sublime, sacred, magical, and mysterious remain an integral part of our experience.

Eternity bountifully drives the mechanics of the everyday machine.

May 5

> "Often we really don't know how best to show compassion in the workplace.... Yet we cannot treat co-workers as if they have no feelings, problems, or personal lives. We must be able to offer them an appropriate measure of compassion as the need arises if we are to build workplaces of support and community."
>
> *Gregory F.A. Pierce*

Personal grief and loss are not normally welcome discussion topics in the workplace. The troublesome teen, the parent with Alzheimer's, the emotionally troubled spouse—these are not considered the stuff of "polite" office conversations.

Years ago, when my beloved brother was in a war zone, my equanimity and my concentration levels decreased greatly as the war clouds thickened. As my fears steadily increased, there seemed to be no way to reconcile the required office place "business as usual" demeanor with my mounting concern. At the time, I was unable to risk exposing the full measure of my humanity to my colleagues, and this deepened my pain.

If trouble looms in our personal lives, we do not have to carry our burdens silently. If we so choose, we have the right to declare who we are, and what we are experiencing, at any given time. While we also have the right to maintain our chosen level of privacy, we do not have to remain silent simply so that our co-workers can feel less awkward. We always have the right to speak our truth.

Carl Jung had a sign over his office door that read: "Bidden or unbidden, God is present." Our whole selves—body, mind, and spirit—are as present in the workplace as they are in our homes. As we become more comfortable with the evolving facets of our authentic selves, we will find we can express who we are, and what we are experiencing, in any appropriate manner. Whether in our homes or the senior partner's office, we have a right to include and express our total humanity. We do not need to don a robotic professional persona upon entering our offices, merely to please others.

> ## "We cannot all be great but we can always attach ourselves to something that is great."
>
> *Henry Emerson Fosdick*

One of my most memorable encounters with the majesty of our legal system occurred unexpectedly, on a Saturday morning, when I answered the call of a distressed neighbor. Her teenage son was being questioned by the police outside their home. As I arrived, the police had just directed the young man to retrieve and empty the contents of his backpack on the front lawn. I introduced myself as the young man's lawyer and directed my "client" (while shaking in my boots, and wondering what to do next!) not to follow the policeman's orders, since no warrant had been produced. To my immense relief, the policemen acquiesced in my direction, and they eventually left the premises without further action.

While this simple example may be a daily occurrence for our criminal defense brethren, I had never personally participated in the awe-inspiring triumph of the exercise of constitutional rights over the opposing police power of the state. This simple encounter, while unspectacular to many, is an example of the true majesty of our legal system. For more than two centuries, untold numbers of lawyers have heroically struggled to ensure the maintenance of the standards of law, freedom, and the individual integrity envisioned by the Bill of Rights. As a result of their diligence and loyalty to the cause, my young friend, and all of us, have been rendered secure in our persons and our property.

The lawyer's calling is to uphold the ever-evolving values of a free and democratic society. The beauty and majesty of the rule of law, when properly mediated by legal professionals who have sworn to uphold its integrity, is an awe-inspiring vision.

May 7

> "There comes a time when the risk to remain tight in the bud was more painful than the risk it took to blossom."

Anais Nin

You are on the train, or in your car, making the same lifeless commute that you have made for so many years. The anomie that surrounds your thoughts of the work-day ahead, and the perhaps equally stultifying evening at home, is suffocating. Does it also keep you awake at night? That aching pain that says you have lost yourself, that somewhere on life's path you made a turn into a complete dead-end.

At such times, we often believe the solutions to our desperation are to be found in a new job, a different spouse, another profession, a new neighborhood. Yet, the title of Jon Kabat Zinn's book of meditations, *Wherever You Go, There You Are*, points to the fallacy of our thinking. For, in fact, we bring ourselves—our restlessness, our irritability, and our discontent—into the new home, the new relationship, the new job. While the novelty and pleasure may temporarily numb our discontent, before long, the soulful yearning and the sleepless nights return. "I have the cash and prizes, but I am still miserable. Now what?"

Theologian Richard Rohr teaches that, during such times of deep questioning, we should allow ourselves to be drawn into sacred, "liminal" spaces where transformation can take place. Liminal space is the in-between space, where we are no longer "this," but not yet "that," just as twilight is neither day nor night. Rohr maintains that liminal space is "always an experience of displacement in the hope of a new point of view. Liminal space pulls us from our private absolute center and revitalizes our experience."

The moments of deep passion experienced in the in-between space can be the staging area for entry into the new life that we are seeking. The wise have always known that pain is one of the most effective motivators for change. While the pain can lead us to the door of new possibilities, we alone must take *action* to open the door.

May 8

> "Listen to your life. See it for the fathomless mystery that it is...touch, taste, smell your way to the holy and hidden heart of it because in the last analysis, all moments are key moments, and life itself is grace."
>
> *Frederick Buechner*

Have you ever made all the correct connections and viewed each blessed moment as imbued with magic, meaning, and mystery? When body, mind, and spirit are well-nourished and you are operating on all cylinders, the possibilities for passion, learning, and creativity are boundless. Your imagination can take you any place you want to go. Put on your spacesuit and shoot for the stars. Don't come down until your head hits the pillow. Learn to leave the prevailing social conventions of fear, doubt, and uncertainty behind. You are better served by experiencing mystery in the mundane, magic in the ordinary, meaning in the daily grind. We are the dreamers who need to live the dream.

May 9

> "These then are my last words to you.
> Be not afraid of life. Believe that life is worth living
> and your belief will help create the fact."
>
> *William James*

It is absolutely possible to make a transition to a type of lawyering that allows us to "soar to the heights," and to experience great satisfaction and joy in the practice of law. If we want to make such a transition from our present mode of lawyering, however, we must be willing to take persistent, daily actions that move us closer to our goal. Dramatic resignations and hastily arranged sabbaticals are not necessary prerequisites. What is required is that we define our goals, and then take simple, steady actions moving toward those goals, today, tomorrow, and the next day.

If we have a desire to represent indigent clients, or small businesses, or the victims of domestic violence, we do not have to take the dramatic step of leaving our steady corporate job in order to do so. Rather, we can take a small first step toward the goal—for example, calling the bar association for information on *pro bono* defense, or speaking with another lawyer who works in the desired practice area—to investigate realistic methods for fulfilling our dream, or, as frequently occurs with accumulating knowledge, to refashion the particulars of our dream.

For today, all we need to do is take one small step toward our intended goals. If we show up for the more mundane tasks of research, speaking with others, checking relevant Internet sites, and so on, great things will come to pass. A sign that hangs in my office states: *"That which you are seeking is causing you to seek."* An already existing inner wisdom, if respectfully consulted, will guide the way that our soul knows is right for us. The path thereto becomes uncluttered by our small, but persistent, actions.

May 10

> ## "Wisdom is nothing more than healed pain."
>
> *Robert Gary Lee*

As a group, lawyers continuously deal with those who have been the victims of violence—physical, mental, emotional, and spiritual. The experience of transgression can be very psychologically damaging, whether it occurs in our personal lives or the lives of our clients. From a motivational perspective, few experiences will inspire lawyers toward the zealous representation of a matter more than personal identification with a direct, willful, and transgressing action.

Violence has predictable consequences and stages. We feel the stinging pain of the hurt as we physically or psychically ward off the initial blows. We spend countless hours mulling over every detail that led up to and accompanied the transgressing event. We scan alternative hypothetical interpretations concerning the mindset of our adversary. We begin to shift back and forth emotionally, assuming the mental position of victim, avenger, forgiver, and mediator, as we attempt to make sense of what has happened. We glimpse the episode from a broader prospective, trying to reclaim an overall context that diminishes the trauma of the experience. Alternately, the situation looms as too large, and then too small, before assuming its proper perceptual space.

Whether we are dealing with such transgressions in a personal or professional context, we should remain cognizant that timing is the key variable in our psychological adaption to the event. Humans are innately self-healing organisms. We ultimately come into accord with an understanding of the transgressing situation that we can initially tolerate, and then accept, and, ultimately, process, and integrate within the entire conglomerate of our life's experiences.

May 11

> "Don't ask what the world needs.
> Ask what makes you come alive and go do it.
> Because what the world needs is people
> who have come alive."
>
> *Howard Thurman*

Are we capable of loving what we do? Is it fair and reasonable to assume that some, if not many of us, might describe our day's labor as pleasurable? Can we go so far as to describe the romance of our labors?

The term "romance" normally conjures up images of lovers lost in the faraway gaze of idealized love, the scent of roses, and the poetry of love's divine inspiration. Yet, in a broader sense, romance encompasses a spirit of adventure, passion, curiosity, awe, and enthusiasm. Romance, whether its subject is one's beloved, one's work, or life itself, elevates mood, inspires hope, creates new vision, and everywhere fosters possibility.

Dreams, ambitions, desires, and goals are the direct by-products of the romantic imagination. Our lawyering, when imbued with romantic passion and purpose, can soar to hitherto unknown levels, where pure creativity resides.

May 12

> "The greatest appointment you have in life is with yourself. Be sure to show up on time and pay attention."
>
> *Laura Teresa Marquez*

Pain is a part of every life. In *The Power of Now*, spiritual author Eckert Tolle describes the "pain body" that resides within each of us. The "pain body," similar to a digital archive, stores, and recalls on command, all past forms of pain that we have encountered. While the "pain body" normally remains dormant within, severe emotional shocks, or the steady accrual of chronic pain, can cause the sleeping giant to awaken and to cause all forms of havoc in our lives.

Pain is real, and pain is part of the human condition. However, while the experience of pain is mandatory in traversing life's journey, misery is optional. When these facts about pain are fully accepted, we can carry on with the job of creatively living within the solution. While confronting and solving problems is a difficult process, one that most of us would like to avoid, as psychoanalyst Scott Peck teaches, if we are willing to accept that life is difficult, we begin to learn life's true lessons, and eventually reach higher levels of self-understanding and peace.

Misery, on the other hand, results from an unhealthy habitation within the center of pain that keeps us firmly entrenched within the problem, rather than the solution. Many mental health experts believe that a purposeful dwelling within a painful situation can provide emotional payoffs that, like an addiction, may be difficult to cast aside. For example, if we choose to consistently focus on the problems of our addicted child, we may "justifiably" postpone or ignore working on some of our own issues. We may rationalize that the existence of the very painful condition allows us to "let up" on our own character development, thus, providing a "payoff" that we consciously or unconsciously seek. Similarly, we might ask ourselves how could we possibly summon the courage and hard work needed to rejuvenate our stagnating legal practice when a friend is in great need, our spouse is ill, or our child is in pain.

The fact is that, while we are sometimes called to accompany others through difficult situations, we should not postpone our own development while awaiting another's healing.

May 13

> "The most satisfying thing in life is to have been able to give a large part of one's self to others."
>
> *Pierre Teilhard de Chardin*

Robert Eaton's book, *Sacred Work*, poignantly describes how the soul suffers if our work is performed in a robotic and mechanical fashion. For those who have tried, and even for those who have not, it is a humbling experience to realize that our souls are difficult things to manage. When, for example, I tried to convince myself that a high salary and a prestigious position were adequate substitutes for satisfying work, my rational side "bought" this, but my soul refused to acquiesce. I became more restless, irritable, and discontent with each passing day. Just as eating too many rich desserts will eventually play havoc with our physical system, so, too, working solely for material gain and self-advancement will cause great psychic pain, as the soul is deprived of its needed nutrients of purpose, connection, and meaning.

Conversely, enthusiasm, passion, and delight in our accomplishments constitute hospitable furnishings for our soul's abode. It is when we live within an ethic of love and service, truly enjoying the work we are doing, that we engage all that is sacred and profound within and around us, allowing, as author Robert Eaton predicts, for the soul of our work to become the work of our soul.

May 14

> "Let me give you the definition of ethics:
> it is good to maintain life and to further life.
> It is bad to damage and destroy life.
> And this ethic, profound and universal, has the
> significance of a religion. It is religion."
>
> *Albert Schweitzer*

In his book, *Letters to a Young Lawyer*, Law Professor Alan Dershowitz properly counsels that the time to create the "black-letter law" of our ethical norms begins long before we ever meet our first client. Dershowitz explains that many lawyers never make an *explicit* choice as to how values and ethics will guide their professional lives. Rather, "they simply drift toward a widely accepted form of elite corruption without ever engaging in the 'to be or not to be' soliloquy. Most lawyers... do not make a deliberate and calculating step over the line. They move closer and closer until they realize...that the line is well behind them."

Have we planned in advance for those situations in which we *must* assert: "I will go this far, and no further?" Do we know the boundaries and limits that our integrity requires? Will we ever intentionally mislead our clients or our opponents in our communications? If so, under what circumstances? To what end? To what extent will I allow the end to justify the means, and thus to deviate from honesty, integrity, and wholeness?

Although complete disclosure may not always be the only appropriate option in deciding our course, let us be faithful in assessing our actual motivations and behavior, always driven by the eternal wisdom: *"To thine own self be true."*

May 15

> "And the work of righteousness shall be peace;
> and the effect of righteousness quietness
> and assurance forever."
>
> *Isaiah 32:17*

There is a steady calm and assurance that flows within when we know we are properly attending to our multifaceted lives. It seems, somewhat paradoxically, that when we keep the focus on ourselves, by practicing intentional physical, mental, and emotional self-care, our relationships work better. When we become calm and centered within, we exude a genuine confidence and assurance that allows us to quietly but firmly say what we mean and mean what we say. We are not frantically trying to assess what we think a situation requires, or to speak the words that we believe others may want us to say. Rather, firmly grounded, we can trust that our own assessment of a matter, and our voicing thereof, will be sufficient. So possessed, the silent refrain, *I am enough, I have enough, I do enough,* seems to underlie our steadfast approach to the challenges of the day.

There is no peace in wrongdoing. When we fail to do the next right thing, agitation, discontent, second-guessing, and an innate disappointment in ourselves, conscious or unconscious, follows. Whether we allow fear to direct our actions, or if we abandon ourselves by alignment with a perceived consensus, thereby temporarily choosing the "easier, softer way," peace will always elude us, since, as the prophet Isaiah tells us, peace, quietness, and assurance are the fruits of righteousness.

May 16

> "The whole course of human history may depend on a change of heart in one solitary and even humble individual—for it is in the solitary mind and soul of the individual that the battle between good and evil is waged and ultimately won or lost."
>
> *M. Scott Peck*

The insightful spiritual program, "A *Course in Miracles*," teaches that whatever we think is lacking in the world is what we are failing to contribute to the world. This adage contains much experiential wisdom, and logically flows from the understanding that, for each human being, the world is not as the world is, the world is as the human being is.

So, we often find that when we are pleased with our performance in a particularly challenging client meeting or court appearance, the world seems more in order, abundant, and properly predictable. Conversely, after a misunderstanding, or a lack of validation in a personal or professional encounter, we may perceive the world as a fearful, menacing, and inhospitable habitat.

The common denominator in all these encounters is the mental, physical, and spiritual "centeredness" of the actor. If we are firmly planted in our own self-understanding and awareness, we do not readily surrender our innate inner power to outer circumstances or "the good opinion of others." Rather, simply stated: "If we think we can do it, we're right, and if we think we can't do it, we're right."

As always, it is an inside job. The "inside job" leads to positive and productive results for all concerned when we are grounded within our inner wisdom, our higher knowing, and our ever-widening web of connectivity with all creation.

May 17

> ## "In a real dark night of the soul it is always three o'clock in the morning, day after day."
>
> *F. Scott Fitzgerald*

The "dark nights of the soul" are not a unique phenomenon known only to saints and mystics. Lawyers and others who consciously seek personal and spiritual growth are only too familiar with the soul-crushing questioning times and the sporadic crises of confidence that can activate our "desert experiences."

Whether we are challenged by personal, relationship, or professional issues, many a legal career has been periodically or even permanently sidetracked by pervasive restlessness, distress, depression, and other disturbing symptoms. Both medical and psychological help may be necessary in navigating particularly murky waters. Trusted friends and mentors may also provide needed support.

Yet, the more profoundly painful crises of confidence require something more. This often involves a searingly honest and painful discussion between God and ourselves, wherein all forms of pretense and rationalization are cast aside, as the release from spiritual and emotional pain is sought above all else. These existential crises and brutally frank conversations between God and self often birth the beginnings of transformation that could not have evolved in any other way.

Stand strong. We will survive hitting bottom and terrifying dark nights of the soul as we come to appreciate even more deeply what the saints and mystics have always known—pain is an extremely effective vehicle of transformation.

May 18

> "Whatever course you decide upon, there is
> always someone to tell you that you are wrong.
> There are always difficulties arising which
> tempt you to believe that your critics are right.
> To map out a course of action and follow it
> to an end requires courage."
>
> *Ralph Waldo Emerson*

How have we defined success for ourselves? It is important that we specify our internal criteria for defining success if we want to live a tranquil and harmonious life. It seems that if we fail to select our own criteria, the criteria will be chosen for us, as the seductive "cash and prizes" that the world so treasures continually call to us for recognition.

Today, material possessions and achievements are so uniformly proclaimed and revered by society, that, like a child in a toy store, we will be unable to resist their magnetism unless we have thoughtfully constructed our own alternative formulation of the measures of success.

Long after my soul realized that it was time to leave a very prestigious legal position, I remained, handcuffed by the high salary and other trappings. When I finally garnered the necessary courage to leave, despite the great approbation of all around me, I found a freedom and peace that I had never before known.

Today I remain energized and challenged by the many facets of my life, and my challenges arise in the context of attempting to live a successful life, *as defined by me.*

May 19

> "To put the world right in order, we must first put the nation in order; to put the nation in order, we must first put the family in order; to put the family in order, we must first cultivate our personal life; we must first set our hearts right."

Confucius

And what of the needs of our children and families? Do we believe that our work is so critically important that our families must understand and accept that work always come first?

While our work is obviously meaningful and necessary, so are the needs and concerns of our loved ones, great and small. Our work is not more vital than the joyous smiles and contented presence that can surround our dinner tables. A large paycheck is no substitute for a large presence.

Compromise and balance are necessary; abandonment is unacceptable.

Sometimes we understandably become overly involved in our work as client presentations and brief filing dates approach. Other times, however, we attempt to use our work as a safe harbor from the emotional challenges of life. For, despite its many challenges, work well done often produces the desired results: satisfaction, success, compensation, recognition, status, self-esteem, and job security. On the other hand, many other life events, particularly those associated with our home life, are less predictable, and often more emotionally jarring.

The tenor of our intimate relationships can go up and down like a seesaw, and the needs of our children change with each stage of development. With each passing year, our children separate from us more, moving closer to the autonomy of adulthood. It is no surprise that we might want to take cover within the more defined, predictable, ego-enhancing milieu of our work.

Yet, our true spiritual task is clear: we are called to form balanced and responsible relationships with our families and each important aspect of our existence. Our families, most importantly, require the presence, support, direction, and love that only we can give. We should appropriately address these needs as we further our individual quests for greater emotional stability or enhanced professional importance.

> "So many of our dreams at first seem impossible, then they seem improbable, and then, when we summon the will, they soon become inevitable."

Christopher Reeve

While attending seminary, I was required to read a book entitled, *God's Yes Was Louder Than My No*, for one of my pastoral formation seminars. This title has always stayed with me, and, when recalled, is accompanied by a wry smile.

While I was a practicing securities lawyer, I can truly say that the thought of ordained ministry had *never* occurred to me. In fact, I had not even attended church for many years when a friend suggested that I might consider the ministry. The "impossibility" and the "absurdity" of the suggestion were quickly overtaken by the "still small voice" within which firmly asserted: "*Yes, this is something you must consider.*"

To this day, I remain amazed and humbled by the impact of my friend's softly delivered suggestion. My entire being resonated in recognition and positive affirmance of the never-before-considered idea. "When the pupil is ready, the teacher appears."

Today, my legal training and ministry are integrated in ways that produce very satisfying work. God's "Yes" was truly louder than my astonished "No."

May 21

> "Thoughts are things; they have tremendous power.
> Thoughts of doubt and fear are pathways to failure.
> When you conquer negative attitudes of doubt
> and fear you conquer failure."
>
> *Bryan Adams*

When uncertainty looms, our natural proclivity toward either negativity or positivity will greatly affect our intuitive decision-making processes. Is the glass really half-full, or half-empty, or, does the answer lie more properly in between?

Curiously, many primitive psychological processes, such as intuitive thought, operate on an "all-or-nothing" basis. At higher levels of processing, after much time and energy have been devoted to realistic problem-solving, we naturally engage in more sophisticated reasoning processes, including the consideration of the likelihood of success or failure in a given situation. This heightened perceptivity is needed to remedy the radical deficiencies of mere intuition. Our primitive neuro-circuitry is hard-wired for on-the-spot decision making, while our brain's more advanced processing enhances our evaluative processes by considering such matters as the likelihood of future outcomes.

It is helpful to know whether we are prone to positive or negative intuitive responses, and, if the latter, to attempt to modulate this tendency as much as possible.

May 22

"…Things fall apart;
the centre cannot hold."

W.B. Yeats

Every lawyer can readily recite several "crash-and-burn" stories that resulted from the clash of unmanaged personal and professional demands. The legal battlefield is strewn with disillusionment, alienation, broken relationships, and the broken dreams of lawyers and their loved ones. What starts out as a "storybook life" often defaults into brokenness and personal despair. Among other indicia of discontent, the divorce rate among lawyers generally appears to be higher than the divorce rate among other professionals. For example, researchers at Notre Dame's Center for the Study of Contemporary Society found that the percentage of lawyers who are divorced is significantly higher than the percentage of doctors who are divorced, and that the difference is particularly pronounced among women.

Many of the salient characteristics of the modern lawyer's work life provide ready rationales for an escalating divorce rate. These are of little comfort, however, to those whose security and well-being have been so pervasively disordered by marital break-ups.

Modern family life is inherently stressful, with even the youngest member's harried schedule coming into conflict with the needs and demands of the others. Long gone are the days of nightly family gatherings around the dinner table, followed by a quiet evening of homework, reading, and TV. Yet, while current family time challenges are what they are, we do not have to become unwitting victims of the extreme busyness that plagues society as a whole.

Following the practices set forth in our reflections, we can bring the busyness issue within the transformative triangle of awareness, acceptance, and action. We might first become mindfully aware of the competing personal, family, and professional demands that put so many claims on our time. Then, accepting these competing demands, we can sort the "wheat from the chaff," attempting to discern how our personal values and beliefs require that we prioritize our time. Finally, we can take the action of firmly but flexibly regulating our own behavior so that our actual use of time more closely parallels our chosen values and beliefs.

May 23

> "The search for meaningful work is no different from the search for meaning elsewhere. It involves a search for grounding—a sense of connectedness to ourselves, to our co-workers, to the environment, and to the ground of our being."
>
> *Rolf Osterberg and Thomas Naylor*

On so many days, in so many ways, we may feel "possessed" by our calendars, our clients, our families, and our responsibilities. Life seems to be an endless series of demanding requirements and responsibilities, leading us to ponder, yet again, *is that all there is?*

When the going gets this heavy, it is time to metaphorically shed our tight-fitting, heavy winter coats, and intentionally don light and breezy attire, the "loose garments" of joyous living. While we rightfully approach our workday with diligence and intentionality, we do not have to totally exclude the fun, lightness, and laughter that can often lighten the course of a rigorous workday. These attributes can be both found in communion with others, or can be self-created, if we are only willing to remain open to the possibilities.

A recent study of over 1,500 law firm associates, conducted by the National Association of Legal Professionals, confirms what many of us have always known: the most important factor for the lawyer in determining whether a legal position is "meaningful" depends mainly on the person's relationship with colleagues. Although compensation, quality of work, autonomy, and other factors are certainly considered within the "meaningful" assessment, the quality of professional relationships is the *primary* factor.

As social beings, legally trained or not, we naturally hunger for acceptance, a sense of belonging, and a feeling of being valued by others. While we readily value traditional professional abilities in the workplace, we might also appreciate the "emotional intelligence" that can contribute so meaningfully and abundantly to the quality, texture, and fabric of our lives.

> "The purpose of life is not to be happy. It is to be useful, to be honorable, to be compassionate, to have it make some difference that you have lived and lived well."
>
> *Ralph Waldo Emerson*

Tom Brokaw reports that the idea for his best-seller, *The Greatest Generation*, blossomed while he was preparing a documentary commemorating the fortieth anniversary of D-Day, when he was intimately engaged with the then-60- and 70-year-old heroes of June 6, 1944. As he listened to the quiet, reverent, and humble telling of their stories, Brokaw came to understand that he was meant to memorialize the heroes' epic tales, and thus, his influential book came to be.

One of the heroes highlighted in Brokaw's book was Chesterfield Smith. On D-Day, despite gunshot wounds already suffered, Smith demonstrated incredible valor in personally dismantling enemy gunnery. Without Smith's actions, the equipment, positioned on a hilltop, could have killed and maimed many more thousands of disembarking soldiers as the invasion of Normandy began.

After the war, Smith became a lawyer, and he exhibited equivalent valor during his fifty-five-year legal career. Even today, Smith is often referred to as "America's Lawyer" and "the conscience of the legal profession." Smith was the outspoken president of the ABA during the Watergate era. Smith's unambiguous manifesto: "*No man is above the law,*" appeared on the front page of *The New York Times* following the infamous Saturday Night Massacre on October 20, 1973.

Smith's words and actions were defining moments in the American legal system, just as his deeds had been on June 6, 1944. Drawing on the strength of a well-nurtured character, Smith made his controversial assertion without benefit of consensus, and without regard to the potentially disastrous professional and personal consequences of his outspokenness.

Many lawyer-statesmen like Chesterfield Smith have sanctified our legal history. The legal profession had and has many heroes. As members of the noble profession, we are each charged with displaying our own brand of heroism, leaving it to greater forces to determine whether that will be of the spectacular or unspectacular variety.

May 25

> "It takes a lot of courage to release the familiar
> and seemingly secure, to embrace the new.
> But there is no real security in what is no
> longer meaningful. There is more security in
> the adventurous and exciting, for in movement
> there is life, and in change there is power."
>
> *Alan Cohen*

"*If you want what we have, then do what we do,*" is just one of the many wise sayings heard in Twelve-Step recovery programs. The directive is used to address the common misperception of newcomers to recovery that all life problems will be solved merely by putting down the addictive substance or behavior. The longer-term members attempt to gently lead the newcomer to understand that, in addition to abstinence, a new way of living must be found and cultivated, and the "causes and conditions" that led to the addiction must be rooted out.

Whether we are dealing with addiction or some other desired change in our lives, we are well-advised to observe those who embody our desired characteristics and actions, and then to seek their guidance on the process needed to attain them. And it is a *process*, since it is the rare transformation that occurs immediately. In most instances, we must be content with trial and error and patient improvement.

All significant change requires courage of at least two types. We first need the courage that allows us to firmly and finally declare: *This I will do no longer.* The second type of courage is that which is needed to maintain our initial decision, after the beginning euphoria has worn off. Whether we are in need of initial courage or maintenance courage, or both, seeking the help of others will always lighten our load.

> **"I've learned that people will forget what you said and what you did, but people will never forget how you made them feel."**
>
> *Maya Angelou*

Kindness is an attitude and behavior that is welcome and appropriate in all of our personal and professional dealings. The few extra seconds involved in holding open a door, letting another car merge into traffic, or listening patiently without interruption—these are the actions and disciplines that benevolently but firmly announce to the world: *I am myself, I own my time and my space in this world, I will not be unconsciously propelled by the angst that surrounds me.*

The rewards of kindness can be immediate, as in a kindly nod of appreciation, or other acknowledgment. At other times, our own soul may be the only witness to the growing wholeness and integrity that results from simply "doing the next right thing."

Clients who seek our advice often suffer greatly from a lack of kindness in so many areas of their lives. No matter how complicated the legal dilemma involved, we should attend to our client's personhood and circumstances not only with legal competence, but also with human kindness.

May 27

> "Do not wish to be anything but what you are,
> and try to be that perfectly."
>
> *St. Francis de Sales*

It is not unusual to dream of "leaving it all" if our workdays are filled with unsatisfying and energy-draining work. Flight fantasies intensify the longer we remain in stress-producing situations, and especially where we see no relief in sight.

In some work situations, where conditions are truly abusive, an actual change of environments may be necessary. An enlightening question to ask ourselves when we are considering such a change is: does this objectionable person/place/thing affect my ego or does it affect my welfare? In other words, is it something that I would prefer changed, or is it something that must be changed in order to assure my dignity and integrity? If our welfare rather than our ego is at stake, a change of environments is probably required.

In many more instances, however, what is called for in response to an objectionable situation is a change in our thinking and actions. The provocative title of Jon Kabat Zinn's work, *Wherever You Go, There You Are*, reminds us that we take ourselves with us when we change jobs, neighborhoods, spouses, or other life circumstances. Since the maintenance of our serenity level is "an inside job," chances are good that the stress and discomfort experienced in one work situation will be transferred to the next, unless we make the necessary inner changes to assure that our own inner house is in order.

May 28

> "We cannot care for the soul of the Law from the outside through transient ideologies or managerial fads. If renewed imagination is called for, it must emerge from lawyers' dedication to recovering the soulful dimensions of their own work."
>
> *Benjamin Sells*

What stories should we be telling ourselves and each other, including the newest members of the profession, as we seek to restore the community and professionalism that the law has so proudly witnessed in prior generations?

Walter Bennett, author of *The Lawyer's Myth, Reviving Ideals in the Legal Profession*, strongly advocates the exploration, reshaping, and transmittal of contemporary mythology as the primary vehicle for restoring the ideals of the legal profession. Against the familiar landscape of the Arthurian myth of Parcival's quest for the Holy Grail, Bennett details how the individual lawyer-hero's quest for greater wholeness and higher consciousness through service to others will constitute a major source of healing for the profession's many ills. Bennett informs us that such restoration can be effected if we undertake to "rekindle the campfires and create new circles in which our new stories can be told."

May 29

> "Set your expectations high; find men and women whose integrity and values you respect; get their agreement on a course of action; and give them your ultimate trust."

John Akers

As lawyers, we often act as if it is a "badge of honor" to single-handedly confront and deal with our personal and professional problems. What's more, we often do not believe that there is any other way to meet these challenges. Who, we ask, could we possibly trust enough to allow them access to our most private fears and concerns? The vulnerability and humility required in asking for such assistance often seems too hefty a price to pay.

Yet, spiritual wisdom and experience strongly suggest that we at least begin to cultivate the "we of it all." What I cannot do alone, often, we can do together, minus the pain of fear, loneliness, and desperation that is so characteristic of single-handed combat.

Years ago, confronted with a very serious medical situation, I found that, despite many years of skilled "legal jousting," I could not strategize, fight, or negotiate my way out of the very painful situation. Emotional and physical survival required that I find a power greater than myself to help me through the situation, since it soon became clear that my personal power regarding the situation was near nonexistent. That greater power was initially found in the support of other people, and ultimately, in a God of my understanding.

They kept me afloat when I perceived approaching annihilation.

May 30

> "To care for anyone else enough to make their
> problems one's own, is ever the beginning
> of one's ethical development."
>
> *Felix Adler*

In the spiritual realm, the term "hospitality" means much more than entertaining people or making them feel comfortable in our homes. Hospitality is a way of living life, and, according to theologian Henri Nouwen, primarily entails creating a welcoming space, where the stranger can enter, feel at home, and become a friend. The purpose of hospitality is not to change people, but to offer them a space where changes they elect can occur.

While Nouwen's book, *The Wounded Healer*, focuses on the manner in which clergy can shape their ministry based upon a true understanding of hospitality, Nouwen's insights apply equally to all persons who seek to serve others in their professional dealings. Lawyers especially can benefit from a deeper understanding of hospitality, since they so often encounter the other, the Biblical "stranger," during times of deep distress, anguish, and tragedy. Nouwen writes: "But it has become very difficult for us today to fully understand the implications of hospitality. Like the Semitic nomads, we live in a desert with many lonely travelers who are looking for a moment of peace, for a fresh drink and for a sign of encouragement so that they can continue their mysterious search for freedom."

Nouwen explains that there are two prerequisites for offering hospitality to others. First, the host must truly feel at home in his own house, that is, must feel "comfortable in his own skin," and second, the host must create a free and fearless space for the visitor. It is only when we become our truly authentic selves that we can reach out to others and invite them onto the broad highway of healing.

May 31

> "The prophet and the martyr do
> not see the hooting throng.
> Their eyes are fixed on the eternities."
>
> *Benjamin Cardozo*

The recently released Carnegie Foundation's *Study on Educating Lawyers* reviewed the teaching practices of sixteen law schools that were chosen as being representative of the approximately 200 ABA-approved law schools. Not surprisingly, the Foundation concluded that the institutions "fail to complement the focus or skill in legal analysis with effective support for developing ethical and social skills." The researchers also found (as most lawyers will confirm from their own training) that law students are frequently criticized by their professors if they allow their innate sense of fairness, justice, and compassion to "cloud their legal analysis." Thus, law students are effectively instructed to leave their souls at the door as they enter the hallowed halls of academia.

Can this possibly be the standard of the 21st century lawyer, who is called upon to provide a corrective for a struggling profession in a very hurting world? The Carnegie Foundation researchers think not, in that they recommend that legal educators devote a significant portion of the law school curriculum to "an explanation of the identity, rules and dispositions consonant with the fundamental purposes of the legal profession."

Just as importantly, we, the existing members of this profession, must demand and work for an educational protocol that will engage not only the rational faculties of our newest colleagues, but one that will also engage what the Foundation terms the "moral imagination" of these students.

> "Remember that fear always lurks behind perfectionism.
> Confronting your fears and allowing yourself the
> right to be human can, paradoxically, make yourself
> a happier and more productive person."
>
> *David M. Burns*

When is less more and when is more less? We learn through experience to refine the impulse, especially common among lawyers, to get things "just right." A "middle-road" approach is our best ally in the fight against perfectionism.

A sense of proportion may not seem intuitive to the "master achievers" who inhabit the legal halls. Yet, just as a song writer follows a formulaic pattern of verse, chorus, bridge, and return to verse, so, too, the legal professional can rely significantly on tested experience and legal formulae when dealing with novel issues. We do not have to reinvent the wheel for each new matter. Instead, when we have come to appropriately value our own legal talents, we can trust that we will properly handle each matter by extrapolating from past learnings, and combining newly crafted and nuanced modifications.

Then, having completed our creative work in a thorough, competent manner, we should appreciate that we do not have to "micromanage" further details to the point of licking the stamp and dropping off the envelope. Our good work is good enough.

June 2

> "A little nonsense now and then,
> Is cherished by the wisest man."
>
> *Roald Dahl*

The story is told of a man who measured the passage of time by the number of summers he lovingly passed with his cherished wife.

Each year, our entire beings open to the seasonal changes that herald the arrival of another golden and glorious summer. Days lengthen, schedules lighten, escapes are plotted, and smiles appear where before there were none.

Take note, fine legal counselor, of the cyclical dance of nature that defines the rhythm of life itself! Vacate, vacate, thy place of legal confinement, and have some fun!

We are not meant to stodgily operate outside of the realm of life's precious engagements.

The warm breezes of summer, a blazing sunset, a romp in the surf with the kids—these seasonal treasures are not to be missed another day, another year, another lifetime.

See, touch, and taste the glory of the summer's day, and become revived in the ocean of life.

June 3

> "Only those who will risk going too far can possibly find out how far one can go."
>
> *T.S. Eliot*

After sufficient reflection, we will discover the exact nature of the dreams that we alone must pursue. The content of our dreams does not always present as a completed picture. More often, an initial idea presents, and, if ignored, presents again. A recurring idea, sometimes sprinkled with pieces of nightly dreams, and supplemented by other happenings and "coincidences," seems to tug at our consciousness, demanding our attention, like a cranky child. If we summon the courage to intentionally name and examine the demand, we are often rewarded with the presentation of the next piece of the puzzle, and the process repeats, until we reach critical mass.

Following through, with even the smallest exploratory action, we will be rewarded as that one small action logically leads us to the next step. Eventually, the force of the increasing momentum allows the dream to appear in tangible form, much as the *Pieta* eventually sprung forth from a block of stone. "The marble not yet carved can hold the form of every thought the greatest artist has," wrote Michelangelo.

Our life has a unique purpose and meaning that takes shape through a unique alchemy of innate desires and abilities, mixed with an intentional and courageous pursuit of the desired mode of expression. The fact is that we *will* reach the dreams that we identify, select as our own, and consciously and loyally pursue. Such achievement constitutes the ultimate expression of our humanity.

June 4

> "The self is not something ready-made,
> but something in continuous formation
> through choice of action."

Mary Daly

The cumulative effect of stressed working conditions, conflicted relationships, and haphazard self-care, is often a sense of being overwhelmed and underappreciated. Even when we have firmly committed to following a path of personal growth, trying always to do the next right thing, we may sometimes look enviously upon others who *seem* to be advancing in the material world with nary a glance toward personal growth or service. Maybe, we say to ourselves, we too should be taking the very same shortcuts.

At times like these, we need to be our own best friend and advocate. Positive self-talk, reminding ourselves that we have chosen a spiritual path to bring greater meaning and joy to our lives, might be coupled with some very nourishing self-care, whether that takes the form of physical exercise, a good book, meditation, dinner with a friend, or a few hours, or a few days, at the mountains or the shore.

All growth—physical, mental, and spiritual—has its ups and downs and includes those times when we become discouraged, and seriously contemplate re-upping with the easier, softer way. Rather than forcefully resisting our doubts and concerns, we can sit quietly with them, allowing them a seat on the committee, so to speak, yet also allowing the voice of our higher selves to chair the "committee discussions."

Being gentle with ourselves, trusting that we will eventually choose to rejoin the road less travelled, is often the comforting companionship that our weary souls crave most during times of discouragement.

> "May the sacredness of your work bring healing,
> light, and renewal to those who work with you
> and to those who see and receive your work."
>
> *John O'Donohue*

What does it mean, or what could it mean, to accomplish "sacred" work? What makes work, or anything else, sacred?

Author and spiritual teacher Rabbi Irwin Kula informs us that the word for work in Hebrew is *avodah*, which is also the word for prayer or divine service.

How might we ever imagine our daily office happenings to parallel a sacred prayer or an inspirational ritual?

Rabbi Kula suggests that we evaluate our work life by asking three questions: 1) Has my work brought me joy? If not, why not, and what can I change so that my life brings me more joy? 2) Has my work contributed to the good, and how can I make my work create more good? 3) Has my work been creative, and has it maximized the contributions I can make to this world?

Periodically revisiting these questions keeps us on track, and allows us to re-imagine work in a manner that blesses us and all those we encounter in our professional activities.

June 6

> "Once men are caught up in an
> event they cease to be afraid.
> Only the unknown frightens men."
>
> *Antoine de St. Exupery*

The actual experience of personal transformation occurs when we finally cross over the line in the sand, from the side that reads: "That is what I want to become," to the side that proclaims "This is what I now am." While awareness and acceptance are the tools which prepare us for this momentous crossing, it is action alone that actually transforms our deepest hopes into our cherished realities. Observe anyone who has spent years in therapy, continuously planning to change careers, or assert himself at work, or leave a soul-crushing marriage, but who leaves the therapist's office with no firm plan or commitment to take even the smallest action to move toward the supposedly desired goal. *If nothing changes, nothing changes.*

The action steps we take toward change need not be major ones, especially as we first start out. Rather, making just one phone call or reading one useful book can be the impetus needed to further open the door to willingness. Once opened, we can proceed, one step at a time, one day at a time, toward the transformation we seek. Action, not *thinking* about action, loudly proclaims to our inner selves and to the universe: *Yes, this I must have, and nothing, no fear or discouragement or other obstacle, can or will stop me.*

When our words and our actions, our inner and outer selves, are so synchronized, we will often be surprised to find how quickly and efficiently the universe responds by providing what mythologist Joseph Campbell terms the "thousand pairs of helping hands" needed to accomplish our desired goals.

> "Never put a period where
> God has put a comma."
>
> *Gracie Allen*

Just when we may be finally ready to give up on another person, a relationship, a professional undertaking, or our ability to achieve a desired goal, that may be just the moment when unmerited goodness and grace appear on the scene, ready to cleanse, renew, and transform that which we are ready to declare hopeless.

Timing, like so many other things, is divine. Changes occur on the time schedule that is right for us; however, this may differ greatly from the time schedule we have set for ourselves. The fact is that human beings are not possessed of the power to set an exact timetable for the important things of life. We learn, we grow, we change, we reconcile, we grieve, and we heal on a schedule that is not of our own making, but that can be enhanced by our cooperative participation. We can, by not resisting the natural flow of these happenings, move through them with greater ease and tranquility, graciously accepting that it is left to a power greater than ourselves to establish our life's mega-timetable.

What we resist, persists, taught psychologist Carl Jung. The tree that is able to sway in the wind flourishes, as does a person who calmly accepts each moment as it is. If we continually attempt to bombard our problems with self-will, we will continue living in the problem. Conversely, when we accept what is, keeping the focus on ourselves, seeking merely to do the next right thing, we will peacefully advance toward the next right outcome.

June 8

"The entire legal profession—lawyers, judges, law teachers—have become so mesmerized with the stimulation of the courtroom contest that we tend to forget that we ought to be healers— healers of conflicts. Doctors, in spite of astronomical medical costs, still retain a high degree of public confidence because they are perceived as healers. Should lawyers not be healers? Healers, not warriors? Healers, not procurers? Healers, not hired guns?"

Warren Burger

With few exceptions, the legal academy has disclaimed responsibility for guiding the development of the young lawyer's professional identity. Having trained its students to "think like lawyers," the academy congratulates itself on having fulfilled its responsibilities. Yet our students need broader support and direction from their professional elders if they are to successfully meet the challenges of modern-day lawyering.

At a minimum, students need to be exposed to the full panoply of alternative paths to a successful and meaningful law practice. It is simply not true that there are only two recognized flavors of lawyering, public service and "high corporate."

Students should be exposed to emerging alternative practice trends, including the comprehensive law movement, pioneered by Law Professor Susan Daicoff. Comprehensive lawyering views law as a healing profession, and takes an explicitly humanistic, interdisciplinary, restorative, and therapeutic approach to law and lawyering. Daicoff identifies the "converging vectors" of this movement as: collaborative law, creative problem-solving, holistic justice, preventive law, problem-solving courts, procedural justice, restorative justice, and therapeutic jurisprudence. Daicoff's work, together with that of other authors in the fields of lawyer satisfaction and alternative law practices, should be required reading for all law students.

Finally, law school leaders are responsible for providing an effective counterbalance to certain unchallenged "cultural norms" that are prevalent in most law schools. These include the idea that only those in the top 10 percent will have successful legal careers, and that the law school experience is "worthless" if the student is not on a law journal or holding some other prestigious position. These self-defeating beliefs, which contribute to the creation of a competitive and alienated student body, will continue unless the school's faculty and administration effectively challenge this faulty "student wisdom."

> "Our deepest fear is not that we are inadequate.
> Our deepest fear is that we are powerful beyond measure.
> It is our Light, not our Darkness, that most frightens us.
> We ask ourselves, who am I to be brilliant,
> gorgeous, talented, fabulous?
> Actually, who are you NOT to be?"
>
> *Nelson Mandela*

Although our legal work can often feel stressful or overly repetitive, most lawyers have experienced those beautifully intense moments when we think: "*Yes, this is why I became a lawyer, this is what makes me feel alive.*"

Creating and manifesting excellent examples of the lawyer's craft can be exhilarating and life-sustaining. In fact, we are charged by no less than the universe itself to explore every nook and cranny of our profession to find those matters that truly ignite our passions.

Of course, different people are passionate about different aspects of lawyering. Some of us find our joy in artful presentations to courts and clients, or in producing such a "tight" memo that a single additional word would dispel the directive's majestic import. Others savor the creativity involved in structuring a settlement that *exactly* addresses the needs of all concerned. Some, through dedicated service, have experienced the truly awesome moments when the legal system operates in its highest and purest form, yielding freedom for an innocent person, or appropriate custody for a hurting child.

Every person's dreams, every person's liberty, and every person's hope for the future is hinged upon the maintenance of a legal system that, through skillful application of the lawyer's craft, permits the exercise of the basic rights and liberties of our democratic society. Surely, in the fulfillment of this monumental and never-ending task, there is room for every lawyer to labor, engaging their unique talents, skills and passions, while providing vital service to others.

To despairingly state that there is no area of the law that interests and excites us is akin to stating that there is no area of life that interests and excites us.

As Nelson Mandela has said, the question is not: who are we to assert ourselves into these quests, the question is: who are we not to, given the backdrop of our professional training, skill, and abilities.

June 10

> ## "We should only do those righteous actions which we cannot stop ourselves from doing."
>
> *Simone Weil*

We were often told in childhood that actions speak louder than words, yet it is only our maturity and experience that allow us to appreciate the verity of the adage. No matter how persuasively we may try to counsel others about "doing the right thing," it is our attitudes, beliefs, and behaviors that "speak" the loudest.

I once knew an ethics law professor who reflected such disdain for his students that I discounted any "great wisdom" that he offered. Conversely, I learned more about ethics from observing a beloved godmother than I learned in law school or since.

Sometimes we encounter such acts of profound courage and nobility that within a matter of moments, our entire lives are transformed. This occurred, for example, as I watched 9/11 videotapes, showing the fire department chaplain, Father Mychal Judge, praying with his men just moments before he and they died, trying to save others in the Twin Towers. This example of the ultimate service is etched on my heart with such precision and freshness that I am continuously transformed by the recollection.

The lawyer's craft is words. Yet, the lawyer's lasting legacy will be found in the example of care and integrity with which the lawyer provides service for others.

June 11

> ## "To be a hero or a heroine,
> ## one must give an order to oneself."
>
> *Simone Weil*

There are more than 6.6 billion people in the world, yet lawyers often complain of feeling alienated and alone.

Surrounded by people or not, lawyers often experience the deepest form of alienation, alienation from our true selves, the person who once laughed, and loved, and who experienced lawyering as a giant, bold adventure, hoping to "be somebody" while helping others.

At some unspecified point, the fullness of life seemed to transform, almost unnoticed, into the humdrum responsibilities of getting to the office, going through the motions, arriving home exhausted, and getting up the next day to do the same thing all over again.

If we have arrived at this point, the immediate question we must address is: *what must we do to gain passage back home to fullness?*

If we are able to honestly appreciate the depth of our alienation and its consequences, we may come to the critical liminal place, the jumping-off point, where we must take one of two forks in the road. We either become willing to go to any lengths to recapture our enervating life force, or we default to joining the dull-eyed legions who have wordlessly committed to making a living instead of making a life.

The journey back home to the fullness of ourselves is the spiritual journey we have been discussing throughout our reflections. The spiritual disciplines discussed throughout—prayer, meditation, mindfulness, self-awareness, honest sharing with others, taking action, moving beyond our comfort zones, relinquishing self-defeating behaviors, service to others, gratitude, amending relationships, connecting with nature and a higher power, being in the moment, experiencing "enough," self-nurturing, and many others—these are the tools that, when properly developed and regularly utilized, will hasten our journey back home to ourselves.

June 12

> ## "The biggest human temptation is to settle for too little."
>
> *Thomas Merton*

Surprisingly, one of the hardest changes to make in life and lawyering is one that involves a move from "good enough" to better. A very wise man taught that "good is the enemy of best." When our life or work circumstances are very painful, we are often less resistant to seek help and summon the courage to change, since it seems that our very survival is at stake. However, when these circumstances are "okay" or "good enough," we often carry on, hoping things will get better or change, but mainly proceeding in a default mode, saying to ourselves, "let's just see what happens."

Reinhold Niebuhr's *Serenity Prayer* encourages us to accept the things we cannot change, and to change the things that we can. "Good enough," especially when it describes several important areas of our lives, does not make for a life that is happy, joyous, and free. Rather, it makes for a life that is "good enough."

Less than optimal situations can provide a vehicle for our development and the exercise of courageous behaviors, which can greatly enhance our lives. Whether a situation is gravely painful, or consistently depleting, the path to wholeness consists of the same elements: honest *awareness* of the true nature and effects of the situation, *acceptance* of such facts and the physical, mental, and emotional consequences resulting therefrom, and *action*, no matter how small the steps, taken to increase the vitality and integrity of our lives.

The bravery needed to change the less dramatic, but consistently depleting, aspects of our lives involves a special type of courage, one that implicitly proclaims to ourselves and others that we will not allow fear to limit our rightful claim to the best that life has to offer.

June 13

> ## "We can only be said to be alive in those moments when our hearts are conscious of our treasures."
>
> *Thornton Wilder*

Just what are our treasures? What people, places, things, institutions, deities, values and beliefs do we hold nearest to our hearts as our most precious treasures?

On September 11, 2001, when Stephen Siler, an off-duty firefighter and father of five, heard that the Twin Towers were under attack, he headed directly to the site to help. When his truck was stopped at the Brooklyn Battery Tunnel, he raced to the Towers on foot, for three miles, carrying more than 75 pounds of equipment on his back.

Siler perished that day, along with 342 other firefighters.

These firefighters, along with so many other heroes, were driven by one treasured value that trumped all others—the desire to help the people and the city they had vowed to protect, no matter what the personal cost. Can we ever forget the stunned, yet awed, recollections of survivors, who, when speaking of these heroes, repeated over and over again: "We were running away from the horror while they were running toward it."

Although our duties vary dramatically, lawyers, like firefighters, proudly claim their place in the list of service professions. Like their predecessors, most incoming law students cite a desire to do meaningful work and to help others, as some of their primary incentives for choosing to attend law school. Yet, by the time they graduate, most students are much more interested in money and prestige than in serving others. Not surprisingly, studies confirm that the students' levels of depression, alienation, and discontent rise proportionately as extrinsic motivators replace the intrinsic desires for meaning and service.

A calling to service attracts most firefighters and lawyers to their professions. Yet, unlike firefighters, many law students are diverted from their desire to serve because the legal culture endorses *only* power, possessions, and prestige as the profession's "crown jewels."

While our society and our profession continue to affirm extrinsic motivators, the more sparkle the better, our souls also long for meaningful service and excellent work.

June 14

> ## "Life shrinks or expands in proportion to one's courage."
>
> *Anais Nin*

Harsh winds can blow strong. Sometimes, no matter how determined our efforts to shed our lethargy, disappointment, sadness, or depression, these conditions can seem intransigent. Other times, the conditions may seem to have abated, only to bounce back with such increased velocity that we despair of ever leaving them behind.

We should try not to project too much as we navigate these emotional storms. Taking it one day at a time, sometimes one minute at a time, is the best we can do. As best we are able, we should continue to suit up, show up, and do the next right thing.

We can also take solace in the fact that no one has ever disproved the spiritual theorem, *"This too shall pass."* While the pain of waiting is very real, and we should rightly consider potentially ameliorating actions, sometimes the best thing we can do is sit with, and embrace the pain. The renowned psychologist Carl Jung taught that everything we resist persists. Conversely, everything that we allow to pass through our lives, uninterrupted, has a beginning, a middle, and an end.

A heart-wrenchingly truthful conversation with our God, however perceived, or with a trusted friend or therapist, may be helpful during these dark times. *Be still and know.* Our inner wisdom will eventually come to the fore, given the appropriate invitation and hospitable welcoming. And, as a good friend always advises in such circumstances, *"Just don't quit five minutes before the miracle!"*

June 15

> ## "Beware the barrenness
> ## of a busy life."
>
> *Socrates*

One of the greatest impediments to our tranquility is the creation of an unrealistic "to do" list. It is not the list itself that is problematic; it is the entry of an impossible number of tasks for any given twenty-four-hour period that triggers our anxiety and discomfort. However, if we are thoughtful and realistic in our planning, we will, in fact, get to everything that *truly* needs to be done today. The rest we will accomplish in due time, or, the entries will be eliminated in other ways.

If we daily take the time to be still and to go inside, we will receive the guidance, the intuitive thought, as to what must be on today's "to do" list, and, equally important, what should be placed on our "not today" list. Properly and realistically structured, a list of tasks can keep us on track. Conversely, if we fail to discern and prioritize our tasks in this simple manner, we will soon be overwhelmed by calls, emails, conferences, and miscellaneous energy-draining "crises" that present throughout our workdays.

We can select and list the items which *must* truly be attended to today, and we can "honor" (and remember!) the others by giving them an entry on the "not today" list. That is the best we can do, and it is truly enough. We are then freed to creatively and mindfully attend to our current tasks, without wasting energy by fretting about what remains undone. Despite management jargon to the contrary, soulful human beings were not meant to multitask, we were meant to be present for the task at hand. We alone manage, or fail to manage, the tasks of our workdays.

June 16

> "One day, after we have mastered the winds and the waves, gravity and the tides, we will harness for God the energies of love. And then, for the second time in human history, mankind will have discovered fire."
>
> *Pierre Teilhard de Chardin*

While few would deny that our world is sorely in need of love, the love that is most needed is of the deeply authentic variety, not merely the love of good intentions, benevolence, or kindness. True love, higher love, derives not so much from kindness and helping others; rather, it springs from knowing who we were meant to be, and acting accordingly. We can believe that we love another, yet if we are conducting ourselves in a self-centered, narcissistic manner, our "love" may constitute little more than attachment and need.

The world's libraries are a treasure trove for those who seek the "ultimate" definition of love. Poets, ministers, philosophers, romantics, and free-lancers of all sorts have memorialized their contribution to the cause. One seemingly workable formulation for lawyers has been contributed by psychologist Scott Peck: *"Love is the will to extend one's self for the purpose of nurturing one's own or another's spiritual growth."*

Peck's definition is helpful in that it specifies the elements of love—the intention, the action, and the results—in much the same manner that the elements of a cause of action might be parsed. Using the formulation as a guide, we are individually accorded the responsibility for determining specific required actions, as well as what constitutes "nurturance" or "spiritual growth," within any given factual setting.

While we are invited to craft our individual formulations, Peck's definition of love provides a foundational understanding of love that is centered in awareness of both the self and other, and that includes elements of discernment, boundary-setting, and action, rather than popular notions of love that center on connection, feeling, sentiment, and pleasure-seeking.

Whatever our personal formulation, we do well to reflect on the properties of the incredible force of love, if ever we desire, as the philosopher envisions, "*...to harness these energies...and for the second time...discover fire.*"

> "At some level, however subterranean it might be, we are always watching ourselves, always monitoring our thoughts, words and our deeds."
>
> *Marsha Sinetar*

With the above words, spiritual author and psychotherapist Marsha Sinetar encourages us to "keep awake" and to deliberately select "elegant choices" for our lives. Sinetar defines elegant choices as those options that tend toward truth, beauty, honor, and courage—choices that are life-supporting in both motive and quality.

We have all witnessed certain extraordinary public events that rightfully claim the label of elegance: Jacqueline Kennedy's deportment at her husband's funeral; the Amish community's reconciliation with the killer of their schoolchildren; Lou Gehrig's unforgettable *"Today, I am the luckiest man alive"* speech; young Sarah Hughes, skating her way to a gold medal, capturing the heart and reinvigorating the soul of everyone who witnessed the elegant transcendence of her performance.

The annals of our noble legal history hold within them events of similar transcendent elegance. Few today, for example, can appreciate the extreme courage and elegance required in defending positions and persons deplored by the societies of yesteryear.

While relatively few of us may become involved in highly notorious legal matters, our daily choices, be they elegant or inelegant, will also have major effects on our character, our family, our associates, and our profession.

Whether we offer a candid response or a dilatory half-truth, whether we draft passable motion papers or those that reflect our full attention and abilities, whether we courageously admit to an oversight or attempt to cover it up by blaming others—in all of these instances, we need to choose wisely, if we wish to bequeath a positive legacy for future generations to behold.

June 18

> "...[J]ust as despair can come to one only from other human beings, hope, too, can be given to one only by other human beings."
>
> *Elie Wiesel*

Life is not meant to be survived, gotten through, wrestled to the ground, or overcome. Life is to be lived. Life is the purpose of life. If our current worldview partakes of a "vale of tears" backdrop, we need to consider what changes are necessary so that we can live more happily. "Happily" does not mean problem-free, or without occasional storms; rather, it means finding peace and guidance *within* the storms of life.

When problems do arise, we can maintain our equanimity if we have taken the time for a "pre-storm" review of our friends, mentors, family members, and acquaintances, to determine, with particularity, who's in our court, and for *exactly* what issues. We seldom find one person who can unselfishly and unconditionally support us as we travel through all of the difficult issues in our lives. So, for example, while we may be blessed to have an understanding and supportive spouse, who normally helps us to keep balance during times of stress, our spouse may not be the person to whom we should turn when one of our children is in great pain. At such times, our spouse may well be experiencing his or her own distress regarding the child's situation, and therefore may not be able to give comfort and aid in this situation.

If we are calmly discerning about this matter, we will often discover, to our great relief, that for every type of issue we may face, we already have a person "in our court," (or one who can be readily located), who has experienced similar issues, and who is perfectly suited to listen, support, and guide us through the storm, if only we are willing to ask.

June 19

> ## "The love of our neighbor in all its fullness
> ## simply means being able to say to him,
> ## 'What are you going through?'"
>
> *Simone Weil*

A recurring analysis in our jurisprudence focuses on what a "reasonable person" would do in a given situation. In the spiritual realm, the "reasonable" is given a wide berth, and each person is afforded great latitude in choosing the exact course of his own life's journey.

When dealing with colleagues, clients, family members, and others, it often helps if we can suspend our critical judgments of others, substituting instead an inclusive, welcoming hospitality. While logic and critical analysis are valued tools of our professional craft, human beings are not "issues" to be analyzed. The human soul is not at home in a conversation that resembles a deposition. Instead, a proper blending of our critical faculties with our soulful humanity provides the proper backdrop for meaningful communication.

It also helps to distinguish the settings in which we are called upon to render professional advice, and those in which we are not. A spouse who describes the difficulty of working with a demanding boss may be seeking affirmance and encouragement, rather than an analysis of employment law. While our professional tools can enhance our dealings with others, they should not be employed as a substitute for an honest sharing of our experience and understanding. Not everything in life translates into a legal theorem; in fact, very little outside the office does. If we are able to listen "with the ear of the ear," it will become easier for us to allow others to voice their own opinions and understandings without our feeling the need to have the final word or to "set them straight."

Negative judgment differs greatly from peaceful discernment. If other people are acting in a reasonable fashion (broadly defined), they are entitled to their opinion and their individual "take" on life and its issues. Giving them the benefit of the doubt helps us to move gently and peacefully throughout our day, while harsh judgments keep us stuck in negativity and turmoil. As a friend advises, *be well enough to let others be wrong!*

June 20

> ## "Sin is humanity's refusal
> ## to be who we are."
>
> *Rabbi Abraham Herschel*

We often hear it said that imitation is the most sincere form of flattery, and to some degree, this is true. It is appropriate to model the characteristics and actions of those lawyers who exemplify the highest ideals of the profession. It is always a good idea to take the best and leave the rest. When, however, we seek, in a chameleon-like fashion, to duplicate another's personality and style—whether it be the very confident litigator, the sage senior partner, or the wise business counselor—we do ourselves and others a disservice. As each fingerprint is singular, so it is with our particular strengths, attributes, and talents. There is a great dignity associated with our being and our work if they are aligned with our inner, unique core.

We should seek to adopt the most noble and excellent characteristics of others, but always as a supplement, and not a substitute, for our own unique manifestation and way of being in the world.

June 21

> "He who believes is strong; he who doubts is weak.
> Strong convictions precede great actions."
>
> *Louisa May Alcott*

"*As you are now, I once was. As I am now, so you shall be, and I will go to the Father…*" This expression, uttered with an Irish brogue, and permanently etched in my memory, was a favorite of my 92-year-old grandmother, who was affectionately known as "Granny." As she spoke these words, Granny would reach across the table, taking the hand of my sister, the youngest family member, and, looking my sister in the eyes, she would continue: "*The young and the old, the young and the old.*" When Granny was unhappy with the behavior of a family member, she expressed herself emphatically, with a left-handed table-pounding, to grab attention, she would then draw a line with her forefinger, in a slow, deliberate motion, uttering "*Produce.*"

My grandmother did not say much, but what she said, and how she said it, remain with me today. She spoke only about what really mattered, and she said it in a way that we all got it. She communicated with words, gestures, and passionate embraces about who she was, who we were, and how she was connected to us. She made her mark permanently, as a woman who would tolerate nothing less than success.

Like the clever farm woman she was, she chose an action verb for success that was both a process and an outcome. "Produce" was what one was supposed to do in one's life space. Granny's goal in life was to live life fully, through all the ages and stages, to make deep abiding connections, and, ultimately, to produce.

Are our convictions so solidified, or are they more transient, subject to our modification and overrule, as convenient?

June 22

> ## "To keep the body in good health is a duty...
> ## otherwise we shall not be able to keep
> ## our mind strong and clear."
> *Guatama Siddharta*

Upon recovering from a serious bout with illness, we often experience a heightened gratitude for the normal daily functioning of our often-underappreciated bodies. Loss of physical capacity, great or small, sets in motion the release of adrenaline and noradrenaline, hormones designed to signal an alarm, coupled with a "fight-or-flight" response, when all is not well with the body.

Many serious ailments, cancer or diabetes, for example, and some commonly occurring maladies, such as a flu or anemia, serve to both lower our immune function and set the stage for the appearance of certain symptoms that mimic depression (fatigue, loss of energy, loss of pleasure and motivation). Consequently, as we recover from physical illness, we may also feel that a significant psychological weight has also been lifted.

Attention to the maintenance of our physical functioning is a primary responsibility of the well-matured adult. When we persistently take the necessary steps to maintain our physical well-being, we prepare ourselves for the full engagement with, and enjoyment of, the panoply of life's offerings.

June 23

> "One of the great undiscovered joys of life comes from doing everything one attempts to the best of one's ability. There is a special sense of satisfaction, a pride in surveying such a work, a work which is rounded, full, exact, complete in its parts...."
>
> *Og Mandino*

What key elements within our work of lawyering can provide for a sense of enhanced satisfaction?

Many of us find that a sense of pride and pleasure in our work normally progresses with each professional advancement, and our well-done work continues to sustain us. Yet, it is often helpful for busy professionals to find a happy medium between the stimulation and novelty associated with new learning in their work, and the confidence and assurance associated with the application of knowledge drawn from the well-grooved tracks of experience.

The nature of satisfaction and contentment is very subjective. If we wish to increase our satisfaction in the practice of law, we might review a recent "portfolio" of work with an eye to assessing what people, what subject matter, and what combination of newly developed and time-tested competencies, produced the greatest degree of satisfaction in our work days. This knowledge can help us to seek out and claim the types of legal work that yield the most personal satisfaction.

June 24

> "He who chooses the
> beginning of a road chooses
> the place it leads to."
>
> *Harry Emerson Fosdick*

Often, in business as in life, we come to the decisional fork in the road where going down one path or the other permanently alters who we are. We choose our path. We make that call. In these situations, it is helpful to have a pre-formed vision that allows us to predict the consequences of our actions and to anticipate the likely probabilities. For those new to the practice of law, it is wise to have the eyes and ears of a mentor figure, to pass along wisdom derived from experience.

June 25

> ## "The quality of a leader is reflected in the goals and standards they set for themselves."
>
> *Ray Kroc*

A lawyer is called by training and vocation to be a leader. This is our individual and collective calling, so, beginning even in law school, we must adequately prepare ourselves to assume the mantle of leadership.

There are at least two types of leaders—the first type rules from afar and from above, seldom "getting their hands dirty" in the rough and tumble of the work that needs doing. The second type of leader, the servant-leader, works with and among the people he or she leads. So, for example, the fire department officer often accompanies the team into the burning building, rather than merely giving orders from afar.

True leadership does not consist of vain displays of power and glory. True leadership is found in able example. The servant-leader humbly executes the task at hand, working beside fellow workers, mindfully employing the leader's long cultivated training and skill. As spiritual writer Parker Palmer phrases it: "Good leadership comes from people who have penetrated their own inner darkness and arrived at the place where we are at one with one another, people who can lead the rest of us to a place of 'hidden wholeness' because they have been there and know the way."

The world does not need more "ruling from afar" leaders; in fact, the world is sorely in need of more servant-leaders. Atticus Finch, the servant-leader lawyer portrayed in *To Kill a Mockingbird*, was not a noble hero because he managed 100 lawyers or because he deployed a SWAT team of young associates into a hostile courtroom. Atticus Finch was a hero because of the character he had developed, and the values he had cultivated, which permeated every aspect of his representation of an innocent, yet controversial, defendant.

The noble execution of the tasks of the noble profession has been ably completed by prior generations of real-life legal heroes. Lawyers of highly developed character and competence are also the needed warriors and heroes of today's legal profession.

June 26

> "For too many lawyers, the goal of success becomes the primary driver. But surveys of working lawyers tell us that a great many of them are unhappy even when their planned goals are realized..."
>
> *George W. Kaufman*

How much money do we really need to live a satisfying life? If we carry unexamined fears of financial insecurity, there will never be enough, even if our earnings are very high. Enough is a state of mind, it is not a dollar amount.

Once our basic needs are satisfied and we are somewhat comfortable, all else becomes a choice concerning how much of our life's energy we will exchange for what we consider valuable, including money, possessions, power, and prestige. There is nothing intrinsically wrong with any of these things; however, we must accept the idea that possessions have the potential to enslave or to liberate.

When gravely dissatisfied lawyers are asked why they have not left an emotionally painful position, the most common answer is that they cannot afford to. The more real and urgent question is *whether they can afford to stay in such a position.*

Do we really need to wait for the family trauma, the critical medical diagnosis, or the death of a best friend before we undertake the changes necessary to live the life we were meant to live? And just how will we answer the poet's ultimate challenge: *"Tell me, what is it you plan to do with your one wild and precious life."*

June 27

> "Self-reflection is the gateway to freedom.
> It also brings greater appreciation and enjoyment.
> We begin to enjoy spending time with our
> own mind, and we enjoy reflecting
> on our own experience..."
>
> *Dzigar Kongtrul*

There is no substitute for living an examined life. An examined life inevitably begins to incorporate enunciated personal values, together with self-assessment and self-correction when we fall short of our closely held values. There is no weakness associated with honest self-reflection; in fact, it is one of humanity's most courageous acts. It is only when we can begin to realistically assess our strengths and weaknesses that we can assume our authentic place in the world. Personal authenticity is the basic ingredient that allows us to be comfortable in our own skin.

If we are new to introspection, we do not need to be overly fearful of what will be revealed. After all, the act of looking does not create the problem. What we are already exists. Rather, the process of self-examination reveals those human tendencies and attributes that need tending. Once recognized and accepted, we can begin to take the necessary steps to eliminate those things that we find troublesome and that prevent us from being all that we can be.

June 28

> "I clean the teapot with the kind of attention I would have were I giving the baby Buddha or baby Jesus a bath."
>
> *Thich Nhat Hanh*

Kindness is an attitude and a behavior that is appropriate and appreciated in all of our professional and personal endeavors. Kindness, in its purest form, is not a proxy for weakness. Rather, true kindness is an attribute of those few who stand strong in their own being, who understand that all is sacred, and who are in touch with an abundant inner source of replenishment. A friend once remarked that her partner was so ungenerous that he acted as if he only had a limited number of "Good mornings" to utter each day. Consequently, he had to frugally allot them with great care. The partner did not comprehend that, as with many of the finer values, one paradoxically has to give kindness away to get it.

Mindfulness is a prerequisite to kindness since mindfulness requires that we be awake and attentive to the present moment. If we are centered in the eternal now, not thinking about tomorrow's court appearance or yesterday's stalled negotiation, we can bring our full attention to ourselves and the persons and things in front of us. Without the rush and drama that is so often associated with our lawyering, we can become gently aware of our own needs and wants, as well as those of others, and act accordingly.

June 29

> ## "If you are here unfaithfully with us, you're causing terrible damage."
>
> *Rumi*

The legal profession and individual lawyers are under increasing public derision as instances of greed, self-aggrandizement, and lawyer-involved scandals regularly bombard the public consciousness. This public derision is troubling, at best, to the legions of lawyers who competently and professionally fulfill their daily responsibilities to their clients and our noble profession. Nonetheless, it is commonly perceived that the most salient characteristics of contemporary lawyering are power, personal wealth, and a sense of being above the law, as opposed to the traditional advocate's characteristics of pursuing justice, fighting for the underdog, service, and zealous representation. Informed commentators seem to be in general agreement that there are three primary maladies that are affecting the legal profession today: 1) professionalism has decreased; 2) public opinion of lawyers and the profession has declined; and 3) lawyer dissatisfaction and dysfunction have increased.

To the extent the above maladies exist, the problem is, as lawyer-author Joseph Allegretti explains, not a problem of ethics or public relations, but a spiritual crisis, in that lawyers and the profession have lost their way. Once having examined and accepted this idea, we do not need to continue to lament the faults of our profession; rather, we may more constructively turn our focus inward, identifying and acting upon the spiritual impulses that brought us to the practice of law in the first place. Steven Keeva explains these spiritual impulses as follows: "To the extent that you enter [the legal profession] as a calling, the practice of law is about hunger—the hunger for resolution; for healing the lives of individuals, organizations, and communities; for enabling society to function harmoniously and productively; and, ultimately, for justice."

June 30

> "Think what a better world it would be if we all—the whole world—had cookies and milk at three o'clock every afternoon and then lay down with our blankies for a nap.... And it is still true, no matter how old you are—when you go out into the world, it is best to hold hands and stick together."
>
> *Robert Fulghum*

It is with much gratitude that I reflect on the fact that so many esteemed spiritual teachers have answered the call to record their experience, strength, and hope, in written form. Consequently, our libraries are literal treasure troves of spiritual wisdom, awaiting only our interest and attention. Due to the existence of this body of work, current-day seekers do not have to continuously "reinvent the wheel," as they contemplate the trajectories of their own spiritual journeys. The signposts have been planted for us, like a well-marked hiking trail.

It is comforting for us to come to understand that, in many ways, "there is nothing new under the sun." Many of the very same principles that constituted the foundation of a well-lived life two millennia ago still apply today, albeit, dressed in modern-day garb.

Robert Fulghum's best-seller, *All I Ever Needed to Know I Learned in Kindergarten*, confirms, in a very contemporary context, that one's life credo need not be complex or novel to be complete and sustaining. Who can forget his very memorable: "*Share everything...play fair...don't hit people...say you're sorry when you hurt somebody...wash your hands before you eat...*" Reviewing his published credo some twenty-five years later, Fulghum confirms it as *elemental, not simple*, saying: "Everything you need to know is in there somewhere. The Golden Rule and love and basic sanitation. Ecology and politics and equality and sane living." Amen.

"…many young people today journey in the dark, as the young always have, and we elders do them a disservice when we withhold the shadowy parts of our lives. When I was young, there were very few elders willing to talk about the darkness; most of them pretended that success was all they had ever known. As the darkness began to descend on me in my early twenties, I thought I had developed a unique and terminal case of failure. I did not realize that I had merely embarked on a journey toward joining the human race."

Parker Palmer

My father was often preoccupied with the idea that life experience needed to be learned first-hand, and could not be passed down from generation to generation. Only now, at the midpoint of my life, do I understand any of my father's perspective.

Imagine the spiritual evolution of consciousness that might occur, if, like the emerging science of gene substitution, we could eliminate the less-healthy behavior patterns of the prior generation, and substitute in their stead more positive adaptive behaviors for the benefit of the offspring. Imagine also if we had the capacity to communicate and transfer the meaning of our life lessons to one another, in a fully synthesized and thorough manner.

Our current methodology of inter-generational and inter-personal critical information transfer is massively flawed. We rely upon faulty memory processes, and a haphazard hand-off process, to convey our most sacred life's learning. Imagine if we spent more time with our children for the sole purpose of communicating to them who we are, who they are, and what we, as a group, stand for.

Imagine if, as lawyers, we attempted to live value-driven lives on a daily basis, and communicated to our colleagues and others, the stories of our challenges and successes, in a candid and fulsome manner.

Along with others, lawyers have become disconnected from themselves, their families, their ancestral lands, their rituals, and their sense of community. Yet, if we could imagine seizing moments to bridge this divide with our families, our colleagues, and others, the spread of positive effect would be enormous.

July 2

> "Death is a challenge.
> It tells us not to waste time.
> It tells us to tell each other right
> now that we love each other."
>
> *Leo F. Buscaglia*

Drawing on their own experience, many mature lawyers refute the idea that a few selected professional developments—high grades and journal participation in law school, working for a prestigious law firm, making partner—will ultimately and profoundly shape the contours of one's entire legal career.

While these matters do, of course, have some professional impact, particularly during the early stages of the legal journey, they have little to do with a person's overall success, as the mature professional defines it.

See for yourself.

Write your obituary now—long before it is due—so that *you* can determine its content. If phrases like "corner office," "managed many people," and "highest paid" are the most important, you should know that, and either change or accept it. If, as is more likely the case, phrases like "trusted friend," "concerned counselor," "loving partner," and "treasured parent" are the most important, you should know and accept that too, and act accordingly.

If you knew that you had six months to live, what would you change about your life circumstances? Who would you contact, to whom would you say, "I love you," "I am sorry," "I forgive you," or, "Let's start again." Consider these questions, and let your life shine with *lived* success.

July 3

"Feel the fear and do it anyway!"

Susan Jeffers

Courage is not the absence of fear. Everyone is afraid of certain things, and, if this is denied, greater self-knowledge should be sought. *To thine own self be true.* Courage comes into play when we feel our fear, acknowledge and accept it, and then take an action step, no matter how small, toward doing the next right thing, notwithstanding our misgivings.

Fear often results from a perceived loss of control over people, places, and things. In such situations, our mistake is in believing that we had *any* control over these matters to begin with. For the fact is that we can control only our own attitudes and actions; we are powerless over others. Although at certain times we may hold leverage over others, such that we can influence their behavior through our power or prestige, this does not equate to actual control over others.

The more we persist in attempting to control outside events, the more fearful we will become. Bombarding our problems with self-will is not the answer. Rather, if we can see a difficult situation for what it is, name our own fears in connection with it, and then summon the needed strength and resources to move forward with integrity, we have acted with great courage.

July 4

> "Every single person has capabilities, abilities and gifts.
> Living a good life depends on whether those capabilities
> can be used, abilities expressed and gifts given.
> If they are, the person will be valued, feel powerful
> and well-connected to the people around them."
>
> *John P. Kretzmann and John L. McKnight*

After time away from the office, we are often capable of viewing life, our legal practice, and ourselves, from an enhanced perspective. Did everything run smoothly while we were away? Were we missed? Did the firm, and the important case, survive without us? Did anyone notice that our special talents were missing from a given matter?

We all play key roles in the smooth functioning of a larger institution. It is often helpful to our understanding of self and others to assess our role within this "quasi-family." Are we like first-borns, the super-responsible types, the rule-bound citizens who operate with great deference to societal constraints? Are we the more wild and rebellious "outside-the-box" second-borns, who simultaneously rebel and creatively re-sculpt the landscape with individualistically driven contributions? Are we the third-borns, the natural mediators who create healthy alliances, thereby assuring the smooth functioning and working order of the entire unit? Are we like single-child loners, always viewing others as protective parents, and expecting privilege and opportunity based on status, rather than achievement?

Maybe we behave less like children, and more as surrogate parents and older siblings, within our firm's social unit. Do we take on the responsibility of smooth functioning, always with an eye to the nurture and supervision of our colleagues?

In considering these questions, our goal is not so much to change, but to understand our "archetypal myth." This awareness provides greater knowledge concerning ourselves, as well as the nature of the interpersonal relationships and functioning of our firms.

> "I was going to buy a copy of *The Power of Positive Thinking,* and then I thought: What the hell good would that do?"
>
> *Ronnie Shakes*

The Power of Positive Thinking, written more than fifty years ago by Norman Vincent Peale, a New York clergyman, contains information that is as cogent and useful today as the day it was written. The author's view, that life unfolds much as we expect and envision that it will, is representative of an ongoing stream of thought that is found in the writings of many philosophers, theologians, and visionaries. The idea that we attract that which we envision, and that we can do that which we think we can do, has much validity in both the experiential and research spheres. While certain derivatives of, and successors to, *The Power of Positive Thinking* overstate (some might say exploit) the core premise of the book (for example, by assuring that anyone can become a millionaire merely by envisioning the thought), we can all attest to the power that our thoughts have, at least in certain areas.

What Peale knew through his accumulated wisdom, experience, and intuition, has now been repeatedly documented by the social scientists. Thus, for example, psychologists today often suggest the "reframing" of a troublesome issue, a shorthand for saying that the meaning of any situation can be found in the frame within which we view it. Reframing is about changing perception by understanding something in another way, and is a key to the puzzle of self-fulfilling prophesies—the concept that our beliefs tend to unconsciously manifest themselves in our actions and decisions.

As lawyers, our professional mission is to define and meet challenges. Our ability to do so is much enhanced by a properly cultivated understanding that a positive, energized attitude is a key indicator of success in every undertaking.

July 6

"To pay attention, this is our endless and proper work."

Mary Oliver

Balancing family and career is one of our toughest challenges. In my early years of lawyering, I can recall enviously watching the administrative staff prepare to leave the office at 5:30 p.m. The lawyers' day was in full swing at this hour; there would be no relaxing dinner for us.

Over time, we may acquire some flexibility in our scheduling; however, few lawyers report a high degree of success in the work/family balance arena. Yet, we should not lose heart, since, as Alan Dershowitz writes in his book, *Letters to a Young Lawyer*, "The Greek philosophers extolled the life of balance. Two and a half millennia later, we still have not devised the perfect balance for achieving it."

Nonetheless, achieving any recognizable form of family/work balance requires reflection, intention, and flexibility. George Kaufman's excellent book, *The Lawyer's Guide to Balancing Life and Work*, contains many useful exercises that encourage us to look at our professional paths, seeing where they intersect with other parts of our lives. In working through the book's exercises, we are consistently challenged to assess whether our values and our actions are in harmony.

When the authors of this book conduct seminars, we use a shorthand version of Kaufman's exercises, asking participants to list, in order of importance, the ten most valued aspects of their lives. They are then asked to indicate the percentage of time spent on each of these activities during the preceding week, to determine if there is congruence between the lawyer's personal values and actions. So, for example, if we consider time with our family to be our most important priority, yet our allocations indicate that we saw our children only once during the week, we may want to examine this issue further. Temporary shifts, such as working longer hours in advance of an upcoming trial, differ from established patterns, and should be given appropriate flexibility in our assessments.

Whatever decisions we make regarding our priorities should be just that, *decisions*. If we allow the professional *crisis du jour* to consistently trump our vaguely desired, but never sacrosanct, family time, or other priorities, we will always be in a catch-up mode, never attaining the work/life balance we seek.

> "May the light of your soul guide you.
> May the light of your soul bless the work you do
> with the secret love and warmth of your heart. May you
> see in what you do the beauty of your own soul."
>
> *John O'Donohue*

My spouse is one of those rare lawyers who, after many years of practice, greets each workday with excitement and pleasure. As both an engineer and lawyer, he thrives in handling the legal concerns of a large engineering and construction firm. His day, the embodiment of life-long passions, encompasses work, play, socialization, moral challenges, calls to excellence, creative brainstorming, managing human relations, judgment calls, disappointments, difficult negotiations, voicing difficult truths, attending to mundane organizational matters, drafting the letter that clearly draws the line in the sand, saying no, saying YES, traveling, presenting, convincing, handholding, guiding, consoling, laughing out loud, going against the flow, wincing in disbelief, adding a dose of perspective, rallying the troops, and, as always, moving one step further than seemed possible.

For lawyers who are passionate about their work, enthusiasm and delight drive the rhythm of their days. When so operating in the "flow," inner and outer dimensions meld; body, mind, and spirit merge into a unified force field, and a joyful playfulness emerges that recognizes little distinction between work and play.

Being present in the moment, navigating the ups and downs of the task at hand, aspiring to excellence, finding sheer joy in the process of creation—this is the way to the promised land of lawyering, where, as the poet tells us, "*...you see in what you do the beauty of your own soul.*"

July 8

"Law school taught me one thing: how to take two situations that are exactly the same and show how they are different."

Hart Pomeranz

Law school provides the one experience that is shared by all lawyers. It is the "novitiate" where legal apprentices are introduced to the norms, expectations, rules, goals, and aspirations of the legal community. Today, approximately 200 law schools have been accredited by the ABA to train our newest lawyers.

Given the highly concentrated and regulated loci of professional initiation, one might expect that each law school would model only the highest standards of excellence in behavior and attitude. Sadly, this is not always the case. While many lawyers have pleasant recollections of particular professors, courses, or other experiences, the more general anecdotal experience is now confirmed by studies that show that the majority of law school graduates are greatly dissatisfied with the law school experience.

Other studies reveal a very high degree of depression, alienation, and competition within the student body, the incidence of which increases with each succeeding year of law school. It is now hypothesized by many researchers that the ever-increasing negative manifestations of dysfunction within the legal profession, and its individual practitioners, have their genesis in the law school experience.

For better or for worse, the legal profession is the driving force behind much of what is right (and wrong) in American society. If law school is actually robbing students of their potentially positive and critical contributions to an ailing society, this is a matter of the gravest concern for all of us.

In light of the perceived crisis in the profession, some of the nation's most esteemed law schools are re-examining their priorities, their curricula, and their teaching methods, in attempting to stem the negative tide. A particularly wary eye is being cast toward the often hard-edged Socratic method, which, throughout the legal ages, has so often been accompanied by infantilizing and demeaning professorial conduct.

While such reform measures are positive, in order to effectively dismantle the institutional inertia that overhangs many law schools, every lawyer should consider increased involvement and activism in requiring that law schools take seriously their responsibilities to properly engage the "moral imagination" of every law student. Given the current level of professional dis-ease, we can no longer accept the oft-heard disclaimer that the law school's job is merely to train students to "think like lawyers." This limited self-understanding was never appropriate, and is considerably less so in the midst of today's professional angst and disintegration.

> ## "To affect the quality of the day,
> ## that is the highest of arts."
>
> *Henry David Thoreau*

I once heard an inmate describe a prison chaplain by saying that, although he didn't remember her exact message, he did remember that she was kind. This description resonates with some of my own experiences, when I heard, during distressful times, the poignantly soothing: *"Sit here and rest," "Tell me about it," "Take your time," "Yes, you can do it, and I'll help you,"* or, *"I'll be there for you."* The greatest gift we can give another is the gift of our time and attention. The second greatest gift we can give another is our expectation of their success.

When was the last time we generously delivered or received these gifts? We were not meant to travel life's journey alone. Yes, we are often rushed and pressured and overscheduled, but being responsible does not equate to refusing the cool drink of water offered by a fellow sojourner. We need to give and take encouragement along life's journey. In the school of life, no one receives a higher grade for struggling alone without the comforting support of others.

July 10

> "Now I become myself.
> It's taken time, many years and places.
> I have been dissolved and shaken,
> Worn other people's faces..."
>
> *May Sarton*

While there is much talk today of the "identity theft" that can deprive us of our material possessions, few stop to consider the spiritual identity theft lurking within much of our everyday beliefs, communications, and understandings. The world entices us to relinquish our true identity as deserving and worthy citizens of the universe when it overtly or covertly communicates: *"You are what you earn; the one with the most toys wins; power is everything."* This unrelenting seduction toward solely materialistic values can lead to true identity theft at depth. We are, the world tells us, succeeding only if we are in the most exclusive jobs, salary ranges, country clubs, and power circles.

This is a lie, but a widely held lie, which is seldom brought into the sunlight for observation and analysis. Rather, the lie tends to slither through the darkness of our deeper, unspoken, and unexamined understandings. Absent the sunlight of the spirit, all forms of darkness and corroding influences can romp unimpeded, leaving in their wake untold confusion and despair. Yet there is a solution.

We are worthy children of the universe, each possessing a uniquely structured humanity. Yes, we have our human limitations and imperfections, but we are called only to be our authentic selves—foibles and all—with all the joy and sorrow, adventure and challenge, that are encompassed within that calling.

July 11

> "We can not live only for ourselves. A thousand fibers connect us with our fellow men; and among those fibers, as sympathetic threads, our actions run as causes, and then come back to us as effects."
>
> *Herman Melville*

How often do we sit in the rocking chair, listening to the drone of the summer crickets as the sun begins to fade into the night sky? Do we take the time to truly hear our heart's inner longings? And, how often do we truly listen and give ourselves over to the needs and wants of our children? And, when was the last time we were wholly available to our partner's musings and scattered concerns? And, what of time and attention for our friends, our colleagues, and the countless others who cross our path?

We were not meant to walk this life alone. We belong to ourselves and others—partners, families, colleagues, professions, communities, the global citizenry—and an ever-broadening web of relationships. We exist within a tapestry of relationships, some of which we have been privileged to weave ourselves. And, every day, we are graced with the opportunity to renew our vows, and rekindle our commitments, to our lives and our loves. Each day we are graced anew with the extraordinary honor to positively impact the lives of all other "web-dwellers."

Could there be a more heroic calling?

Just as the clouds sometimes seem to hide the glory of the sun, there are times in our lives when we lose sight of what really matters. We mistakenly believe that the brief we are writing, or our next court appearance, or our involvement in the latest office power play, should rightfully trump all other happenings in our lives.

As happens on any heroic journey, we will sometimes become disoriented, and lose our way. Temporary missteps are to be corrected, and then set aside, as we continue our heroic journey toward true wholeness and meaning.

July 12

> "Nurture strength of spirit to shield you in sudden misfortune. But do not distress yourself with imaginings. Many fears are born of fatigue and loneliness. Beyond a wholesome discipline, be gentle with yourself."
>
> *Desiderata*

There are times in our professional lives when, despite our best efforts, many situations seem positioned to be our undoing. We inadvertently miss a non-negotiable filing date, we become embroiled in a self-defeating argument with a superior, or we lose an important client through misunderstanding or error.

At these times, most of us have a tendency to deal harshly with ourselves. How could I have done such a thing? How could I have been so irresponsible? Maybe I am not cut out for the demanding road of lawyering. If thoughts such as these occupy our minds as we inevitably encounter the realm of our own human error, perhaps we can seek another way of perceiving our situation. Just pausing, breathing deeply, and asking: *"Spirit, is there another way to see this?"* can break the domino effect of fear, anxiety, and worrisome imaginings.

We can also choose not to be such harsh taskmasters and judges when we are humbled by our humanity. The words humbled and humanity both derive from the same core, *"humus,"* meaning decaying plant and animal remains. We are not saints, and we are not perfect. While we may rightly aspire to excellence, our humanity is, by its nature, limited.

We can be gentle with ourselves at these times. If a friend had come to us to discuss similar errors, we would most likely be filled with compassion, caring, and reassurance, acting with a sincere desire to restore our friend's inner peace. We must do no less for ourselves.

So, we made a mistake. Welcome to humanity. Let us calm ourselves first, and the storm will eventually settle. As *Desiderata* advises, *"Beyond a wholesome discipline, be gentle with yourself."*

> "Integrity is not a conditional word. It doesn't blow in the wind or change with the weather. It is your inner image of yourself, and if you look in there and see a man who won't cheat, then you know he never will."
>
> *John D. MacDonald*

What does it mean to be a person of value and integrity?

On average, people spend more than fifty hours a week working on income-producing matters, and lawyers' hours often greatly exceed this average. Yet, being a person of value requires so much more than earning money. To be a person of value, one must fully develop and evolve, both internally and externally, so that the world is unquestionably left a better place by our having been here.

We are each called upon to find that singular overlap of our unique skills, and the world's greatest needs, in order to elevate ourselves and all others. The nature of the evolved person is to contribute to the universe in the unique manner that only he or she can.

July 14

> "The reality of the other person is not in what he reveals to you, but in what he cannot reveal to you. Therefore, if you would understand him, listen not to what he says but rather what he does not say."
>
> *Kahlil Gibran*

Attorney-client relationships are just that—they are relationships. While our clients often present themselves to us in the midst of tumultuous circumstances, our clients, like us, are whole persons, worthy of full respect and recognition. We must resist the urge to view our clients as problems themselves, as the medical doctor might refer to the "broken leg in Room 242."

Each client is a full human being with a past, a present, and a future, traveling the same road to wholeness that we ourselves walk. Although our circumstances may differ at any point in time, both the client and the lawyer, and the relationship between them, are important pieces of life's landscape. As in our personal relationships, attorney-client relationships are enhanced by mutual honesty, respect, care, and attending to responsibility.

The over-stressed, over-scheduled, and overwhelmed lawyer is often not capable of bringing these attributes to the encounter with the client. The result: unhappy clients, unhappy lawyers, and unresolved legal issues.

When we speak with a client on the phone, we should do nothing else but give our undivided attention to the matter at hand. We should not be simultaneously checking emails, signing letters, or looking for a paper on our desks. While the client's matter may seem commonplace and mundane, we must be present in the moment, sensitive to the fact that the client may be experiencing fear of economic loss, emotional insecurity, or other potentially serious and life-altering consequences. Our clients deserve our very best, and that *always* begins with providing our *undivided* time and attention.

> "Sure, intuition can develop with experience.
> But trusting your hunches has perils, too."
>
> *David G. Myers*

Intuition is a shortcut in thinking that leads to a simplistic understanding of complex events. Although our intuitive sense is an invaluable tool in providing certain insights and immediate diagnoses of legal issues, overconfidently relying on intuition alone can dangerously mislead us. David Myers, author of *Intuition: Its Powers and Perils*, cautions: "Smart thinkers will also want to check their intuitions against available evidence. Our gut instincts are terrific at some things, such as instantly reading emotions in others' faces, but not so good at others, such as guessing about the stock market, assessing risks, and predicting football outcomes."

When examining a new legal problem, we can greatly benefit from superimposing an anti-intuition filter onto our problem-solving schematic. So, for example, we might try formulating five competing hypotheses for why any set of events has occurred. This strategy compels the lawyer to incrementally and fundamentally consider alternate approaches in attempting to arrive at the "truth."

Truth reveals itself in bits and pieces, and, according to the wisdom of the ages, completely exposes its essential form in "God's time." However, such ultimate timing is hardly convenient for the fact-finding lawyer. Like any good scientist, we have to work with the tools at hand, in our determined pursuit of understanding situations *as they truly are*, and proceeding accordingly.

July 16

> "One day you finally knew
> what you had to do, and began,
> though the voices around you kept shouting
> their bad advice....
> But you didn't stop....
> It was already late enough..."
>
> *Mary Oliver*

Many lawyers are dissatisfied with their work simply because they are not involved in matters that suit their interests and talents. If, for example, we become passionately energized when analyzing corporate business plans, and how they fit within the scheme of applicable legal requirements, we will never be "at home" in professional work that involves answering calendar calls in landlord-tenant disputes.

Life charges us with finding and following our own interests and desires, not those of others, nor those that merely pay well and offer job security. Our professional identity cannot be at odds with who we are as individuals if we are to find true satisfaction and meaning in the practice of law.

July 17

> ## "Money and success don't change people;
> ## they merely amplify what is already there."
> *Will Smith*

How do we accept and properly manage success in our legal careers? When professional success begins to be perceived as a fact, *by us*, it is most often the result of a long series of successfully negotiated challenges. But, we now ask, are we prepared to assume our starring role?

How we assimilate and "wear" achievement speaks volumes about who we are. We are responsible for selecting, identifying, and deeply cherishing the components of our success that we alone most value.

Do we remember the moments when our strengths, gifts, and positive attributes first came to our attention, and that of others? Or do we focus instead on the outcomes and accomplishments themselves? Do we mentally or emotionally deny the validity of our accomplishments, lacking the necessary esteem to embrace our positive experiences? Do we attempt to distract ourselves from our successful undertakings with overeating, drinking, or smoking? Do we remain alienated from others because of an uncomfortable feeling we have in relation to the good work we have done? Alternatively, do we unctuously impose ourselves on others, immediately proffering note of our achievements, as a badge of honor?

What we think about our success and how we "wear" those thoughts, is an area ripe for investigation in coming to better know who we really are. It is an important hallmark of professional maturity that we experience congruence between the good experiences which we have achieved, and the emotional responses we have in connection with them.

July 18

> "You can bend it and twist it.
> You can misuse and abuse it....
> But even God cannot change the Truth."
>
> *Michael Levy*

What can happen in a conversation, but the revelation of one person to another? To know and be known in truth by another is a highly complex human undertaking, for, as far as we know, only humans have the necessary reasoning and thinking for conversational exchange. Dialogue, the back-and-forth question-and-answer process that deepens learning and broadens knowledge, represents a cornerstone of Western thought, originally cultivated by the philosophers of ancient Greece as a formula for coming to know the truth.

We, as lawyers, obviously place value on truth ascertained through conversation, since truth-seeking is a primary goal of the judicial system, and a daily undertaking of the legal professional. When listening to others, particularly our clients, we should be attuned to subtle, fine-tuned statements and distinctions that may indicate that bias, misperception, and even untruths, have entered the conversation. If we can help others sift through apparent distortions, omissions, and confabulations, we can then properly shape a correct statement of the problem needing resolution. And, as the sages have taught, a problem well-framed is near-solved.

July 19

"Although the world is full of suffering, it is full also of the overcoming of it."

Helen Keller

There are many times in our lives when we have thought that our "hour had come." Perhaps it was the day we graduated from law school, or the day we got married, or had our first child, or the day we made partner—oh, the feeling of elation that victory was finally ours and our hour had come!

These were very joyous times. But these high points were not final destinations. Rather, they were the new beginning points of our life's journey, portions of which would hold joy, and portions of which would hold pain. As William Blake so sagely wrote: "Man was made for joy and woe, and when this we surely know, through the world we safely go. Joy and woe are woven fine, a clothing for my soul divine."

In our current days, punctuated by news of war and starvation, terror and hate, fear and scarcity, it is sometimes very difficult to view our lives as set against a backdrop of uninterrupted grace. But, in fact, they are. Yes, life can hurt, but in the hurt and powerlessness, there is always the potential for healing.

As an author friend of mine says, "You have realized your powerlessness, now realize your power." This is our hour as lawyers. This is our hour to work together to revitalize the noble practice of law so that it once again constitutes a creative and healing force in a hurting world.

An ancient story parallels our current situation as lawyers who strive to restore the legal profession to its rightful status.

The story goes that a very holy man was traveling a great distance. Along the way, he encountered men and women, and even children, who were oppressed and starving and beaten, who had suffered every kind of torment. In his anguish, the holy man looked up to heaven, crying out, "How could a loving Creator allow such torment to exist and do nothing about it?" After several moments of silence, God responded: "I did do something about it. I created you."

The spiritual life is not a theory; we have to live it. The hour has come to pay attention, to stop procrastinating, and to live who it is we say we want to be.

Now is the hour to be still and know. Now is the hour to recommit to wholeness, whether or not it is clear to us what that means at any given moment. Now is the hour to be honest and open and willing to receive guidance. Now is the hour to reconnect with our highest purpose and to let our light shine. Now is the hour, says Joseph Campbell, to "…stop sleepwalking through our lives, refusing to listen to those who speak of the eternal values that have to do with the centering of our lives."

Now is the hour to honestly ask whether we are living the lives we were created to live, and, if the answer is no, to start making the necessary changes. Oh, yes, our hour has come.

July 20

> **"You only have to have
> two loves in your life:
> God and the person in front of you."**
>
> *Eloy Cruz*

Sometimes, when we speak of an ethic of love and service, what comes to mind are overly extravagant images—Mother Theresa ministering on the streets of Calcutta, or the harried lawyer slaving away, penuriously, in a storefront clinic. These perceptions are unnecessarily exaggerated, in that, as lawyers, we *are* already living an ethic of love and service if we perform our work in a mindful, compassionate, and caring manner.

Every client we represent, whether the CEO of a large company or an indigent tenant, is worthy of the same attention and care. Remaining fully present with each client, we can look deeply into their eyes, and connect with the fear and concern that we have been called to help alleviate. Our narrow thought patterns, suggesting, for example, that a particular client's matter is not worthy of our best efforts, can be properly reframed, if we allow ourselves to connect with the humanity of each individual involved.

When we begin to view our profession and our own lawyering as a healing balm in a sorely hurting world, we can begin to share our gifts more genuinely and more generously, at once benefitting both the giver and receiver.

July 21

> "You must have a room, or a certain hour or so a day, where you don't know what was in the newspapers that morning...a place where you can simply experience and bring forth what you are and what you might be."
>
> *Goethe*

When times get *really* hard, when we believe that even our best friends cannot understand what we are going through, when we ourselves are tired of reviewing the contours of our dark inner landscape, it is a blessing to have a sacred space that we can escape to, much as we might have sought refuge in a childhood hideout when emotional storms were brewing. The solitude, the quiet, the familiarity, the "nothing bad ever happens here" feel, are the essentials of a true sanctuary.

A necessary retreat from the world can take the form of an actual getaway to a restful place, or, when an immediate respite is needed, we can "bloom where we are planted," and select a nearby quiet place for our "hideout." Houses of worship are available and usually have the advantage of proximity to our homes and offices. The weary soul can also find comfort in a small park, a tree-lined trail, a small café, a dusty bookstore, an unused office, or the quiet lobby of a nearby hotel.

Notwithstanding the nature of our chosen space, our retreat from the maddening crowd honors our soul's weary call for refreshment, for a needed chance to *be still and know*. Abiding in respectful silence, we can remember and re-member, who and what we are. We often emerge from our sanctuaries possessed of a quiet calmness and assurance that seem to convey, *"Yes, yes, we can do this day."*

July 22

> "It is often said that stress is one of the most destructive elements in people's daily lives, but that is only a half truth. The way we react to stress appears to be more important than the stress itself."
>
> *Dr. Bernie Siegel*

Our lives are often filled with very productive and desirable events, yet, even these gifts can cause stress in our lives. Periods of creativity, good work, peer recognition, and financial success are truly gifts to be cherished. Yet, sometimes it seems that we become "cursed by our blessings," as we begin to sense that we are too "out there" in the world of things—creating, performing, and accomplishing. And, despite the world's accolades, we feel like we are off the beam, that we have lost our center.

Mental health professionals remind us that even "good stress" is stress, and all unhealthy levels of stress take a toll, emotionally, physically, and psychologically. Stress is a consequence of any force or event that upsets balance. Our need is to return to our balanced center, whether in the midst of accomplishment and excitement, or in the midst of an over-scheduled calendar and financial insecurity.

Psychologist Amiram Elwork, author of *Stress Management for Lawyers*, and creator of the *Law and Psychology Program* at Widener University, advises that, due to the unique stressors of the legal environment, lawyers are 3.6 times more likely than other workers to suffer from depression. Whether we judge the causes of stress and imbalance to be "good" or "bad," we are well-advised to act in a thoughtful manner in dealing with the stressors in our lives. Proper nutrition, restful sleep, regular exercise, flexible time management, allowing for "quiet time," and the other practices described in our reflections, will help us keep the stressors at a healthy level.

July 23

> ## "I long, as does every human being, to be at home wherever I find myself."
>
> *Maya Angelou*

When a friend's cat died prematurely, several family members lamented their loss, using very similar words: "Sammy never got to grow into his [rather large] ears."

Their unusual expression of lament reminds me of the stature that each of us is called to fill when we allow ourselves to broadly open to life; not only to the tried and true, but also to the novel, the incredible, the awe-inspiring, the terrifying, the magnificent; in short, to the absolute adventure of it all.

On my best days, I can experience my comings and goings as occurring in a virtual camp—my personal slice of heaven on earth. I play, I laugh, I work, I eat, I sigh, and I exclaim with the simplicity, joy, and delight of an unself-conscious child in a warm and secure environment. This, it feels, is my natural state, my natural home—joy, delight, achievement, belonging. Living at my virtual camp does not equate to an absence of responsibility or exertion, since, as the Buddhist Masters teach, even in a more enlightened state, we must still "chop wood and carry water." And similar to living amid the delights of a true camp, we are still required to clean our bunks and write letters home.

We can grow into the fullness of life as we imagine and design it, to just about the extent that we choose. How much longer will we remain content to reside within too narrow a spiritual dwelling, to partake of too few of our souls' delights?

The price? Awareness, choice, and committed action. Moving *way* beyond our normal comfort zones. The result? Being at home, wherever we find ourselves.

July 24

> "What you see and hear depends a good deal
> on where you are standing; it also depends
> on what kind of person you are."
>
> C.S.Lewis

It is sometimes helpful to stop and examine the quantity of negative messages that we often encounter in our daily rounds, so that we can limit or eliminate their dispiriting effects on our day. "Look to this day…for it is the very life of life…" directs the ancient Sanskrit poem.

I have personally chosen to journal, pray, and meditate immediately upon arising, so that I can enmesh myself in a positive attitude in beginning the day. This is often followed by thirty minutes of exercise, during which I reflect on some of the ideas that have surfaced during the journaling and meditation. I have also chosen to deliberately restrict the amount of radio, television, and newspaper intrusion into my personal space, knowing that so much of this communication is distracting, at best, and demoralizing, at worst. In other words, I try to be aware of those people, places, and things in my life that tend to bring me down, or distract me from my primary focus of living a happy, joyous, and free life. Although it is not practicable to eliminate all disturbing elements from my life, I limit my encounters to brief intervals, and, when possible, plan them at times when I do not feel particularly vulnerable.

It has been said that we can determine who our friends should be by assessing how we feel about ourselves when we are with them, and after we leave them. Anyone who has spent even a few minutes with a gossiping, critical, and negative person can readily attest to the energy drain that follows the encounter.

It is a very positive choice to seek the company of the persons we admire, people who are also interested in personal growth, and who enhance the positive in life. By identifying and naming that which is attractive in these people, we can appropriately model these characteristics and enhance our own positive drive for wholeness. Likewise, we can appropriately anticipate and limit encounters with those persons and activities that tend to activate the darker, more negative sides of our personality. *Lawyer, know thyself, and thy surroundings!*

> ## "There's a world of difference between truth and facts. Facts can obscure the truth."
>
> *Maya Angelou*

"I can't talk backwards, but can adults do that?" asked my 8-year-old nephew one evening. After some interesting back-and-forth, he ran off to solve the next mystery in his world.

Yet, his question set in motion a flurry of thoughts on the effects of the direct disclosure of information, and the circumlocutions that lawyers often deliberately employ. For example, we consistently advise clients to say as little as possible, and to answer only the question that was asked. And, when a requested answer is not supportive of our cause, we often parse through alternative readings/interpretations of a distasteful question with such intensity and creativity that one almost expects the inanimate typed page to transmute itself to offer up the question we would prefer to answer.

I remember one particular litigator who, when considering an "unfortunate" question in an interrogatory or otherwise, would poll as many colleagues as necessary concerning the question's meaning, until that magical moment when more than a majority of those polled concurred with his preferred interpretation!

While there are many times when circumspection is both appropriate and necessary in our legal practice, what is the effect of the disclosure of limited facts, rather than truth, on one's inner self?

Do we learn to cordon off portions of our internal world because no one has been astute enough to ask the right questions? Do we take the same "don't ask, don't tell" approach when engaged in *supposed* self-reflection? And do we consider it our spouse's responsibility, for example, to ask exactly the right questions about the family's financial situation, before we share disturbing information that only we know, but are too afraid to disclose?

While full revelation of truths is not always called for, or appropriate, our souls benefit when, as much as possible, we mindfully practice the art of living open, candid, and truth-centered lives.

July 26

> "We have what we seek,
> it is there all the time,
> and if we give it time,
> it will make itself known to us."
>
> *Thomas Merton*

It is important for us to recognize that every time we say yes to one thing, we are saying no to another. This recognition allows for the inclusion of the proper mixture of interesting and diverse experiences in our lives, while also allowing for realistic balance and flexibility. A wise friend always says that, although we can have much of what we want in life, we cannot have it all, or at least not all at once!

So, for example, if we intend to devote substantial additional time to building or enhancing our law practice, we will, of necessity, have to lessen our involvement in other activities. In making this decision, we should consider whether this is the right time to lessen our family participation, or whether there is a particular situation brewing at home which may require added involvement on our part. Achieving balance in our multifaceted lives is an ongoing challenge, requiring frequent adjustment and recalibration as we experience the pushes and pulls of the many segments of our lives.

If attempts at balancing become overly stressful, we can recall that we *do* have enough time to accomplish the goals we thoughtfully set for ourselves, as long as we are willing to realistically plan our day and make necessary adjustments for the natural ebb and flow of events that occur in our lives.

July 27

> ## "There is no greater agony than having an untold story within you."
>
> *Maya Angelou*

Cultivating gratitude for our past and current relationships is an important spiritual practice. A life partner, a supportive colleague, a mentor, a therapist, a really good friend—each of these people is an indispensable thread in the incredible tapestry that is our lives. Mentally enumerating the specific aspects of others' understanding and support infuses our relationships with joy and refreshment.

When a particular issue arises in our life that requires honest discussion with another, we should be selective in choosing the right confidant for the particular issue. At a minimum, the person chosen must be able to appreciate the confidentiality of our communications. Often, it is best to select someone who has encountered and effectively dealt with similar situations.

We should be sensitive not to involve a confidant who might be hurt or upset by our revelations. So, for example, deep-seated fears about the future of our law partnership might be better shared with a close friend, rather than our partners, who may be equally fearful about the future. Although in certain circumstances, intimacy is increased with soul-bearing honesty at depth, at other times, deep sharing about a mutual problem can deepen the pain of the other person and should be avoided.

If we "go where it's warm" for the particular matter, we will obtain appropriate guidance from concerned guides, while causing no harm to others.

July 28

> ### "When we love and allow ourselves to be loved, we begin more and more to inhabit the kingdom of the eternal."
>
> *John O'Donohue*

As we progress in our emotional and spiritual maturing, we may sometimes find ourselves pensively questioning, *Who are my friends, my real friends?*

It is always comfortable to have friendly dinner companions, or a dedicated colleague who is always willing to lend advice regarding a troublesome case. These co-journeyers make our days more enjoyable, and their companionship eases some of the inevitable bumps in the road of life.

Yet, when the truly harsh winds blow—death, illness, deep loss, unbelievable betrayal, or a deep crisis of faith—nothing but the shelter of deeply forged and cultivated relationships can provide a safe harbor for our very troubled souls. There, we can be enriched, when our own resources seem so desperately inadequate for the task at hand. Sacred ground becomes consecrated where two people gather in *radical* honesty, acceptance, and love. Profound revelations of the most authentic type can occur there.

The rich Celtic understanding of this sacred friendship is described by author John O'Donoghue, who writes: "In everyone's life there is a great need for an *anam cara*, a soul friend. In this love, you are understood as you are, without mask or pretension. The superficial and functional lies and half-truths of social acquaintance fall away, you can be as you really are…. When you really feel understood, you feel free to release yourself into the truth and shelter of another person's soul."

We should look around in our world to discern who is or might be our own *anam cara*. If no candidates readily appear, we can today begin the process of first looking within, and then initiating desired relationships by acting ourselves as the friend that we would like to have. *If you want a friend, be a friend.*

July 29

> ## "Grief is so often the source of our spirit's growth."
>
> *Rainer Maria Rilke*

Perhaps every lawyer has experienced what might be considered professional failures. The important case that was decided against us, the prestigious partnership offer that we did not attain, the client who sued for malpractice, the vibrant law practice that precipitously disintegrated—the list could go on indefinitely.

"Failure" seems to appear in varying degrees of magnitude: *the small daily doses*, often associated with such stressors as a losing day in court; *the larger life events*, such as the failure to get a hoped-for position; and, finally, *the extremely critical variety*, including the alcohol problem that eventually results in disbarment, or the fraud charges that effectively decimate a firm.

The pain that results from these situations, no matter what the magnitude or notoriety of the situation, has the same potential as any other type of pain: it can constitute the most effective motivator for change. In choosing to live a more spiritual life, the layers of internal pain can be peeled back and examined, allowing us to see the situation and our part in it for what they really are, and then, to clean our side of the street, to the best of our ability. If the painful event did not result from our actions, we can employ our spiritual practices to determine how we might peacefully adapt ourselves to those situations that we cannot change.

With this newfound perspective, self-appraisal, and purposeful action, we can move forward in the important business of living our new lives, exercising heightened vigilance to sidestep any potentially derailing pitfalls.

July 30

> "There is nothing heavier than compassion...
> pain intensified by the imagination
> and prolonged by a hundred echoes."
>
> *Milan Kundera*

It sometimes happens that the matters that summon lawyers into action are not of the most righteous variety. A transgression may have occurred, a dispute may have arisen, an extreme injustice may remain unaddressed. Each of these conditions may contain elements of trust shattered, discontent aroused, and material and emotional security stripped away.

The dark emotional twists subsumed within these situations, while primarily affecting the actors, can also have secondary effects on the lawyers involved in the matter. No matter how intentionally we attempt to remain professionally detached, compassionate human beings will absorb some portion of the unfolding emotional pain. The technical term for this interaction is "reciprocal inhibition," the process by which we affect others, and they affect us.

If we do not mindfully consider the emotional backsplash that can result from interactions with our clients, we run the risk of unintentionally becoming distrusting, cynical, and alienated from others.

Consistent self-reflection, awareness, and the establishment of appropriate boundaries will restore our perspective, and will act as effective antidotes to these conditions.

July 31

> "It doesn't interest me to know where you live or how much money you have. I want to know if you can get up, after the night of grief and despair, weary and bruised to the bone, and do what needs to be done to feed the children."
>
> *Oriah*

With the above words, spiritual author Oriah offers a deep invitation to action that will clearly "separate the men from the boys, and the women from the girls."

As I write this passage, I am enveloped in emotional pain and concern for a deeply hurting loved one. My inclination, upon awakening, is to avoid the world, to deliberately "hunker down," dedicating myself to the sole cause of shielding my loved one and myself from further pain. Numb, forget, reanalyze, blame, allow my mind to obsessively seek reasons, and then more supposed solutions—in short, to stay securely wrapped within the problem, shutting out every real chance of guidance, perspective, balance, and positive action. "Bruised to the bone," the last thing I want to consider, literally or figuratively, is "what needs to be done to feed the children."

And, yes, there are the many reassurances that it is "only natural," when in such pain to seek a quiet place to lick our wounds. Yet, I know, even in my befogged state, that what is deemed "only natural" by our spiritually ailing society is often neither healthy nor productive. So, while debating whether to continue to imprison myself within the problem, I am also called to decide whether I will admit my spiritual cowardice in following such a path.

"*And this above all: To thine own self be true,*" wrote Shakespeare some 400 years ago, and the directive is just as urgent today. And what is my truth, today, in this situation? I know that to choose self-pity and fear will yield just that—a day of self-pity and fear. Today, my protesting soul demands that I choose courage instead. Thus, I choose to take the actions that my soul *needs* to take, driven not by a spirit of martyrdom, but through a deep understanding that life demands that "the children be fed." Today the road less traveled is the one my soul must take.

So, here, at the writing table, I sit, and there, in the sheltering bed, I do not lie.

August 1

> "To every thing, there is a season, and a
> time to every purpose under the heaven."
>
> *Ecclesiastes 3:1*

As lawyers, we are accustomed to performing the roles of advisor, advocate, and adjudicator. We pride ourselves in being able to secure for others those things that are rightfully theirs, in the eyes of the law, and in the name of all that is right. We perform our lawyerly duties with aplomb, grateful that we can meaningfully contribute our talents to enriching the lives of our clients and society as a whole.

Yet, as exhilarating as such service for others can be, spiritual maturity requires an acknowledgment that, as finite creatures, there are also seasons for us to ask for and accept assistance. We were not meant to travel the road of life alone, yet, our accustomed role as "fixers" may make it very difficult to ask for help for ourselves when it is needed.

All healthy relationships—including those with a single intimate other, those occurring in the professional sphere, and those between ourselves and the world generally—each contain a healthy dose of mutuality, where each relationship partner participates in the ebb and flow of relational happenings on a give-and-take basis. Such partners are able to give support when needed, and to graciously receive it as well. In asking for and accepting another's support, we inherently acknowledge our standing as one among many, understanding that we do not always have to rise above the rest of the crowd, and that we too are sometimes in need of the comfort and support that only others can give.

While our professional training and demeanor cast us in the role of "the strong one," true strength of character requires that we ask for help when needed, thereby fostering mutuality and growth in all of our relationships.

> "You may be a construction worker working on a home,
> You may be living in a mansion or you might live in a dome,
> You might own guns and you might even own tanks...
> But you're gonna have to serve somebody, yes indeed
> You're gonna have to serve somebody..."
>
> *Bob Dylan*

Most human beings work in the service of others. This is not a negative factor; rather, from an evolutionary perspective, a strong argument can be made that this is the natural state of affairs. The ability to serve others and delay gratification, holding our personal desires in abeyance, represents a fundamental aspect of the advancement of civilization.

Sacrifice for a higher cause was an essential element that contributed to the survival and furtherance of our ancestral tribes. It is a relatively modern development that our capacity for altruism is perceived as related to personal, familial, professional, religious, or other ideological underpinnings.

A desire to please is often a concomitant of service. As with a child's delight in the praise of a parent, few things are as pleasing to the individual as the recognition and esteem received from peers for a job well done. In the well-matured adult, however, the desire to meet one's own standards generally becomes more important than satisfying others. Thus, healthy lawyers eventually learn to "parent" themselves, both with respect to their personal and their professional undertakings. The ability to seek one's own inner direction and approval, with appropriate, but not superseding, regard for the needs and opinions of others, is a defining characteristic of the self-actualizing person and lawyer.

August 3

> ## "Leadership without character is unthinkable— or should be."
>
> *Warren Bennis*

As busy professionals, we often make lists to help us keep track of our responsibilities. Many of us carry our to-do lists with us everywhere we go. But, do any of us keep lists to remember our relationships? To keep track of our hobbies? To tune into our interior lives? To uncover any of life's deeper truths? Are we, as lawyers and human beings, responsible for knowing more than the law and our next task? Is good lawyering not, at least partially, the by-product of good living?

Human beings are the only creatures born with free will and who exert a positive or negative impact upon one another. As lawyers, we have an obligation to not only observe professional ethics, but, as officers of the court, we are also called to observe high ethical norms in our personal lives. We should select our companions judiciously, resisting the "herd mentality" that consistently edges us toward the path of least resistance, lest we become morally diminished in the process.

As lawyers, we are called to be societal leaders, acting as, and associating with, value-driven individuals, as powers of example.

August 4

> ## "We can do no great things, only small things with great love."
>
> *Mother Theresa*

Contrary to popular mythology, we do not normally become "great" by a single heroic undertaking or discovery. Rather, we become "great" by mindfully doing a series of small things on a daily, consistent basis. Once we have established an effective personal regime that fosters and enhances our physical, mental, and spiritual growth, it is essential that we persistently perform these tasks on a continuous basis.

A person becomes "great" when, day after day, week after week, the person executes the everyday disciplines that constitute the foundation of a mature character. Such a person is truly a power of example, and the world is a better place simply because that person lives in the world.

If, in the course of human events, the light of public notoriety shines upon an impeccable character, we are all enriched and can claim a true hero in our midst. In the more frequently occurring event, however, where a good person's light shines in smaller circles—among friends, family, colleagues, and community, we are similarly greatly enriched by that person's dwelling among us, offering a sure and steady example of excellence.

August 5

"When it is dark enough, you can see the stars."

Charles A. Beard

Although many people seek and find meaning through connection with God or other higher power, many have also developed a deep sense of purpose in life without the connotations of a Divine Other.

Victor Frankl, a psychotherapist, made substantial contributions in this regard when he wrote about the development of life's purpose over forty years ago. Frankl's initial ideas of meaning or purpose in life were developed prior to World War II, and were reinforced by his experiences as a prisoner in a concentration camp, the horrors of which are related in his epic, *Man's Search for Meaning*. Frankl believed that an individual could find meaning in several ways: by creating a work or doing a deed, from the individual's vocation, from experiencing nature and culture, or "by experiencing another human being in his very uniqueness—by loving him." Frankl lived out his beliefs in the concentration camp, demonstrating that a person could find purpose and maintain dignity, even in the most hopeless situation.

In *Man's Search for Meaning*, Frankl relates that at one particularly brutal and deadly time in the camp experience, he was called upon by his comrades to speak to the group in an attempt to alleviate the overwhelming despair. At first Frankl wanted to refuse, since he was also cold and hungry and tired and frightened. Yet he finally rose to the occasion, and later described his speech as follows:

"I said...whoever was still alive had reason for hope. Health, family, happiness...position in society—all these were things that could be achieved again or restored. Whatever we had gone through could still be an asset to us in the future.... I estimated my own chances [of survival] at about one in twenty, yet...I had no intention of losing hope and giving up. For no man knew what the future would bring.... Having been is also a kind of being, and perhaps the surest kind."

Present-day researchers, building on the work of Frankl and others, continue to confirm that developing sources of our own personal meaning in life is a strong and consistent predictor of well-being throughout our life span. Having a sense of purpose is a primary building block in establishing positive characteristics, strong values, and healthy mental attitudes.

> "In the history of legal education in the United States, there is no record of any concerted effort to consider what new lawyers should know or be able to do on their first day in practice or to design a program of instruction to achieve those goals."
>
> *Roy Stuckey*

The above words are alarming for all lawyers who are concerned with the state of their profession, especially since the person quoted is Roy Stuckey, an expert on legal education, and principal author of *Best Practices for Legal Education*. Comparing the research contained in his book, and that of the Carnegie Foundation's Report, *Educating Lawyers (2007)*, Stuckey reports that, despite the use of very different methodologies, the conclusion resulting from the two projects was identical: *law schools overemphasize teaching legal analysis and doctrinal knowledge, and virtually ignore teaching professional skills and values.*

Stuckey is unrelenting in his indictment that law schools have consistently ignored recommendations from interested groups of lawyers, judges, and academics, who, since the 1970s, have concluded that law schools are not preparing students to provide effective and responsible legal services. According to Stuckey, the reasons for such intransigence include: 1) the fact that law schools are faculty-centered, not student-centered, thus allowing for the faculty's unilateral control of the organization and the content design of the curriculum; 2) law professors are rewarded more for scholarship than for teaching; and 3) there are no incentives to motivate faculty to move beyond their present pedagogical comfort zones.

Stuckey predicts that the recommendations to improve legal education contained in *Best Practices* and *Educating Lawyers* will, like its progeny, fall on deaf ears, *unless practicing lawyers, working in conjunction with bar associations, provide incentives for law professors to change their practices and attitudes.* He sets forth ten suggestions for effecting such a paradigm shift, which include: encouraging lawyers to read the reports to better understand the issues; forming a bar association committee to research and report on the local law schools' commitment to best teaching practices; meeting with law school representatives to discuss findings; and taking appropriate action if an underperforming school is not responsive, such as withholding contributions (and letting the school know why!), and encouraging other members of the bar to do the same.

Most importantly, Stuckey advises, "Do not accept law teachers' claims that they are experts in educational theory or curriculum design, or that they know better than practicing lawyers what students need to learn in law school. *This is simply not true.*"

"To do nothing is also a good remedy."

Hippocrates

During those times when our searing soul-pain seems truly unquenchable, with practice, we can learn to wait in positive expectancy, and do that which is absolutely abhorrent to most lawyers: *we can do nothing.* Even during non-crisis times, in our practice of law, as in our practice of life, we might also discover that doing nothing is the best "action" that we can take in a given situation.

Those master lawyers who can mindfully and selectively employ the practice of "doing nothing' will immediately attest to the complexity of the practice. For, at a minimum, the practice entails the Hippocratic directive to *do no harm.* Restraint of pen, tongue, and email, especially during times of high tension and emotion, is a spiritual practice that only the most determined practitioners can master. Yet, if we can sit silently and peacefully, we will often be surprised to find how often life and its complexities will naturally unfold and resolve themselves, without our involvement, our intervention, or even our anxiety.

Sometimes our silence will make room for others to engage, to move beyond their comfort zones, in such a manner that they rightly assume leadership in a matter needing resolution. At other times, our respectful silence provides the needed creative space for an evolving solution, much like the heated incubator provides sustenance for the premature infant. Finally, doing nothing, in the sense of suspending a left-brain takeover of a situation, may constructively invite and allow emotional intelligence and other ways of knowing to positively influence the problem-solving process.

Don't just sit there, do nothing!

> ## "Talent comes with an individual name tag."
>
> *Charles Handy*

Our unique combination of gifts, talents, interests, and passions is a once-only occurring phenomenon in this universe. The appreciation of our uniqueness, coupled with an active cultivation of our gifts, is the only appropriate response to this phenomenon. Each of us, fully expressed, is a necessary thread in the exquisite tapestry of creation. That is why we are here. We are meant to shine through our unique expression. Fear often blocks the full flowering of our gifts, fueled by the misguided perception that if we don't climb too high, we won't have far to fall.

This competitive and scarcity mode of thinking presupposes that if one of us wins, another one has to fail. This is just not so. The world does need another hero, and each of us is called to the role. "*I am enough, I have enough, I do enough*" is an empowering mantra that allows each of us to take center stage and to shine as we alone have been called to do.

August 9

> ## "If you would only recognize that life is hard, things would be so much easier for you."
>
> *Louis Brandeis*

Are we just expected to keep following others' marching orders till we drop, like the valiant yet ill-fated troops in a military charge? When do we turn rank, and abandon the mission whose cause we question? When do we reframe, in our mind's eye, exactly what it is that we are doing in life?

Well, there are three principal pathways for resolving these and other inner conflicts: walking, talking, and spinning. We walk away from a problem that temporarily cannot be solved, to perhaps return another day, to find, or further seek, the solution. We talk our way through most of life's travails, applying reasoning, logic, and hypothetical problem-solving. This is, of course, the standard method of choice in therapy.

That which seems impervious to walking and talking, and which we must endure, we can reframe and spin to a more suitable mental vision. Spinning is a strategy for the resilient of mind and spirit, and is the most difficult of all three tactics, since it entails changing perception by understanding something in another way. So, for example, one of the first things a mediator does in the mediation process is to get the parties to explain their view of the problem. This allows the sides, as well as the mediator, to see how each is framing the conflict. The mediator then attempts to reframe and restate the nature of the conflict in such a manner that the parties mutually desire to seek a resolution.

All three methods of resolution are necessary tools in the arsenal of life, however, spiritual maturity requires that we judiciously decide when, where, and how to utilize the appropriate problem-solving approach.

> ## "Do not go where the path may lead,
> ## go instead where there is no path and leave a trail."
>
> *Ralph Waldo Emerson*

It is very rare in our materialist culture generally, and in the legal culture specifically, to find a trusted mentor who embodies and exemplifies the values and beliefs that we hope to nurture and develop. Yet, rarity does not equal non-existence. Rather, like a treasured jewel, it simply makes more precious the encounter with the person who has firmly committed to live in a manner that best comports with his or her values, beliefs, and convictions.

The legal profession was once a treasure trove for those who sought wise mentors who understood the value of service. Anthony Kronman, esteemed author of *The Lost Lawyer, The Failing Ideals of the Legal Profession*, poignantly describes what he considers the near-extinction of "lawyer-statesmen"—those formerly ubiquitous role models who were not merely legal technicians, but persons of practical wisdom and prudence. In previous generations, the lawyer-statesmen cared so sincerely for their fellow citizens that personal well-being was regularly subordinated to attending to the public good.

When I first started practicing law in the 1970s, each large law firm had its own parade of ancestral heroes, who were reverently described and revered as exemplars of the highest values of the noble profession. On a less-grand scale, but just as importantly, respected neighborhood lawyers, including a beloved uncle of mine, were regularly consulted, not only for legal advice, but for every significant matter that demanded "superior attention and judgment." Almost none would charge for these "extra-curricular" counseling sessions, as they were deemed to be an ancillary professional service that the lawyers were honored to provide.

The legal profession of the 21st century has within its ranks legions who are, or who can become, the modern ideal of lawyer-statespersons, and who can again lead the profession into a contemporary "golden age of lawyering."

August 11

> "A man would do nothing if
> he waited until he could do it so well
> that no one could find fault."
>
> *John Henry Newman*

When is enough enough? When does satisfaction of mind, heart, and body become firmly established? When are the standards of perfectionistic impetulance finally quieted, and a softer, more reasonable voice of moderation honored? Like sandpaper to wood, we too often scrape away at our inner core with each new bout of perfectionistic insanity

Why are we perpetually fooled by the supposed goodness of this corroding influence? How do our minds become warped into believing that continuous, unrelenting effort is needed to yield a required outcome?

Perfectionism is comprised of a fear that drives the wagon of obsession, and a doubting that pervasively erodes our confidence and sense of perspective. These demons will be laid to rest, however, not through obsessive overwork, but only through the time-honored tradition of facing the fear, seeing it for what it is, and then taking the small steps needed to walk through the dreaded challenge.

August 12

> "There are only four questions of value in life....
> What is sacred? Of what is the spirit made?
> What is worth living for? What is worth dying for?
> The answer to each is the same.
> Only love."
>
> *Don Juan DeMarco*

Can we possibly imagine dying for a cause?

One of my most treasured family legacies concerns my Belgian grandfather, who was incarcerated as a political prisoner in Berlin during the 1930s. A surviving compatriot reported that, before he was killed by a firing squad, my grandfather's last passionate words were: *"Long live freedom. Long live Belgium."* It is always humbling to recall that, along with my grandfather, countless millions, before and since, have surrendered their precious lives so that we might dwell in freedom.

As a child, and even to this day, I often try to imagine my grandfather's last hours—that sleepless night, that sense of ultimate fear and dread, that clinging despair of an unfinished life, that heart-wrenching break from beloved family. I wonder what words I would have said...what deeds of heroism, if any...would mark my grave?

If we are to honor the heroes who made the ultimate sacrifice, we should not take one day of our precious freedom for granted. For this ultimate gift has been purchased with no less than the humanity of our heroic predecessors.

August 13

> "And as we let our own light shine,
> we unconsciously give other people
> permission to do the same."
>
> *Marianne Williamson*

We are so much more than we think we are. While we might be tempted to value our legal abilities and talents based solely on current net "wins and losses" (especially when we are in a "low" cycle!), the fact of the matter is that we *are* so much more, and know so much more, than we might appreciate at any given moment. Our greatest legal teachers, perseverance and experience, have prepared us for whatever matter is presented, on a much deeper level than we normally appreciate.

A recent encounter brought this truth home for me. In advising a friend on how she might respond if a potential action were filed against her, the wisdom within, born of long years of study and legal practice, seemed to take on a life of its own. While quite properly advising that she seek a specialist's advice on the matter, I was very able to preliminarily outline the information that was needed at the moment. Until the exact moment of that conversation, I had not been in touch with the depth and breadth of my procedural and substantive knowledge regarding the particular matter. We acquire "legal common sense," even in those areas of law in which we do not ordinarily practice, as the natural outgrowth of suiting up and showing up for our daily practice of law over many years.

Appreciating our limits *and* our gifts, we can go forth boldly, for we most certainly do know what we are talking about!

August 14

> "In everyone's life, at some time, our inner fire goes out. It is then burst into flame by an encounter with another human being. We should all be thankful for these people who rekindle the inner spirit."
>
> *Albert Schweitzer*

There may be no pain as deep as the feeling of extreme alienation and isolation that casts an unbelievably bleak pall over every aspect of our lives. Whether we call this pain sadness or depression or extreme loneliness, it can be so excruciating that we feel that we may never survive.

These are very critical times; however, *there is a solution*. The solution is three-fold: physical, mental, and spiritual, and each of these dimensions must be attended to.

If we are having thoughts of suicide, we must IMMEDIATELY inform another and get in contact with a health professional. This is *non-negotiable*.

The saddest day of my law school teaching occurred the day a bright and beautiful young student took her life because, from what we could assess, the pressure was too overwhelming, the resources too few, and the hope non-existent. It does not matter whether we believe we can be helped or not, what matters is that we reach out for help. We do not have to suffer alone. Many thousands of people have been at a similar fork in the road, yet they live happily today because they did the "impossible"—they reached out to another person, even when the act itself seemed futile.

When dealing with less urgent mental and emotional issues, many people have sought and obtained great relief from putting themselves in the hands of a caring health professional. Our pain is very real, and we are not being cowardly by seeking relief from it; in fact, just the opposite is true.

The rates of depression in the legal profession far exceed that of the general population, and are significantly higher than among other professional groups. Fortunately, the legal profession is beginning to take steps to recognize and deal with the issue of depression. Many of the Lawyer Assistance Programs maintained by local and state bar associations have resources for dealing with lawyer depression, as well as substance abuse and other issues.

We do not hesitate to speak up for our clients when they are in need of help. We must do the same for ourselves if we are to be the lawyers and the people we were meant to be.

Feel the fear, but do it anyway!

August 15

> "The way to build self-confidence is to start
> doing things you're not sure you can do...
> seize the day and get started and stay with it,
> and things will get easier and easier from here."
>
> *Paul Williams*

Once we have enlisted the proper health professionals to help us with the physical and mental aspects of our alienation and depression, we must also begin to work on the spiritual aspects thereof if we want to achieve full healing. Today, many thoughtful therapists employ a three-fold, body, mind, and spirit, approach to treatment, and this is most effective.

Our healing actually begins when we assume full responsibility for obtaining the help we need, and then follow through with recommended action. Our active and continuous participation in the healing process, including, as appropriate, engaging in the practices outlined in this book, is essential.

We do not get well merely by visiting a therapist's office once a week. Action, not self-knowledge, is the key to right thinking. We do not think our way into right acting, *we act our way into right thinking*. And, we gain self-esteem by doing esteemable acts—the next right thing, not just the next comfortable thing—in a given situation. Problem-solving is itself an esteemable act, and, as we become more able to deal with the challenging situations in our lives, the resulting satisfaction will provide further momentum.

August 16

> ## "Myths are clues to the spiritual potentialities of the human life."
>
> *Joseph Campbell*

Somewhere between the ages of 18 and 24, most of us set out to pursue our personal and professional journeys, our unique quest. This process has both practical and mythological components, as we pursue a larger-than-life path in attempting to secure our life's dream.

This ambitious quest is fueled by our neuro-circuitry, since, at this developmental stage, our brains have matured to their final adult form, and our memory formation processes are more effective and efficient than during any other phase of life. Later on, in the last stages of life, our most salient and intact memories will be those associated with this questing and journeying phase of our young adulthood.

There is much "mythological" about leaving home, finding our path, securing our economic niche, unpacking our unique talent sets, finding our life partner, and then presenting this amassed composite to ourselves and the world. For, in a mere few years, we have exited the nest of childhood and crossed the treacherous bridge into adulthood, experiencing and processing the full range of emotions, impulses, and urges attendant thereto. Hazards, adventures, and challenges test our mettle, and allow for unlimited exploration of psychology, friendship, loyalty, honor, innovation, and intelligence. Our journey bespeaks a combination of terror, heroics, romance, absurdity, error, and grace.

Along the way, we tell and embellish our personal tales to friends, family, and passers-by, to help us herald our own arrival at center stage. We are here. We have arrived. We are the new conquering heroes and heroines, capable of slaying dragons and demons of all sorts. We ride in glory, for we are now the world-changers, the world-shakers, the world-achievers, here to spin our individual dreams, while bettering the world in which we live.

Is it any wonder these memories remain so clear until our dying day?

August 17

> ## "One of the symptoms of an approaching nervous breakdown is the belief that one's work is terribly important..."
>
> *Bertrand Russell*

Although practicing law is a very serious business, and is properly treated as such, we should not take ourselves too seriously, or we run the risk of priggish self-righteousness. In the face of the majestic history of the law, we are, in fact, mere bit players in the grand scheme of things. This majesty has been unfolding for millennia, and will continue to do so long after we are gone. While our individual attitudes and actions certainly affect the current and future status of our beloved profession, and of the world, many of us might benefit from allowing a dose of humor into our workdays.

While the service we perform for our clients is targeted for excellence, the funny, and sometimes hilarious, moments of "non-excellence" that we encounter along the way, are very worthy of our light-hearted attention.

Laughter, especially that which derives from our own foibles and follies, is a very therapeutic tonic that can readily readjust our perspective and refuel our energy.

August 18

> "Instead of running away from our loneliness and trying to forget or deny it, we have to protect it and turn it into fruitful solitude. To live a spiritual life we must first find the courage to enter the desert of our loneliness and change it, by gentle and persistent efforts, into a garden of solitude."
>
> *Henri Nouwen*

The emotional "first responder" to pain is often additional busyness and other forms of attempted escape from the painful circumstances. So, for example, if our child is acting out, we may spend more time at the office or schedule a vacation. If we perceive that our job security is threatened, we may increase our alcohol intake. If our life partner is experiencing increased stress, we may spend more time at the gym, or out with friends.

As psychologists will readily explain, our hard-wiring for the "fight-or-flight" response, which evolved at a time when "eat or be eaten" was a physical reality, continues to drive us, even as we sit comfortably in our corner offices in modern high-rise buildings. When our brain registers a threat to our body or psyche, similar to our evolutionary ancestors, the body's automatic response is to decide between fight or flight, and act accordingly.

Since lawyers are intelligent people, however, our "flight" response is often camouflaged by layers of denial, rationalization, and justification. We tell ourselves that our absence from our troubled homes is warranted by our upcoming trial or client presentation. Through such defense mechanisms, we attempt to avoid confronting what William James termed our "torn-to-pieces-hood." While such flight behavior may be "normal," it is not always healthy, and often serves to prolong and intensify the emotional pain of the neglected, underlying situation.

We do in fact possess what we need to "accept the things we cannot change" and act with the "courage to change the things we can." We did not get this far as lawyers without accumulating sufficient moral fortitude and courage to deal with adversity. The problem *du jour* is not going to unravel us, it only *feels* that way because it looms large *today*. If we are honest with ourselves, we will see that we have gotten through much worse in the past. We can be thankful that today, through the practice of the principles discussed here, we have discovered an inner compass that leads us, with today's troubles in our hands, to a transformation triangle, where each of awareness, acceptance, and action, constitutes the proper directive to doing the next right thing.

Our fear of facing a particular problem is similar to a child's fear of the dark. Like the child's bogeyman, fear reduces to a manageable commodity when exposed to the light and parsed into its component parts. Then, taking an action, no matter how simple, we begin to move toward the healing horizon.

This, my friend, is nothing other than courage of the highest order.

> "Everywhere I go it seems people are killing themselves with work, busyness, rushing, caring, and rescuing. Work addiction is a modern epidemic and it is sweeping our land."
>
> *Diane Fassel*

There are actually very few things that we must complete in a given twenty-four hour period. Yet, whether driven by fear, greed, or unreasonable ambition, we often attempt to incorporate an unreasonable number of tasks into a given day. This practice cannot add peace to our lives; in fact, it can only make us more restless, irritable, and discontent. Doing "less'" in a thoughtful and intentional manner, is, in fact, "good enough" for today, and this mode helps to foster a life of peace and meaning.

No human being, whether a Supreme Court justice, a renowned trial lawyer, or a prolific author, can accomplish eighteen hours of work in ten hours. If, however, we more reasonably schedule our day, allowing a sufficient cushion for the unexpected, and comfortably leaving undone that which exceeds our reasonable efforts, we will be "working smart" in a manner that honors body, mind, and spirit. If we further allow for periods of relaxation and "regrouping" during our workday, for example, a refreshing walk to the café, where we can sit undisturbed for a few minutes, we will be able to resume our craft, not running on empty and surviving by true grit, but calmly anticipating the next part of our day.

When we move into the natural rhythm of our work, good-naturedly accommodating some inevitable detours, we will come to know a peace of mind that even the busiest times cannot disturb. And, when evening comes, upon leaving the office, we can try to sketch a reasonable plan for the next work day.

> ## "There is a crack in everything
> ## God has made."
>
> *Ralph Waldo Emerson*

Sometimes we ponder why every time we seem to straighten out one aspect of our lives—perhaps a work issue or trouble with our child—another problem immediately assumes its place.

The answer that often accompanies our musing sounds something like this: *Because this is life—the very life of life.* Although life holds much joy and pleasure, it also holds daily challenges. As one friend says, the reason we are here is to learn the lessons that this "earth school" presents. And it is in the responsible facing of these successive challenges that we are permitted to move to higher levels of consciousness and the experience of being alive.

Yet, when we are not in such an expansive frame of mind, our immediate response to problems may be to blame others, or to attempt to instantly fix, or eliminate, some caustic factor in our environment. While we continue to look outward, rather than inward, we will remain part of the problem and not a part of the solution.

The simple yet oft-elusive fact is that living life is mainly an inside job. Whenever any person, place, or thing is disturbing, we must look within for calmness and insight. We should try to define our role in the situation, and, if necessary, clean our own side of the street, before trying to otherwise affect exterior conditions. Once this is completed, we can allow others to behave and think as they will, without losing our most precious treasures—our inner peace and serenity, for we can then *live and let live.*

August 21

> "You will never do anything in this world without courage.
> It is the greatest quality of the mind next to honor."
>
> *Aristotle*

Martin Seligman, prominent psychotherapist and pioneer of the "learned optimism" movement, advises that the use of psychotherapeutic treatments and medicines for mental and emotional issues is roughly 65 percent effective. Current therapies seldom "cure"; more often, they ameliorate symptoms and support a person's ability to better function in the world. Seligman believes that, given the less than maximal recovery rate of existing therapies, those suffering mental and emotional ills should be encouraged "to live in the best part of their psychological symptoms."

Whether Seligman's assertions are statistically precise or not, we can be sure that, except with respect to a discrete number of maladies, full "healing" seldom occurs by sole reference to external agents, medicinal or psychotherapeutic. Health professionals have always known that the patient's active commitment and involvement is required if healing, rather than amelioration, is to occur.

Seligman's approach to filling the "healing gap," which is supported by his many years of research and clinical experience, is in complete harmony with many of the themes that we have been discussing. So, Seligman notes, "An old-fashioned virtue must be coupled to these interventions. It is called courage: the courage to understand your psychological problems and manage them so as to function well in spite of them."

Seligman is far from alone in confirming that, while mentors, friends, medicines, and therapists can assist and support our journey to wholeness, our well-being is ultimately an inside job. No matter how rigorously we might try to "externalize" both our problems and their solutions, we will not find lasting wholeness until we commit to going deeply within, piercing through every strata of fear, denial, and rationalization, to ultimately find and address conditions as they are. As theologian Paul Tillich wrote, the good life is the courageous life we have when we let ourselves "surpass ourselves."

> "We do not grow absolutely, chronologically. We grow sometimes in one dimension, and not in another; unevenly. We grow partially. We are relative. We are mature in one realm, childish in another. The past, present, and future mingle and pull us backward, forward, or fix us in the present. We are made up of layers, cells, constellations."
>
> *Anais Nin*

Long ago, I read a poem that spoke of experiencing temporal age as a circular, rather than a linear phenomenon. The thought was that, although a person might be 40 or 60 or 80 years old, every experience of every prior age still lived within. So, as a middle-aged lawyer, smartly dressed on the courthouse steps, I carry within my fractious 4-year-old, my enthusiastic 22-year-old, and my temporarily defeated 37-year-old, together with every other age and happening my being has experienced. Each of these iterations of self accompanies the "current me," dragging its own time-stamped joys and concerns, triumphs and failures, ordinary times and extraordinary times.

Today we are responsible for owning, honoring, and attending to our current life circumstances. However, we might also give due notice and respect to those other phases and times when previous life lessons were learned. Some of those times were painful, but we survived, perhaps mining new sources of courage, perspective, and strength. Some of those times were exhilarating, others were ordinary, but each of those times brought us to exactly where we stand today.

While we eagerly attempt to live our best lives today, one day at a time, we should not hesitate to appreciatively glance back at those formative experiences that brought us to this moment.

August 23

> "Your pain is the breaking of the shell
> that encloses your understanding."
>
> *Kahlil Gibran*

When we sometimes find ourselves in the despairing depths of "*Is that all there is?*" or "*I really can't take it anymore,*" we can pause, take a deep breath, forgive ourselves, and trust that maybe, *just maybe*, we are exactly where we are supposed to be for the present moment.

Perhaps the restlessness and pain is calling us, and moving us, to a deeper and more satisfying way of living our lives, and to a more meaningful expression of self. Just as a beautiful pearl comes into being as a result of the caustic irritation of the oyster's shell, so, too, the most bountiful aspects of our existence may lie below unearthed strata, awaiting necessary, but painful, excavation. Thus, the medical community consistently confirms that alcoholics and addicts almost never voluntarily relinquish their life-threatening behaviors, absent an extraordinarily high degree of pain, often referred to as the "gift of desperation."

On a more ordinary level, many of us would not consider leaving a legal position without experiencing the caustic rub of *grave* dissatisfaction. While some others may plot and plan their next professional moves using a higher calculus, many require a high degree of emotional and psychic pain before dismantling the status quo.

Just as physical pain calls our attention to a potentially serious condition, emotional and psychic pain emit their own "pay attention" signals, which we ignore at our peril. Pain is considered by many to be the greatest motivator for needed change, thus deserving our mindful attention, as demanded.

August 24

> ## "What we say with our words is so much less important than what we live with our lives. Only our lives give weight to our words."
>
> *Mary Jo Leddy*

Lived gratitude is much more than a virtue, a feeling of gratefulness for blessings received, or a felicitous reaction to life's events. Lived gratitude reflects a chosen orientation, a thoughtful and intentional decision to live one's life in a spirit of positive, mindful remembrance. Such gratitude can create a much more meaningful life for ourselves and others, and can be further cultivated by specific gratitude practices, many of which have been enunciated by saints and everyday mystics throughout the ages. With conscious practice, a life of lived gratitude even permits us to appreciate the situations that come packaged within seeming adversity. The "why me?" approach to life can eventually evolve into the more spiritually mature and tranquil "why *not* me?" response.

With lived gratitude, our lawyers' lives of abundance are no longer taken for granted, as we freely choose to stand in reverent recognition of all that we have been graciously given. We begin to deeply appreciate that forces greater than ourselves have always been generously involved in our existence, for, after all, we did not call forth the sun, or design photosynthesis, or strategize to combine hydrogen and oxygen to produce water. No, we are merely the recipients of these incredible gifts, and so many more.

Too often, lawyers stand ready to lay claim to our "earned" accomplishments, often citing years of study, perseverance, and hard work. Yet, honest reflection readily reveals that, had we been born in one of the many countries in the world where extreme poverty is the norm, or, if we did not enjoy our present levels of physical and mental health, we could never have known such "earned" accomplishments.

Author Mary Jo Leddy advises that we can break the "vicious cycle" of dissatisfaction with our lives by cultivating a sense of radical gratitude. We can then begin to appreciate what we have, rather than what we lack, and who we are, rather than who we are not.

> "We probably have wondered in our many lonesome moments if there is one corner in this competitive, demanding world where it is safe to be relaxed, to expose ourselves to someone else, and to give unconditionally. It might be very small and hidden. But if this corner exists, it calls for a search through the complexities of our human relationships in order to find it."
>
> *Henri Nouwen*

What is the purpose of relationship and how does it serve us?

As human beings, we were fashioned for relationship. As infants, we form permanent attachments to our caregivers, upon whom we are completely dependent for the first five years of life. Once we are capable of separating from our parents, we begin to form connections with siblings, surrogate caregivers, and friends.

Relationships have both intrinsic and extrinsic properties. In choosing our best friends, for example, we initially attempt to find people like ourselves, to better understand who *we* are. Later, in the phase of cliques, we continue to sort out who we are, and whether we are leaders or followers. In our mid-teens, relationship takes on new complexity as sexuality elevates the emotional investment in relationships. Ultimately, we pair off, separating from acquaintances and our family of origin, as we proceed toward the creation of our own families. During our school years, we can form connections that last a lifetime, and, often, these close friends play a more critical role in our lives than family. The identification and bonding inherent in close relationships allows us to simultaneously connect and individuate, allowing for the further development of the mature personality.

Relationship also helps to position us in both careers and community. Our professionalism as lawyers is enhanced when we bring well-developed relationship skills to our work. Our ability to effectively communicate with others is a core requirement of lawyering. Affability, openness, sociability, and other personal relationship skills favorably influence professional advancement and one's positioning within an organization.

Relationship-building should continue throughout one's life span, since good relationships, in addition to being essential to our happiness and emotional health, are also an excellent indicator of better long-term physical health.

> "Every decision you make—every decision—is not a decision about what to do. It's a decision about who you are. When you see this, when you understand it, everything changes. You begin to see life in a new way."

Neale Donald Walsch

If we have made a decision to move forward in a new direction, and later discover that it is not totally right for us, we need not despair. Rather, all we need to do is regroup, breathe, and get ready to make another decision.

Closed doors often provide better direction for our earthly journeys than open doors do. Throughout my career, I many times believed that desired pathways promised to be the "ultimate" ones for me. When I did not get the coveted job, or when the doors would not swing open upon my other desired goals, I often felt deflated, discouraged, and despairing of ever finding my "sweet spot" in the practice of law.

However, as I continued to "suit up, show up, and do the next right thing," other paths appeared where before there had been none. Looking back, I see that every step, those joyfully taken, and those not, were a part of the great mosaic of my life, planned by a power much wiser and more powerful than myself. Only my cooperation and persistence were required, insofar as I needed to cultivate awareness and remain active in my quest for personal and professional growth.

August 27

> ## "Live so that your friends can defend you but never have to."
> *Arnold H. Glasow*

What is involved in leading a principled life, and how does this add to your stature as a lawyer? Recently, in referring a lawyer to someone in need of legal help, I described the lawyer as an honorable and honest man. This principled lawyer obtained new business because of the honorable way he conducted himself.

You are known not only for your lawyering skills, but for your humanity. What principles do you profess to lead your life? How do these principles express themselves in your daily behavior? Are you kind, warm, empathic, caring, emotionally available, reliable, generous with your time and energy, honest, and a person of integrity? Or, are you cunning, deviant, competitive, unscrupulous, detached, Machiavellian, manipulative, and ruthless? Which adjectives describe a good lawyer? Which set of adjectives will define your lawyering?

August 28

> ## "Do not let loyalty and faithfulness forsake you;
> ## bind them around your neck,
> ## write them on the tablet of your heart."
>
> *Proverbs 3:3*

Loyalty is a noble yet often overlooked virtue. To stand gratefully with others, united in the shared exchange of experiences and values, is to glimpse heaven. Loyalty to one's family, school, teachers, friends, mentors, church, employers, neighbors—past and current—enables us to appreciate and further cultivate the beneficence of the universe. In honoring the other, we ourselves are lifted up in gratitude for the love, service, and excellence that the other has given us.

We have held an annual family reunion at my home each year for about fifteen years. When we began, we were about thirty people, and this number has nearly tripled in recent times. From the matriarchs and the patriarchs to the youngest children, the ritual of anticipation, assembly, witness, and sharing has few affective counterparts or rivals. For better or worse, we are family, united by genetic material, united by common heritage, united by love, service, and admiration. Of course, we have our petty rivalries and likes and dislikes, yet these pale by comparison to the immense values secured by "tribal" loyalty and reverence.

We can also engender and cultivate a culture of loyalty in our work lives through the conscious recognition and celebration of all that is noble about our profession: the ancestral giants of the legal profession, the everyday heroes, and the majestic rule of law itself, which allows, in its own imperfect way, for the preservation of our treasured American way of life.

August 29

> "It's not hard to find the truth.
> What is hard is not to run away from it
> once you have found it."
>
> *Author Unknown*

As much as we may try to avoid the issue, a portion of our job as lawyers involves delivering "bad news." While a lawyer may listen well to a client's situation, properly analyze the legal issues involved, and then enthusiastically "fight the good fight" for the client, in too many cases, the lawyer does not adequately prepare the client for an adverse, or partially adverse, outcome.

An important aspect of spiritual maturity involves seeing and naming matters *as they are*, and not merely as we would have them be. We must admit these things, first to ourselves, and then to others. While many of us naturally recoil from unpleasant situations and conversations, as lawyers, we are charged with properly counseling our clients during all stages of the representation cycle. Proper counseling involves managing the client's (and our own) expectations concerning anticipated outcomes.

Discomfort is not an excuse for not doing the right thing. Personal and professional integrity requires that we report to our clients all developments, as well as all possible outcomes, in a candid manner. I was once involved in a situation where, after a very competent and zealous representation in a criminal matter, the lawyer was literally unable to report to the client the court's guilty verdict, which carried a lengthy period of incarceration.

Facing and speaking difficult truths can be done when we operate from within our transformative triangle of awareness, acceptance, and action. As we properly supply the complete truth to our clients, they, too, can become similarly empowered to handle the information from within their own transformative triangle.

> "Do you really want to look back
> on your life and see how wonderful
> it could have been had you
> not been afraid to live it?"
>
> *Carolyn Myss*

It all comes down to this. Pull in the reins, tighten the focus, and streamline all of your potential into this momentous "big now" snapshot in time. How often has your credibility, your reputation, your pedigree as a lawyer been determined during a twenty-four- to forty-eight-hour window of opportunity? Are you ready for the dance when the challenge presents itself? Are you equal to the challenge posed by a judge, a jury, or the unique hallmarks of a case? What defines the inner workings of your being? Is character one of the words that comes to mind when describing your work? Could you live your life any other way than to be the best at your game?

August 31

> "Love alone is capable of uniting living beings
> in such a way as to complete and fulfill them,
> for it alone takes them and joins them
> by what is deepest in themselves."

Pierre Teilhard de Chardin

We cannot navigate this world alone. Remaining solitary, there is a wayward drift of spirit, potentially ranging far off-course, if left too long untethered by connection to others.

Human beings attempt to piece together meaning, purpose, order, and unifying themes wherever they journey. If we lose our way in life, it can be arduous to reclaim our forsaken path without the help of others. Although a lucky few seem to dance in the footsteps of God, predicting and making all the right connections, most of us experience more trial and error as we navigate life's journeys.

It is at these times that our friends and mentors come to our aid. Not blinded by the passions of the moment as we are, they are able to analyze our situation with clarity. They can also help us to reset our own compass, and reinvigorate our higher reasoning capacity to journey forth again.

September 1

> "In the depths of winter,
> I finally learned there was in me
> an invincible summer."

Albert Camus

Letting go of summer overflows with pathos. The child within us urgently grasps at the long sweet, golden days, and the carefree nights filled with star-hewn skies. Our hearts resist letting go of the deep reassurance of summer that seems to whisper: *No matter how harsh the winds may blow, there is a place that remains ever-protected and sweet, where the fragrance of eternity lingers in the softened glow.*

We can go home again. Home to the place within that is always safe, and always allows us to be just as we are.

September 2

> ## "I wake expectant,
> ## hoping to see a new thing."
>
> *Annie Dillard*

The amber hues and the crimson-rimmed leaves of autumn remind us, like each change of season might, to journey inward and experience the altering landscape of our souls. The unique seasonal qualities add invitation and depth to an already examined life.

For many of us, ever-attuned to the school calendars of our childhood, autumn is the psychological beginning of the new work year. The lightened load of summer is nearing an end, and a burgeoning, challenging fullness, awaits. Like the ancestral harvesters of yesteryear, we are called forth from the hazy, timeless pace of summer, and are propelled into the crisp urgency of fall's necessities.

New beginnings are, perhaps, life's most tender mercy.

September 3

"This moment contains all moments."

C.S. Lewis

If we find ourselves becoming entangled in the complicated web of a full and active life, we can stop, breathe, and check where our feet are, in order to regain our bearings. The present moment requires our full attention. Multitasking may be an admirable activity on the corporate barometer, but it is the archenemy of the serene life.

We can remain present in the current moment and still accomplish all that needs to be done in a given day.

Let us sketch, for example, the possible mindful use of our time as we prepare to attend a client meeting outside the office. Traveling to the client meeting, we might focus on the earth's natural gifts, the air, the sky, the breeze. When arriving at the client's building, we might stop for a moment of gratitude, appreciating the professional gifts that allow us to engage in creative problem-solving, and to use our talents and training to bring clarity and order to a situation where before there was none. Gratitude can also be found in the recognition that our financial remuneration derives from such meaningful and creative work. We might then envision the imminent meeting as producing the best outcome possible.

During the meeting, we can keep focused on the topic at hand, and during moments of concern or indecision, we can breathe deeply, garnering the courage and inspiration needed for the present moment. We can truly listen to others, quietly seeking to ascertain the client's true needs and concerns, perhaps ascertaining the "sub-script" that lies beneath the spoken words. If we remain open-minded to all possibilities, we may see issues not yet anticipated, and potential solutions not yet imagined. We can leave the meeting knowing we have given it our best, ready to move on to doing the next right thing.

None of these things would occur if we were preoccupied with remembrances of yesterday's stalled negotiations, or tomorrow's troublesome court appearance.

For everything there is a season, and for every small but meaningful encounter, there is a moment. Our lives are made up of nothing but moments, well-lived or not, and as the poet Annie Dillard advises, how we live our moments is how we live our lives.

September 4

> "There is a sacredness in tears. They are not the mark of weakness, but of power. They speak more eloquently than ten thousand tongues. They are messengers of overwhelming grief...and unspeakable love."
>
> *Washington Irving*

A swell of tears can arise in us, when, for example, we contemplate the journey ahead without our beloved beside us. Such a significant loss, or anticipated loss, often moves us to tears. Why does this happen, and is there not some way to avoid this uncomfortable and often unintended display of emotion?

The act of crying is hard-wired into our systems. Crying biologically realigns our homeostasis and restores our internal equilibrium. Additionally, of course, crying serves to communicate to the world around us, and to ourselves, that we are struggling with an important issue of loss, grief, or abandonment, or that we are moved beyond words by positive emotions of joy, gratitude, and awe.

Depression, death, and the loss of a relationship or opportunity are the primary reasons why our tears flow. Each of these situations requires tender attention and care from ourselves, and those who care about us. Depression is an illness that requires treatment, and should not be ignored and allowed to linger, for instead of benignly departing, depression often takes root, biologically and cognitively, thereby predisposing the brain for future depressions. Death and loss are universally times of great despondency, and we require significant support and space for healing.

Our lives intermingle and flow together in mysterious ways. We need not be afraid of our tears, for although crying usually signals a time of sadness, it is often followed by reflection and an inner restructuring, which allows us to journey forward in an enriched and healing manner.

> "National Alcohol and Drug Addiction Recovery Month provides an opportunity to underscore our commitment to stopping alcohol and drug abuse before it starts and to helping citizens in need overcome addiction and rebuild their lives. Alcohol and drug addiction can ruin lives and devastate families. We must continue working toward a society in which our citizens can lead lives free from the influence of alcohol and drugs. Friends and family members can play a vital role in the fight and prevention of abuse by discussing the dangers and consequences with loved ones."

2007 Presidential Proclamation

Since September is National Alcohol and Drug Addiction Recovery Month, we will spend some time this month reflecting on how alcohol and drug addiction negatively impacts lawyers, their families, their colleagues, the legal profession, and society as a whole.

It is estimated that 20 percent of lawyers, *one in five*, have a substance-abuse problem. Imagine convening at the annual retreat of your 200-lawyer firm, when the managing partner announces that forty of your colleagues are in various stages of this life-threatening and baffling disease!

The *one-in-five* ratio means that almost every lawyer is involved with substance abuse on some level during the course of the workday: either the lawyer is chemically addicted; one or more of the lawyer's close colleagues are addicted; or, the lawyer is in contact with judges or other legal professionals who are drug or alcohol abusers.

If a family of five had one addicted member, we have all experienced enough and read enough to calculate the negative impact that this disability would have on the entire family. Yet, except for those who are no longer able to keep up even the appearance of propriety, 20 percent of the lawyers showing up at the office are suffering from the disease of addiction.

For those unfamiliar with the workings of addiction, these scenarios may seem impossible to believe, since we very seldom encounter a lawyer who is actually slurring his words or stumbling around the office. Nonetheless, we should remain aware that the physical, mental, and spiritual disease of addiction may be silently corroding the body, mind, and spirit of 20 percent of the apparently functioning lawyers that we encounter every day.

> "None of us like to think that we are bodily and mentally different from others. Our drinking careers have been characterized by countless vain attempts to prove that we could drink like other people. This delusion that we are like other people has to be smashed."
>
> *Alcoholics Anonymous*

Denial is a primary attribute of any addiction, and is a particularly insidious barrier to a lawyer's seeking help. The experts define denial as a series of psychological maneuvers designed to reduce the awareness that drugs or alcohol are the cause of the individual's problems.

Due to environmental factors, the lawyer-sufferer is often able to keep the reality of addiction a secret from himself or herself, and from others. Since lawyers are sophisticated, and often materially well-positioned, they encounter difficulties in admitting to the problem since, they reason, a true alcoholic or addict could not possibly maintain their level of power, possessions, and prestige. Since they have so many "things," and appear at the office on a near-daily basis, they believe that they could not possibly be trapped in the cycle of addiction. In fact, they often believe that the drug or the drink is the only thing that is "holding it all together" for them.

The fact is that many, if not most, addicted lawyers *appear* functional in their legal positions. A lawyer does not have to be obviously abusing a substance during the course of the workday to be a full-blown addict or alcoholic. The addicted lawyer's behavior can run the full gamut from the outspoken trial lawyer, to the withdrawn and fearful office worker who barely comes out of his or her office. There is no "one size fits all" behavioral role for the substance-abusing lawyer. However, in quieter moments, the lawyer, as well as astute and caring observers, may question why there are many "unexplainable" events in the lawyer's life—personal, family, relational, and professional difficulties—that just don't add up.

In the midst of such baffling circumstances, we do ourselves and others a great service by being mindful of the possibility of substance abuse, the afflicter of so many lawyers.

> "We have an allergy to alcohol. The action of alcohol on chronic alcoholics is a manifestation of an allergy. We allergic types can never safely use alcohol in any form at all."
>
> *Alcoholics Anonymous*

The American Medical Association has classified alcoholism as a primary disease since 1966. Nonetheless, many people still believe that the use of alcohol is a moral question, and that if people simply exercised more willpower, they would not abuse it. While these "facts" may have some truth for the person who occasionally overindulges, they are not correct for the true alcoholic.

Medical authorities advise that preoccupation with alcohol, coupled with a loss of control over the amount consumed, are the salient characteristics of alcohol abuse. Research establishes that the physical and mental responses of an alcoholic differ from non-alcoholics, in that, once the substance is consumed, the "phenomenon of craving" for more alcohol develops. Without treatment, this craving can be stronger than the need for food or water, and can be relieved only by taking another drink, notwithstanding the devastating consequences that often follow. It is also the case that alcoholics can sometimes abstain from drinking for long periods of time, thereby "proving" to themselves and others that "they can stop any time they choose." For the true alcoholic, however, even long periods of abstinence are usually followed by deeper advances into alcoholism.

Alcohol has long been a staple of the law school culture, where the "victories are celebrated and defeats are forgotten" mentality often initially takes hold. Thus, in a 1993 study of 3,400 law students conducted by the American Association of Law Schools, it was found that 3.3 percent of the law students admitted that they needed help to control their substance abuse, and approximately 12 percent more stated that they abused drugs and alcohol during law school.

Law schools have generally ignored these problems, and, except for possible mention in professionalism classes, offer little instruction or support in dealing with substance abuse. Adding fuel to the fire, law school-sponsored social events support the legal culture's acceptance of drinking.

As officers of the court, we are called to break the chain of silence with respect to active addiction encountered within the profession. Local Lawyer Assistance Programs can supply the information needed to responsibly respond to this matter.

September 8

> "While alcoholics keep strictly away from drink,
> they react to life much like other people. But the first
> drink sets the terrible cycle in motion. Alcoholics
> usually have no idea why they take the first drink."
>
> *Alcoholics Anonymous*

In the last few days we have been speaking about the disease of alcoholism, and the high incidence of the disease among lawyers. While the general public experiences an approximate 10 percent rate of alcoholism, that rate is closer to 20 percent among lawyers. A person is probably an alcoholic if, when they honestly want to stop drinking they cannot "stay stopped," or, when drinking, they have little control over the amount they consume.

Whether or not the medical profession ultimately classifies alcoholism as a "genetic" disease, ample evidence, both scientific and anecdotal, confirms that alcoholism is certainly familial. Yet, even with the very common familial occurrence of alcoholism, many lawyers, sober for a long while, report that they are the only known or "suspected" alcoholic in their family of origin. Alcoholism is no respecter of pedigree; it is an equal-opportunity disease, affecting people from "both Park Avenue and the park bench."

For some lawyers, alcoholism is already well-established during their law school days; for others, the onset comes later. When finally recognized, few lawyers reach out for help, since, as the "ultimate problem solvers," they hope that they can fight the battle on their own. The fact is that very few people have been able to single-handedly recover from alcoholism. While they may seem to be succeeding for a while, the time usually comes when there is no effective barrier between the alcoholic and the first drink.

There are effective and confidential ways to deal with a lawyer's alcoholism and appropriate guidance is a mere phone call away.

September 9

> "We had but two alternatives; one was to go on
> to the bitter end, blotting out the consciousness
> of our intolerable situation as best we could,
> and the other was to accept spiritual help."
>
> *Alcoholics Anonymous*

If you believe that you or another is alcoholic, there is much cause for hope, since alcoholism is a treatable disease. Although there is no known cure for the disease, lawyers in recovery often speak of the one-day-at-a time "daily reprieve" that they experience when involved in a program of recovery.

The alcoholic law student or lawyer can follow numerous avenues when seeking help for alcohol or drug addiction. They can follow a specialized path for legal professionals by calling the local bar association, or the Lawyer's Assistance Program hotline. Alternatively, they can follow a path that is open to lawyers and non-lawyers alike, such as speaking with a recovering alcoholic or health professional, or by calling the local number for Alcoholics Anonymous, and receiving directions as to how to proceed. The inquiries will be treated confidentially, and most people will graciously assist the caller in finding direction. Those who have reason to know what they are talking about may sincerely counsel, "You never have to feel this way again." By following a few simple suggestions, seekers will be put on a path to wholeness.

We have spoken much in these pages of the powerful "awareness, acceptance, and action" triad that is the paradigm within which our lives can be transformed. Nowhere is this formula more powerful and effective than when a lawyer confronts his or her alcoholism.

Once we have become aware that our drinking is no mere habit, and have begun to realize and accept its devastating consequences in our lives, we can then courageously decide to take that one small action that allows others in to guide us toward recovery. The only next right thing to do is to ask for help.

> "The bravest are surely those
> who have the clearest vision of what is
> before them, glory and danger alike,
> and yet notwithstanding,
> go out to meet it."
>
> *Thucydides*

On this day, we remember very dark hours. We especially remember those who have given all, so that we might live freely today.

Try, if you will, to imagine a day without freedom. Conjure the images that derive from a life devoid of self-agency, an existence stripped of meaning and choice.

We must tread lightly upon that hallowed ground where heroes fell, and recall that, at this very moment, in many lands, others give their utmost so that we may live unencumbered by oppressive restraints.

September 11

> "Love is our true destiny.
> We do not find the meaning
> of life by ourselves alone—
> we find it with another."
>
> *Thomas Merton*

I am privileged to have had several mentors in my professional life. Each of these people lives their life, professionally and otherwise, in accordance with their chosen values. Each of these people defines how their time will be allotted in accordance with those values. Each has a chosen form of regularly reconnecting with their higher power, however defined, and aligning their activities accordingly. Each has a significant degree of peace and serenity in their workdays, since their lives are not totally dictated by the "news of the hour and the crisis of the moment." Very importantly, each of these people is available for me when I am in need of their counsel.

We do not have to travel troubled (or even untroubled) professional waters by ourselves. Some of our most creative and successful undertakings are achieved through collaborative work with others. When we engage with people who share similar attitudes and energy, work can be productive, creative, and will sometimes even resemble the play of our childhoods.

If we are not able to find such a mentor in our own workplace, a similarly situated colleague, a retired lawyer, or a trusted friend might be willing to journey with us as we voice our professional concerns, dreams, struggles, and successes. When our energy ebbs, or our dreams seem nearly drowned in a sea of cynicism, our mentors can provide comfort, perspective, advice, and hope, while restoring our sagging spirits. The greatest gifts we can give one another are our time and attention, and our genuine expectation of their success. *Have a mentor, be a mentor.*

September 12

> "Truth sits on the lips
> of dying men."
>
> *Matthew Arnold*

Parker Palmer, a Quaker philosopher and author, poignantly asks, "How shall we now live?" in the aftermath of the September 11th debacle. Palmer recounts a news story of a Twin Towers survivor who was seen stumbling from the rubble, apparently mumbling about what had just happened. When a policeman compassionately suggested that the man might be confused, the survivor forthrightly asserted that, no, in fact, he had never been more clear and focused in his life.

Palmer interprets this scenario as evidencing the inner clarity that remains after all the normal "protections" of health, security, and strength are stripped away. In light of the enormity of the trauma just suffered, this survivor had "the eyes to see and the ears to hear" so much more clearly and accurately than ever before, much in the same manner that those near death often seem possessed of a deep knowledge of eternal truths.

We certainly do not have to await the occurrence of unspeakable trauma before seeking our own clarity as to how we now shall live. Rather, as of this very moment, we can consciously begin to select and live those values and beliefs that are definitional for each of us as individuals.

September 13

> "The most important thing in life is to learn how to give out love, and let it come in."
>
> *Morrie Schwartz*

I recently attended a creativity workshop where, among other assignments, the participants were challenged to quickly write, without reflection, the three things that they would like to have said about them at their funeral. Composed so quickly that the normal ego filters had not yet been activated, I wrote the following words in my course workbook:

1. She loved her family
2. She had a great sense of humor
3. She was kind

Whether I might have, in another time and place, more eloquently enunciated my desired eulogy, I believe these few words adequately sketched my soul's mission statement.

The time is always right for us to consider what will be said, and what we want to have said, at our funerals. As Morrie of *Tuesdays with Morrie* fame advised, when you know how to die, you know how to live.

Lawyer-educator George W. Kaufman assigns the task of writing one's own obituary when assisting lawyers who are trying to live more balanced lives. In giving voice to the specific qualities we want acknowledged at the time of our death, we write much of our own life's mission statement.

September 14

> "When you do something,
> you should burn yourself completely,
> like a good bonfire,
> leaving no trail of yourself."
>
> *Shunryo Suzuki*

Is there anything in this lifetime that you must do before you die? My best friend, a lawyer, told me that he always wanted to write a country music song. I gave him one of my guitars, a Fender. That was years ago, and he hasn't written that song yet.

Life is short; we are here for a purpose. We are here to leave our mark upon this earth. Cast your net wide. Set your goals. Keep your eyes on the prize. Move systematically and emphatically in the direction of achieving your dreams. Pursue your passions. Accept your God-given talents as the starting point, and then take them over the moon.

September 15

"Through the Thou
a person becomes I."

Martin Buber

True relationship always entails the giving of our time and attention. We get to know another almost as well, and, in some ways, better, than they know themselves. What compels us to do this?

We have many developmental jobs in life. The first is to understand ourselves, and to become familiar with all the rooms of the house in which we dwell. Importantly, in relationships, we get to privately "screen" our life before publicly experiencing it.

Relationship, by definition, entails an "I" and a "Thou." For true connection to occur, we must be capable of caring for both intimately.

Once we sufficiently understand our own behaviors, attitudes, motivations, and thought processes, we are in a position to "cohabit" within the inner sanctum of another's being. The measure of another's suitability and preparedness for relationship can often be glimpsed through their behavior toward animals, children, subordinates, and the elderly, since, how we handle the "outer ranges" of relational connection is representative of our response to more important relationships.

Trust, openness, generosity, and respect for diverse perceptions help us to pass through the early stages of relationship development.

We will eventually reach a critical juncture, where the more immediate concerns of our relationship partner require that we temporarily relegate our own needs to a subsidiary status while we attend, in compassion and empathy, to the immediate, deeper concerns of the other. The nature of our response at this juncture, and whether it is reciprocated, will determine the depth and the meaning of the I/Thou connection.

September 16

> "You might experiment with using the cultivation of generosity as a vehicle for deep self-observation and inquiry as well as an exercise in giving. A good place to start is with yourself."
>
> *Jon Kabat-Zinn*

Generous actions in our modern-day culture often stand out as unusual events that defy our current understanding of how the world really works. We attempt to find a reason for the action, or a context that might explain the generosity, for we question whether a truly selfless gesture could possibly be part of another's daily repertoire.

What would the world look like, what would our home or office look like, if generosity of spirit and action flowed freely? What changes could we create and observe?

Our environment massively affects how we feel about ourselves. We are responsible for, and have the ability to improve, our environment. If each day we make a conscious effort to express kind gestures toward self, others, and the world around us, our positive effect will enhance the world, one person at a time.

September 17

"Crossing this river is difficult: it means leaving behind some of your own ideas."

Dick Raymond

Once we decide to join the legal profession, we immediately become recognized as lawyers-to-be in the public consciousness, perhaps long before we attend our first law school class. So, for example, in many university towns, some landlords will rent apartments only to law students, thereby implicitly acknowledging that, from the very beginning of their training, the law student is identified more by reference to "law" than to "student." Similarly, as soon as proud parents announce to family and friends that their offspring will enter law school, there is a near-unanimous favorable nodding of the head, as images of intelligent, hard-working, and socially adept professionals-in-training are benignly imaged.

While others readily project a positive professional identity upon us, the beginning law student is often clueless regarding the upcoming law school experience, never mind the professional trail that flows from it. (I remember not being clear about the difference between criminal law and civil law upon the commencement of my studies!)

The beginning law student often views law school solely as the required credentialing mechanism, where "dues must be paid," *never* appreciating that there will be a major identity restructuring during the critical law school years. This restructuring is a profound one, in that, on some very basic levels, the student will be asked to leave behind long-held values, beliefs, and idealistic tendencies concerning justice, service, and the majesty of the rule of law, without being given assurances as to what will replace these critically important attributes. Beginning with the first orientation speaker, and ending with the final commencement speaker three years later, students will hear, again and again, about the importance of "thinking like a lawyer," yet only the exceptional law school professor will provide any meaningful guidance as to what it means, or could mean, *to be the best lawyer possible,* given the unique talents, interests, and desires of each student.

Should not this topic also be discussed at orientation, and thereafter?

September 18

> "Don't aim at success—the more you aim at it and make it a target, the more you are going to miss it. For success, like happiness, cannot be pursued; it must ensue... as the unintended side-effect of one's personal dedication to a courage greater than oneself."
>
> *Viktor Frankl*

Happiness is…

How differently we might have completed this sentence at different points over the years. As children, we might have completed the sentence with dreams of summer vacations, obtaining a prized toy, or being in the "cool" group. Later, the right car, the right spouse, the right neighborhood, the right legal job, all took their turns in filling our anticipated happiness quotient.

Today, for many of us, happiness is none of these things. While the company of loved ones and interesting work and creature comforts certainly enhance our lives, they are not themselves the creators of happiness. Rather, happiness is the by-product of living a good life, albeit, not a perfect life. The first fruits of this form of authentic happiness are self-esteem, peace, tranquility, and a sense of genuine meaning and purpose in our lives. Life is no longer a dead end, or something to be survived or endured. Life takes on new meaning as we greet each day with a renewed sense of purpose and hope.

Lawyer, know thyself! Do not let "good enough" be a substitute for obtaining and living the best in life. When we are living our authentic lives, we come to know an inner happiness and a new freedom that no amount of possessions, power, and prestige can match. Today is the day to intentionally seek these priceless gifts, as today is the only day we have to suit up, show up, and do the next right thing.

> ## "What we need is more people who specialize in the impossible."
>
> *Theodore Roethke*

We have all met these people, yet, usually without stopping to reflect, we have categorized them as aberrational, having a unique emotional temperament, or as somehow existing outside the "normal range" of expected behavior. Who are they? The few and precious individuals whose very being exudes a genuine and unself-conscious desire to help and serve others. The hospital aide who engages in a genuinely caring exchange with a patient as she adjusts the patient's bed. The bus driver who softly coaches the elder to "take her time" getting up the steps. The doctor who reassuringly tells us that help *will* be available, day or night, until the crisis passes. The lawyer who agrees to delayed payment until the client "can get back on his feet."

When we are privileged to witness such events, or, even better yet, when we ourselves are the beneficiaries of such tender mercies, we should savor the encounter and not rush by unaware, unheeding. In fact, we should reverently stop and observe the sacred ground that has been consecrated by the love and caring of the passing angel.

Rabbi Irwin Kula tells the story of meeting an ophthalmologist, who, upon learning that he was speaking with a rabbi, announced, "I'm not religious." Later, the ophthalmologist casually related how, every year, he and some doctor friends chartered a plane to go overseas to perform surgery for people who otherwise would have no access to eye care.

Rabbi Kula writes: "I was blown away. This is a guy who told me he wasn't religious. I said, 'Wow, now I understand a blessing in the Jewish tradition that I never understood before: "Praised are You God Who makes the blind see." I tell him this and the guy begins to cry.'" Ever since that conversation, the ophthalmologist begins his workday by reciting the affirmation (*written on a post-it*, no less!), "*May my work today be a blessing.*"

While that ophthalmologist would certainly disdain the accolade of monk, mystic, or even "religious person," the story is a precious reminder that there are many angels in our midst, performing very sacred work, whether they deem themselves religious, or not!

> "Lawyers are...operators of the
> toll bridge which anyone in
> search of justice must pass."
>
> *Jane Bryant Quinn*

Life, we are told as children, can be unfair. Yet our challenge as dwellers of the world community, and as the toll-keepers of the bridge to justice, is to see to it that some semblance of fairness, sound judgment, and the possibility for a better tomorrow, remain within the grasp of each member of society.

The reality of different circumstances dictates the motivational explanation for behavior. We must be cautious to not judge harshly, as we operate from within the elite vantage point of lawyering, and, as the saying goes, we have not walked in the shoes of the ones we presume to judge. Ours is not to critique and mentally discard those we deem as being society's castoffs. As lawyers, we have been called to provide a service of healing and reconciliation, not condemnation and rejection.

As the sole operators of the justice toll bridge, lawyers must hold sacred their heightened responsibility to both acknowledge and respect the unique integrity of every person.

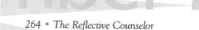
September 21

> "Keep your feet on the ground,
> but let your heart soar
> as high as it will."
>
> *A.W. Tozer*

Research reveals that specific psychological processes enhance creativity, one of the most salient characteristics of the self-actualized lawyer. These processes include an openness to new experience, flexibility, an unconventional, non-conformist approach to problem-solving, and an enthusiasm that gives way to reasonable risk-taking. While a nurturing environment can certainly enhance the creative process, the self-actualizer can still thrive in less-than-optimal conditions.

Talent arises from the combination of innate abilities, coupled with training, knowledge, practice, and motivation. The maturing process also enhances overall performance by allowing for an increasing appreciation of the limits of our knowledge and abilities. Thus, while aiming for our most lofty and idealized dreams and ambitions, the well-matured professional will also remain grounded by frequent reference to our earthly moorings.

September 22

> ## "What we thought was the horizon of our potential turns out to be only the foreground."
>
> *Tom Roberts*

If we could choose to change the world in some extraordinary way, what direction would our life take? Would we separate from our "tribe," advancing and elevating our individual selves far beyond the plane of the ordinary, or would we continue to belong, and, connecting to the roots of our collective heritage, work with others to effect changes that would significantly benefit all of humanity?

Our work is brought to an elevated level when, in addition to reflecting legal knowledge and technical skill, it is soulful, passionate, and directed by the heart. The solitary legal genius is, of course, a major contributor to our profession by virtue of his or her unique capabilities alone. Yet, the fullest gifts to humanity combine our individual level of ability and passion. With few exceptions, our greatest contributions are made when we remain entrenched in the heartbeat of our personal and professional communities.

If we are to bequeath a compelling legal legacy, it is not sufficient to merely contribute to the law's present trajectory and technology. Rather, we must see far beyond the status quo, far beyond the current legal horizon. Are there not legal Einsteins within and among us, who could envision and work their way through accomplishing the "impossible":

- *the redesign of our court systems from the ground up, so that truthful fact-finding and expedient justice became realities,*
- *the reconstruction of our prison systems to achieve rehabilitation at depth,*
- *the engineering of radical societal and structural change, such that the poor and the vulnerable might actually experience equal justice under the law?*

Are these and related goals to be deemed impossible for a profession that counts within its ranks so many of America's "best and brightest"? *We think not.*

> ## "It is not every question which deserves an answer."
>
> *Publilus Syrus*

There are times in life, love, and the law when we find ourselves in the desert, wandering and searching for direction, for answers to unanswerable questions, for the meaning where there appears to be none. In these moments, we turn inward for that "conversation with God" that we hope will shed some light on the subject. Sometimes even God seems vacant and far away, and we cry out in rage that we should suffer so. Moments of deep pain and anguish are fertile ground for rebirth. We re-form our identities around these cornerstone moments in our lives. We carve the initials of who we are by first wandering through the barren wasteland known as the desert experience.

September 24

> "Other than medicine and the clergy, no profession
> can compare to law in the narrative richness it offers.
> The human pageant comes daily through the office door."
>
> *Steven Keeva*

Although we might realistically plan for the future, it is also productive to mindfully examine the experiences that lie behind us. In our extreme busyness, we often rush from one situation to the next, without time for reflection and discernment. Yet, the wise have always known that much is to be learned and savored from even a cursory review of the hours just passed.

While training for ministry, we were encouraged to engage in the art of "theological reflection" as a part of our professional ministerial formation. The primary form of reflection required the writing of case studies that derived from our field-work experiences. After relating the facts of a particular pastoral encounter, we were called to create a "conversation" between the actual experience, and the underlying values, beliefs, attitudes, and goals, that we brought to the experience. In so doing, we were called to assess the deeper meaning of the encounter, as well as our attitudes and behavior. Going forward, we would attempt to incorporate the learnings gleaned from our theological reflection into our subsequent counseling sessions.

In lawyering, as in ministry, we are called to accomplish much meaningful work during the course of our daily rounds, since the subject of our work is the incredibly diverse area of human relations. Some enlightened law schools are today using different methods of professional reflection in connection with clinics, externships, and courses so that the neophyte lawyer will be better able to properly engage in the fullness of attorney-client encounters.

Most of us did not have the benefit of such training. Yet, if we are willing to allot the time, we can reflect on our professional encounters, tallying up those things we have done well, and examining those areas that need improvement. We can reflect on the participants' needs and motivations, seeking to gain a better understanding of ourselves and others. In so doing, we can further our goal of finding meaning and satisfaction in the practice of law by viewing our practice within the context of human relationships, rather than solely by reference to legal issues.

> "My research has shown me that when emotions are expressed...all systems are united and made whole. When emotions are repressed, our network pathways get blocked, stopping the flow of the vital feel-good, unifying chemicals that run both our biology and our behavior."
>
> *Candace Pert*

Has a special day occurred in the recent past that stands out as memorable? What was it about that day that set it apart? Were we surprised in some unpredictable fashion? Were we abruptly and deliciously unburdened of the daily yoke of responsibilities, like the magical snow days of our youth? Did we feel a deep sense of belonging? Did we become active in unfamiliar ways, casting aside our routine, and, without knowing or caring why, become able to laugh with abandon? Did we freely and unself-consciously participate in the unplanned happenings of the memorable day? As evening approached, did we seem to reach some resolution of a lurking concern, even if we were not even thinking about it during the day?

Peak experiences are seldom calculated or pre-planned life events. Most often, they are experienced as a by-product of stress release, especially when we are unconsciously carrying high levels of unrelieved tension.

With the awareness that results from consistent attention to our spiritual practices, we can better appreciate the cause-and-effect nature of stress release and peak experience. We can then begin to mentally and emotionally create the space necessary for these seemingly accidental "mini-vacations."

September 26

> ## "Self-esteem is the reputation we acquire with ourselves."
>
> *Nathaniel Brandon*

Various external and internal stimuli invite or coerce us into believing that, if the world saw us as we truly are, we would surely be deemed "not good enough." The insistent refrain, "If only they knew who I really am…," can accompany us on even our most productive days. These painful, self-defeating thoughts can make us feel like failures, no matter how much good we actually accomplish.

We enter this world with no material possessions, and that is just the way we leave it. Yet, the normal infant, after mere minutes on this earth, can suck, breathe, digest, and perform all the bodily functions needed to sustain life.

Assuming that we have sufficient resources for enjoying minimal comforts, the human journey through the world in which we live, is characterized by "enough." Although material pleasures can be satisfying, especially when savored with others, they are not required components for a sense of being and having enough, nor are they necessary to experience the full joy of living.

"Enough," as in the affirmation, "*I am enough, I have enough, I do enough,*" is a spiritual, not a material attribute; it cannot be purchased, acquired, or desired into existence. Like happiness, "enough" is a by-product of living a good life, a life characterized by awareness, acceptance, and action.

When we hide the truth of who we truly are from the world, fearing we will be deemed not good enough, we deprive the "great mosaic" of essential pieces. We can dare to be exactly who we are today. Yes, we have imperfections, but that is the nature of the human condition. Our life's mandate requires only that we seek progress, not perfection, along the way to becoming the person we were born to be. We are enough.

September 27

> "The very first condition of lasting happiness
> is that a life should be full of purpose,
> aiming at something outside itself."
>
> *Hugo Black*

What unique factors play host to the treasures of our soul?

Mysterious questions for average, everyday people appear as simple equations for the self-reflective. It is perhaps startling to realize that a few key words, laden with meaning, constitute the foundation stones that collectively form our identity and destiny.

Energy must be maintained above a threshold level in order to fuel the desires, achievements, creations, and productions that outline a life. *Responsibility*, a code word for acting as a mature adult, is the vehicle that brings us to the place where we willingly participate and give ourselves over to a variety of chosen life experiences, an essential component of completing one's personal quest. *Service*, or the sacrifice of one's individual self to meet the greater needs of others, represents the ultimate pathway toward the furtherance of our own and others' humanity.

These factors—energy, responsibility and service—are the foundational keys to the unique treasures that allow us to fulfill our personal contribution to the tapestry of being.

September 28

> "The grace of God means something like:
> 'Here is your life. You might never have been,
> but you are, because the party wouldn't
> have been complete without you.'"
>
> *Frederick Buechner*

The concept of being "right-sized" is an important one. The unique combination of abilities, interests, and passions in each one of us, is a once-in-a-lifetime occurrence. The intentional cultivation and application of these attributes allows each individual to shine at just the time, place, and situation where most appropriate. While one lawyer may be a skilled diagnostician and strategist, able to astutely choreograph the elements of a trial defense, another colleague may be better-suited and exquisitely skilled in presenting the very same defense to the jury. A realistic assessment of our special attributes will allow each of us to shine in our areas of excellence, thereby doing ourselves and the world a great service.

There is an ancient Hasidic tale in which a holy man, Rabbi Zuysa, laments the fact that he is not more like Moses. He is quickly reminded by his superior that the proper question is not whether he is more like Moses, but is he like Zuysa? While the near-universal tendency to want to be like someone else has existed throughout history, the matter of ultimate importance is to become oneself.

Thus, each of us is challenged to authentically seek, identify, name, and develop the attributes of the full personhood for which we were created. An individual's unique gifts are not fungible; they are singular threads in the exquisite tapestry of creation. We are called to respond to the needs of life that we alone can satisfy, not with pride and grandiosity, but with humility and gratitude for the unique talents that allow us to properly assume center stage as appropriate.

> '"Think simple' as my old master used to say—
> meaning reduce the whole of its parts into the simplest
> terms, getting back to first principles."
>
> *Frank Lloyd Wright*

As lawyers, we are called upon daily to mastermind complex legal issues, business questions, and strategic plans. While our probative judgments and analytic skills serve us well in such circumstances, we should be cautious of the tendency to engage in overly complex analyses and discussions, especially when simplicity is clearly the preferred order of the day. The simpler approach is particularly appropriate when we are dealing outside the professional arena. Spouses, mechanics, friends, soccer coaches, and children are not usually interested in hearing complicated analyses, when a simple answer is all that is called for.

The Shaker dictum "'Tis a gift to be simple," contains great truth, and should be heeded whenever possible, including, as appropriate, in our professional dealings. While we may be well-prepared to advocate, defend, refute, and cross-examine as needed, most situations require only that we deal in an honest and direct manner to avoid confusion and further our client's cause.

Achieving simplicity in an age of ever-increasing legal complexity is a gift that only the mindful professional can bestow, for making legal language and analyses "plain" is not a simple task. It requires a thorough understanding of the subject matter, coupled with the astute ability to "separate the wheat from the chaff." Most importantly, it involves a judicious commitment to avoiding gamesmanship, in favor of advancing the rightful understanding and resolution of legal matters.

September 30

> ## "Creation is not a
> ## hurdle on the road to God;
> ## it is the road itself."
>
> *Martin Buber*

As law students and lawyers, we consistently strive to achieve many excellent things. Yet, we can all attest to the strong forces that endanger our intended progress. The fact is, as Scott Peck boldly began his much-loved classic, *The Road Less Traveled*, "*Life is difficult.*" No matter how disciplined our characters, or how pure our goals, we will encounter difficult people and situations as we travel toward what we rightly label as success.

Yet, many wise teachers have cautioned against frustration in confronting these seeming obstacles, suggesting instead that they contain "the very life of life." Rainer Maria Rilke, in his poignant *Letters to a Young Poet*, counseled the passionate novice "…to have patience with everything unresolved in your heart and to try to love the questions themselves.…Perhaps then, someday far in the future, you will gradually, without even noticing it, live your way into the answers."

As we intently focus on our upcoming trial, the car still breaks down, and we still have to attend to minor household emergencies on the eve of the *voir dire*. Life happens. Life is life, and it is imperfect. Sustained and patient effort is required if we are ever to meet these life situations with grace and nobility. Only regular attention to our chosen spiritual practices—whether they be prayer, meditation, reflection, time spent in nature, or otherwise—can empower us to "prioritize in the moment," with dignity and grace, when our goals seem stymied.

October 1

> "For every beauty there is an eye somewhere to see it.
> For every truth there is an ear somewhere to hear it.
> For every love there is a heart somewhere to receive it."
>
> *Ivan Panin*

Beauty comes in as many forms as there are eyes to see it. The beauty of a pensive child's thoughtful question, the beauty of a perfectly crafted legal argument, the beauty of justice mercifully applied, the beauty of the bountiful Thanksgiving table—each manifestation of beauty comes folded within its unique wrapping. We find beauty in nature, in human character, in art, in music and literature, and we find beauty in the law. Jurist William Bootle observed: "…[E]verything that is well organized is beautiful. Everything that functions well is beautiful. All harmony and proportion are beautiful, and so is every success in pursuit of a noble objective. By these exacting standards, law certainly qualifies."

A lawyer is privileged to labor within the order, harmony, exactitude, evolution, aliveness, and mystery of the law. As all mindful legal practitioners come to appreciate, the law is as much art as science. Each member of the legal guild adds an individual contribution, for good or ill, to the majestic tapestry that is the law. If our actions detract from our profession, the majesty of the law will be forever diminished thereby. If, however, we respond to the call to excellence inspired by the rich history of the law itself, our noble legal predecessors, and the instinctual desire to protect and preserve all that is beautiful, we will be doing our part to restore the dignity of the noble profession.

While the profession's many detractors often noisily assume center stage in the public consciousness, we, the legions of responsible practitioners, need keep silent no longer. Many currents of healthy change are beginning to emerge within the legal sphere that portend a reclaiming of our proud heritage from the few who have tainted its glory. The simple fact that we meet together on this page heralds the swelling reclamation of the golden age of legal practice. *We will not be silenced.*

October 2

> "When the spirit of people is strong,
> focused and vibrant,
> wonderful things happen."
>
> *Harrison Owen*

When you look in the mirror, do you like what you see? Are there any gray hairs? Are the wrinkles at the edge of your eyes a sign of aging or the gravitas of a seasoned lawyer? Do your tired eyes reflect the ravages of time, or perhaps the penetrating gaze of a wizened professional?

We grow into our roles in life until they fit just right, and we are who we profess to be. How we see ourselves affects how we think, feel, and conduct our professional lives. Keep in mind, we are not only the subject experienced within our minds, but also the object viewed, experienced, and judged by the world around us. As legal professionals, our role is to know some about our world and how it operates, enough about ourselves to maintain a firm foothold in reality, and much about the majesty of law in whose realm we are privileged to labor.

So prepared, we are positioned to transcend the barren wasteland of unexamined lawyering. The troika of worldly knowledge, self-awareness, and legal acumen can lead us to a highly imaginative and creative realm of professional practice.

October 3

> "You don't have a soul.
> You are a Soul.
> You have a body."
>
> *C.S. Lewis*

At certain crucial moments in our lives, we become forcefully aware that some-one or something is doing for us what we could not do for ourselves. At such moments, we intuitively understand that there is a spirit or force responsible for the orchestration and intertwining of events that the human mind alone could not effect.

The great psychologist Carl Jung coined the word "synchronicity" to describe "meaningful coincidences," or what he called "acausal connecting principles"—patterns of connection that could not be explained by direct causality. We have all experienced the phenomenon, whether or not we have given it a scientific label. For example, we finally decide we will do *pro bono* work, and the next day, we meet a person who runs the local legal services clinic at our child's soccer game. Or, hav-ing tirelessly researched a matter without satisfactory results, we review an unre-lated client's file, only to find a colleague's memorandum that directly answers our legal question.

When these events occur, we often experience an inner knowing that appre-hends deeply that we are not solitary persons or lawyers standing against the world. Rather, we are part of a unified tapestry that gives enhanced meaning to all we are, and to all we do. In such moments, truth, wisdom, and unity simultaneously meet and flow into a single stream that waters the holy ground on which we stand.

October 4

> "What we really want to do is what we are really
> meant to do. When we do what we are meant to do,
> money comes to us, doors open for us, we feel useful,
> and the work we do feels like play to us."
>
> *Julia Cameron*

When we stress our bodies to the max, we run the risk of losing our sense of balance and proportion in allocating our finite energy supplies. As we age, one "all-nighter" can disturb the body's bio-rhythms for up to a week. Thus, as the attributes of adulthood and responsibility accumulate, we can no longer "burn the midnight oil" with the fury and intensity dedicated to college finals.

A balanced professional life requires that we learn to work smarter and more efficiently. One component of this balance entails purposeful efforts to carve out a specialty niche in today's very specialized practice of law.

From the client's perspective, there is a significant advantage to employing a law firm of size, since it has the capacity to assemble many specialists to solve a single but complex issue. As we become more seasoned, if alert to the task, we can perceive which of these subject matter areas are most compelling for us, and which we might master with confidence. These pockets of confidence, when knitted together in the course of a day's labor, allow for efficient, effective, productive, and joyous work.

With the passage of time, as we become more involved in, and better known for, the able practice of our chosen specialty, our reputations and our work product will become even more valued, both inside and outside our firms.

Making sense of our own practice area affinities, and successfully claiming participation therein during the course of our workday, are very important competencies for those seeking satisfaction and joy in the practice of law.

> ### "There is no moral precept that does not have something inconvenient about it."
>
> *Denis Diderot*

Some of the most disturbing words we encounter on the spiritual journey are "persistent," "daily," "regular," "continuous," and "sustained." Anyone who has ever gone on a diet is familiar with the initial, enthusiastic state, when the healthy food is purchased and the portions are strictly monitored. Yet, often after just a few days of such orthodoxy, we are ready to throw in the towel, and go to our favorite coffee shop to indulge in the Burger Supreme.

Spiritual practices, like effective weight-loss efforts, require daily and persistent practice. We must engage these practices on a regular, consistent basis if we are to achieve the peace and tranquility we seek within a very busy life. Sporadic practice results in sporadic progress in achieving our goal.

It may be hard for sophisticated lawyers, who deal with very complex matters, to believe the oft-repeated maxim that 90 percent of life is just about showing up and doing the next right thing. Yet, hard-won experience bears out the truth of this maxim. How many client meetings and presentations have we attended, where, walking in the door, we were sure we would fail, believing that we had neither the appropriate preparation nor the skill to adequately handle the matter? Yet, one hour later, we emerged from the meeting room, once again, having more than adequately fulfilled our role.

Each day presents another opportunity for us to consistently show up—first for ourselves through our morning quiet time, and then for others. Doing the next right thing, not dramatically, but consistently, one step at a time. The more persistent, regular, and sustained our practice, the more peace and tranquility we will know.

October 6

"If you were all alone in the universe with no one to talk to, no one with which to share the beauty of the stars, to laugh with, to touch, what would be your purpose in life? It is other life, it is love, which gives your life meaning."

Mitsugi Saotome

In a relatively short period of time, many Americans have significantly separated themselves from family, tradition, religion, traditional institutional allegiances, and cultural restraints. While healthy individuation and self-determination characterize the self-actualizing lawyer, as in all our important undertakings, balance should prominently characterize the individual's relationship to self and to others.

If we totally cast aside all but our individual needs and desires, we may find ourselves very much alone when life's inevitable harsh winds blow. If ever the true meaning of alienation is to be understood, imagine sitting in a medical office, unaccompanied, and on hearing the critical medical diagnosis, realizing that there is no one whom we can call to say, *"Please come, I need you."*

Money and power can carry us only so far. It is our relationship to others, our connection to a power greater than ourselves, our commitments to service, and our attention to character development, that keep us afloat, no matter how battering the tempest.

October 7

> "You are a child of the universe,
> no less than the trees and the stars;
> you have a right to be here."
>
> *Desiderata*

Sometimes it is hard to trust that we are good enough, that we are loved, or even that we are lovable. We may equate loving and being loved as conditioned upon being kind, being successful, doing well, and overcoming our innate human limitations—areas where we often judge ourselves lacking.

Yet, thankfully, our worthiness to exist and thrive is not dependent on others' opinions of us, or even our own opinion of ourselves. Our worthiness derives from the fact that we are children of the universe, created and maintained by love, intrinsically loving and loveable as a matter of birthright, not merit. We do not need to convey to the world the equivalent of a warranty of merchantability. Our worthiness derives from an all-encompassing love that is not earned, deserved, owed, or available for purchase. It is a matter of essence, not attribute. Although we can enhance our sense of worthiness by doing esteemable acts, there is no *quid pro quo* involved. Like the trees and the stars, we have a right to be here, as is. We were not born to struggle through life. Rather, we are meant to live and work in ways that are enjoyable, suitable, and productive, and that unfold in accordance with our natural desires, proclivities, talents, and abilities.

October 8

> "None of us got where we are solely by pulling ourselves up by our bootstraps. We got here because somebody— a parent, a teacher, an Ivy League crony or a few nuns— bent down and helped us pick up our boots."

Thurgood Marshall

It does us well to take the time to identify those people and impulses that directed us to, and allowed us to assume, our place in the legal profession. Once we have identified the people, groups, and institutions that helped us to our current path, we can then consider how to express the gratitude that naturally flows from such identification and recollection.

When I was struggling in law school, a beloved aunt and uncle would often pick me up after a long day of studying and take me to a comfortable restaurant for dinner. Another couple often had me to their house for Sunday dinner, which was preceded by several quiet hours of studying, cosseted away in their warm library. Other friends and relatives helped me to secure interviews that led to my employment with a prestigious law firm. And how can I ever thank my sister and brother-in-law for assuring that I timely appeared at the right place, well-slept and well-fed, for the bar exam? No champagne ever tasted sweeter than that which I drank at the celebratory dinner they held for me after the exam was completed.

Countless people acted as mentors, counselors, and friends throughout my legal pilgrimage, particularly in the early years. When I firmly declared my commitment to undertake the study of law, the "thousand pairs of helping hands" that mythologist Joseph Campbell speaks of became ready to graciously and generously assist me on my chosen path.

We do well to remember and honor those who generously traveled ahead of us, and beside us, and to offer the same assistance to those who follow behind us.

> "Believe nothing just because a so-called wise person said it.
> Believe nothing just because a belief is generally held.
> Believe nothing just because it is said in ancient books....
> Believe only what you yourself test and judge to be true."
>
> *Buddha*

We often state that we seek to live the truth in love, yet what does this mean in a practical sense? Truth has many levels, including that which is objective, subjective, situational, contextual, social, existential, and personal. But if there are such innumerable layers of truth, how can we live our lives by reference to such an elusive standard?

If we honestly seek truth, our internal assessment and alignment of events need to be calibrated in a manner consistent with external reality, and, our attempts at understanding must be driven by a force supported by kindness and service. So equipped, as the Buddha taught more than two millennia ago, we will come to know the truth through our lived experience and reflection.

October 10

> ## "But to know how to use knowledge
> ## is to have wisdom."
>
> *Charles H. Spurgeon*

When you feel the oppressive weight of sleeplessness upon your shoulders, and you are burdened by an unsatisfying feeling resonating from your soul, seek counsel from the higher organizing principle within. If your unmet needs are physical and biological, attend to these basic life essentials first (sleep, food, physicality, contact with nature, recreation). If your needs are psychological in nature, tune in to the control panel of your interior life. When we lose contact with that still, quiet voice within, disquieting results may occur.

Our inner experience provides a template for how we navigate the external world. Without the guidance of this internal organizing principle, we may become disconnected from the core sense of that which we treasure and hold sacred (including family, life partner, children, and friends). The disconnect may eventually lead to a feeling of disillusionment that erodes the meaning and fabric of our lives. Ultimately, if left unchecked, estrangement from ourselves and the stabilizing forces that make life worthwhile will result in immense loneliness. Our job is to see the handwriting on the wall, to anticipate the potential for our personal undoing prior to a major upheaval, and to take appropriate action.

October 11

> ## "If there was nothing wrong in the world there wouldn't be anything for us to do."
>
> *George Bernard Shaw*

No matter how much we try to keep the focus on ourselves, and do the next right thing, there will always be people who invade our peaceful and productive space. The fearful boss who intermittently micro-manages our caseload, the spouse who irresponsibly blames us for his or her problems, the co-worker who continuously harangues us with cynical judgments—these are very real challenges to our peace and serenity which, unrecognized and unchallenged, can chip away and erode the good life we are trying to create for ourselves.

When these situations present, a good first response is self-restraint. If we respond impetuously, we can make a bad situation worse. Perhaps after discussing difficult situations with a friend, we can begin to distinguish which annoying, yet relatively benign, situations might be ignored, and which more detrimental situations must be addressed. A shorthand formulation for this assessment involves asking whether the situation involves "our ego or our welfare." If a matter merely conflicts with our preferred approach, we may be better off ignoring it, or giving it cursory attention. If, however, a person or matter is truly affecting our physical, mental, or spiritual well-being on a persistent basis, our welfare is involved, and additional discussion or other action is probably required.

Spiritual maturity includes the development of an inner knowing as to when we must speak up for ourselves, and when we should do otherwise. While all troubling situations deserve our awareness, only mature discernment will ultimately reveal which require acceptance, and which others demand change.

October 12

> "Not to take possession
> of your life plan is to let your
> existence be an accident."
>
> *Irvin D. Yalom*

If you were to create a snapshot of a meaningful life picture, what would it look like? Would your body look as it does now? Would you be living in the house and neighborhood where you currently reside? Would you be involved with the same life partner and share the same dreams you currently live by? Would your economic status, stability, and future equal that which they are today? The definition of who you are tends to undergo radical changes in accordance with your age and stage in life. Are you at peace with who you are and how you currently live your life? Is your time spent in a way that makes intuitive sense to you? You are the master of your own destiny; lead the life you choose to lead.

October 13

> "I will not die an unlived life. I will not live in fear
> of falling or catching fire. I choose to inhabit my days,
> to allow my living to open me, to make less afraid,
> more accessible, to loosen my heart,
> until it becomes a wing, a torch, a promise."
>
> *Dawna Markova*

Some days, particularly when life seems to be more struggle than joy, we instinctively want to "hunker down," to do the bare minimum that life requires, and to keep ourselves hidden from anything that beckons us beyond our personal comfort zones. In this mind frame, anything that is novel or challenging equates with threatening. Deep down, we may feel unable to handle even the most ordinary matters, and we wonder if we will ever regain the thrill of the challenge, the victory over our fear.

An occasional dance with the devil of fear need not be met with great angst. Our batteries do wear down if they are not regularly recharged with a personal regimen of self-care, including exercise, solitude, reflection, time in nature, time with friends and family, and other soul-refreshing activities. This is particularly true when stress increases in our work lives due to an upcoming trial or client presentation, negative financial events, a change of responsibilities in the workplace, or conflicts with colleagues, clients, or supervisors. Although time pressures may be particularly heightened during such periods, this is *not* the time to ignore the activities that bolster our positive energy. One hour spent in self-restorative activities can do much more to enhance the flow of the workday than many hours spent working under half-steam.

If we keep open to life, this too (whatever the particular *this* is) shall pass, and one day in the near future, we will again awaken with unanticipated joy to meet the new morn.

October 14

> "We are here to supervise [our children's] development, not dictate their reality. They are their own beings. We must not seek to impose our own rhythms on them, but, rather, help them find and maintain their own. We can be the space in which a child's way of being is so respected that he or she finds a greater inner ease. This is the priestly function of [parenthood]."

Marianne Williamson

Parenting is a very complicated issue for most people in modern-day America, and this undertaking becomes all the more complicated as parents struggle to also fulfill demanding professional responsibilities. Nonetheless, we journey as tenants-in-common with all other parents who seek to provide both "roots and wings" for their offspring, the *sine qua non* of parenting.

The "roots" part of the equation—the love, the time, the attention—requires our consistent involvement in family life. However, an equally compelling parental challenge involves permitting our children the space to use their "wings," to find their own way, in an age-appropriate manner. This latter challenge may be particularly difficult when we see a burgeoning independence that we do not believe our child is ready for, or when we do not agree with the path our older children are following.

The conflict that results when our desire to guide and protect our children collides with the reality of our powerlessness to change another human being, is the source of acute parental suffering.

Psychoanalyst Scott Peck offers genuine solace to parents by describing the necessary "healthy suffering" involved in parenting our children. Peck writes:

"Life is difficult. This is a great truth, one of the greatest truths...it is in this whole process of meeting and solving problems that life has its meaning...let us teach ourselves and our children the necessity for suffering...the need to face problems directly and to experience the pain involved...[then] we are teaching them and ourselves how to suffer and also how to grow."

Peck goes on to assure us that healthy suffering is not "wasted time"; in fact, it births the beginnings of self-discipline in the child, whose realization goes something like this: "If my parents are willing to suffer with me, then suffering must not be so bad, and I should be willing to suffer with myself."

The experience of parenting, one of the most spiritually challenging undertakings of our existence, will be greatly enhanced by our consistent attention to our own personal development.

> "…our gifts are the many ways we express our humanity.
> They are part of who we are: friendship, kindness, patience,
> joy…gentleness, love, hope, trust and many others.
> These are the true gifts we have to offer each other."
>
> *Henri Nouwen*

The expression "misery enjoys company" presents an intriguing look into human nature and our psychological makeup. We are biologically endowed with fine-tuned instrumentation for sensing discontent. While the pleasure centers of the brain are relatively few, the human organism contains at least five million receptor cells for pain. This fact, coupled with humans' superbly developed speech capacity, leaves much room for complaint!

During our formative years, we become socialized so that we mentally filter which complaints are suitable for public consumption. This function of socialization is variously referred to as manners, politeness, refinement, and social intelligence. With age, disease, stress, or specific disorders, the capacity to filter our thoughts can become greatly diminished.

Lawyers often encounter their clients at the crossroads of life, where the client's vulnerability is most intense. In times of grief and crisis, our normal defenses can slip away and, depending on the intensity of the crisis, we can become as defenseless as children. As lawyers of compassion and integrity, we should make every effort to accept our very vulnerable clients as non-judgmentally as possible, seeking, as the St. Francis prayer teaches, "…*to understand rather than to be understood*…"

October 16

> "The search for the Holy Grail of miraculous power—humanity's instinctive understanding that we are meant to soar above the limitations of our physical world—has been going on for ages. Yet now the search has become a popular yearning not just among monks or adventurers in far-off places, but among many of us living very practical lives."
>
> *Marianne Williamson*

Some people seek contact with the Sacred through nature, or meditation, or prayer, while others seek that connection through the appreciation of beauty, the arts, creativity, or service. As so many traditions attest, there are innumerable paths to the divine, each one there for the taking. Thus, I well recall a sign that hung in my seminary library: "When I pray, I speak to God. When I study, God speaks to me."

The fact is that spiritual and mystical experiences are not found only in monasteries and ashrams, and other places where we withdraw from ordinary life. Rather, such experiences can be readily found at home, in our workplace, during our commute, and in dealing with a sullen teenager, if only we can recognize them as spiritual experiences. It has been wisely said that the true measure of a person's spirituality is most clearly demonstrated by how they deal with lost luggage, a "no-show" repairman, and a car that won't start.

The spiritual principles that we claim and make our own do not have to equate to Aquinas' *Summa Theologica*. As over-stressed human beings in a chaotic world, we do best to keep it simple, especially during times of emotional disturbance. Think: *Breathe—do no harm—restraint of pen and tongue—move a muscle, change a thought—gratitude—acceptance—compassion—how important is it?—do you want to be right or do you want to be happy?*

We should write these simple instructions on our hearts for easy access in fearful and troubling situations.

> ## "The soul is dyed with the color of its leisure thoughts."
>
> *Dean Inge*

How do you spend your Saturday morning? Do you call the shots, or do your responsibilities dictate your movements? This morning, above all others, illustrates how choice and responsibility interface in our life. For the first time all week, we can separate from our lawyering responsibilities, and review and attend to the other aspects of our lives.

But do we?

Is Saturday morning a time of relaxed choices, family responsibilities, or just another day at the office, albeit in dress-down mode? If we do not go to the office, do we savor our personal and family time, or does it come upon us with a thud, activating that ponderous "what do I do now" thinking? Some of us, like good soldiers, follow the marching orders handed down by the field generals in our lives, while others separate from duty and familial connection to attend to personal needs and desires.

What is the correct balance for navigating this mini-holiday? By taking an honest inventory of personal appetites, familial needs, and professional responsibilities, and recalibrating as necessary, we will find the necessary balance for living our best lives, even on Saturday!

October 18

> ## "Most of us have jobs that are too small for our spirit."
>
> *Studs Terkel*

Some of us have had the odd experience of recovering from an illness that we did not even know we had. Upon awakening one morning, able to breathe and move more easily, we suddenly realize that we had been living with unrecognized, but quietly debilitating symptoms for a considerable period of time.

A similar emotional phenomenon may occur when the work we are doing, or the manner in which we are living, is, on some level, deeply dissatisfying to us. We become emotionally sick from a disillusionment of spirit. Sickness does not have to take a readily recognized form, such as cancer, to have credibility as sickness. Being deeply unhappy is a sickness, as is feeling numb, restless, bored, dissatisfied, and irritable, whenever these supposedly "minor" disturbances adversely affect our overall sense of wellness and psychic equilibrium. We were intended to feel well, and to experience joyous moments, each day of our lives.

When we notice the return of our spirit and our emotional wellness, we should pause to take note of the factors that alternately caused the departure, and the subsequent return, of our treasured well-being.

October 19

> ## "If you want to make enemies,
> ## try to change something."
>
> *Woodrow Wilson*

A paradigm shift is needed in legal education and the legal profession if we are to re-envision the role of the lawyer as prophet, visionary, leader, and trailblazer in creating a just and sustainable legal order. Although much hard work will be required to awaken legal professionals from their lethargic inaction, this shift is possible, and we need not be overwhelmed by the enormity of the task.

But lawyers are *not* trapped in a profession that has irrevocably lost its moorings. While many correctives are obviously needed at each of the individual, academic, and professional levels, we need not walk around wringing our hands, bemoaning the irretrievable loss of the noble profession.

Powerful and energetic lawyers can either be attracted to restructuring the profession's infrastructure for the benefit of all, or they can be coerced into doing so by recognizing what will happen if change is not initiated.

Important trailblazers are already sounding the war drums as a wake-up call to the profession. The legal authors quoted in these pages, including George Kaufman, Steven Keeva, and Anthony Kronman, have greatly contributed to our understandings of the current status of the legal profession. Other harbingers of change include Larry Krieger, Susan Daicoff, and others, mostly law professors and deans, who are developing and communicating to the profession proposed methods of humanizing legal education and the practice of law. In fact, many models of transformative and alternative methods of practicing law are being examined and implemented by law schools across the nation.

These positive efforts are rapidly evolving, as even the most cursory Internet search will confirm. Such efforts are powerful examples of how the legal profession can be re-visioned through creative insights, research, and formulations that are responsive to modern-day concerns. The world always needs its pioneers and prophets, and the legal profession must now support, applaud, and respond to those seers within our ranks.

> "Philosophy begins in wonder.
> And, at the end, when philosophic
> thought has done its best,
> the wonder remains."
>
> *Alfred North Whitehead*

What maxim or motto most clearly articulates our personal philosophy? If all the rules for how to live life could be synthesized into a single unifying principle, what would that be?

Examined and articulated or not, we all carry fragments of a philosophy that greatly influence our lives. The nature of humanity, the causes of evil, the existence or nonexistence of a deity, the nature of courage, the essence of love, the meaning of "last things"—we each hold inclinations, thoughts, convictions, leanings, and impulses deep within us concerning these issues in our never-ending attempts to make meaning of our existence.

Why not rummage through the dusty file cabinets of our souls, carefully lifting out the quickly sketched "memos to file" that contain the scattered fragments of a personal philosophy? Maybe the time is right to begin to collect, analyze, synthesize, and revise those bits and pieces, as we continue traveling the road of increased self-awareness.

October 21

> "Want is a growing giant
> whom the coat of
> Have was never large
> enough to cover."
>
> *Ralph Waldo Emerson*

And just when will we have enough money, possessions, relationships, recognition, and celebrity? How many more books do we have to read, seminars do we have to attend, clients do we have to attract, trials do we have to win, diets do we have to go on, and people do we have to please, before we are and have enough? The fact is that if the pursuit of external cash and prizes is our motivation, we will never have enough. There will always be one more hill to climb to wrest satisfaction out of this worrisome and threatening world.

Like so many things we have been discussing, the concept of having enough is an inside job. There is a yearning within, a hole in our soul, that can be filled only by a deep spiritual connection with ourselves, a power greater than ourselves, and other people.

Often, those who are near death are a privileged spiritual group, in the sense that their situation allows them to see with great clarity that which is important, real, and true.

Through regular spiritual practice, we can come to "die before we die" and select, name, and live those truths that we know in *our* hearts to be true. This includes the idea that we are already enough in every way.

Spiritual satisfaction can be found and developed through conscious contact with the God of our understanding, the source and giver of all peace. St. Augustine rightly explained that our souls are restless until they rest in God. As long as we continue to deny our spiritual thirst, or seek to quench it by acquiring more possessions and prestige, the "big empty" within will grow unabated.

October 22

> "Ninety percent of the world's woe comes from people not knowing themselves, their abilities, their frailties, and even their real virtues. Most of us go almost all the way through life as complete strangers to ourselves."
>
> *Sydney J. Harris*

Different feelings move us in different motivational directions. Feelings rarely occur as isolated events; rather, they most often present in combined patterns that can be difficult to decipher and navigate without a professional's help.

Guilt, for example, is an emotion that is the learned aspect of shame. While shame is comprised of an instinctive feeling paired with inappropriate conduct, guilt serves as the signal to change our behavior to more socially accepted norms. On a more advanced level, guilt can move us toward altruism, when, for example, we realize that if we do not undertake a certain action to enhance the common good, no one else will.

In the demanding milieu of the legal profession, we will better persevere and thrive if we continue to examine our emerging feelings, attitudes, and resulting behaviors, since it is only from such knowledge that we can become lawyers of stature.

October 23

> "Positive images of the future are a
> positive and magnetic force....
> They draw us on and energize us,
> give us courage and will to take
> on important initiatives."
>
> *William James*

When we deeply encounter the legacy of those who have come before us, we can be greatly inspired by their accomplishments, and the noble tradition that we have inherited.

We tread in the steps of legal giants such as Brandeis, Llewellyn, and Holmes, yet we ourselves are no featherweights. What, then, is our place, but to strive to the pinnacle of excellence, personal and public, to restore confidence within and among our fellows in the halls of justice?

We aim to one day be remembered as good people, who proudly etched our names and deeds in the annals of legal practice, and in the larger context of life itself. Our goal is to live a life where we give more than we take, where we think more than we say, and where we combine both heart and mind in attempting to solve complex legal issues.

We have been summoned by a cause that demands we transcend individual needs in order to sculpt a new vision of how to lead a life in the law that is good, true, whole, and noble.

October 24

> "The truth is that our finest moments are most likely to occur when we are feeling deeply uncomfortable, unhappy or unfulfilled. For it is only in such moments, propelled by our discomfort, that we are likely to step out of our ruts and start searching for different ways or truer answers."
>
> M. Scott Peck

Studies of animal fighting behavior reveal complex patterns and rituals that are enacted when one animal is overwhelmed by an opponent. For example, social scientists have documented the observed ritual of "complete surrender," where the overpowered animal ritualistically presents a vulnerable body part, such as its belly, to the opponent. The dominant animal generally accepts the submission and discontinues the attack.

The human species sometimes experiences a similar phenomenon when "emotional demons" attack our most vulnerable points. Softening the heart, rather than attempting to "overpower" and subdue our emotions, is often the most effective way to proceed. Carl Jung sagely taught that "…what we resist, persists." By surrendering to the dominant predators of our life's energy, rather than continuing to "bombard" the threat, we can eliminate, or at least reduce, extreme emotional turmoil. As the author Melody Beattie expresses it, once we accept our powerlessness, we can begin to accept our power, leaving us to focus on those matters that we can in fact change.

Our legal training often encourages aggressive responses to challenge, whereby we "take the bull by the horns" and wrestle it to the ground. While this approach *may* be appropriate in limited situations, it may more properly be viewed as a single, non-exclusive response that exists amid many alternatives. Especially when dealing with issues that stimulate profound inner pain, surrender, and the accompanying admission of powerlessness, can be the most effective means of beginning the necessary healing process.

October 25

> ## "Let no one ever come to you
> without leaving better and happier."
>
> *Flannery O'Connor*

Some poignant remembrances reveal that, during my young adulthood, I often had little sense of my intrinsic self-worth. In particular, I ruefully recall that I actually envied a very self-centered and judgmental colleague. The root of my envy was the perception that, despite her alienating behavior, she seemed not to care one whit about what others thought of her, and, more disturbingly, she seemed to be very selfishly, but assuredly, winning at the game of life.

Today, in addition to questioning the validity of my assumptions about this colleague, I have come to accept that I too, am "a deserving child of the universe, with an absolute right to be here." I no longer need to be a chameleon, desperately attempting to be who others want me to be, or frantically assuming the characteristics of others. I can admire, without envy, the worthy attitudes and behaviors of others, and I can integrate and adapt for myself those traits that I deem noble and excellent. I can do all of these things without compromising the integrity of my unique presence on this earth, now able to "take the best and leave the rest."

If we are open, we have much to learn from others. Whether for good or ill, each one of us is a power of example for others. My beloved father, a beautifully loving and wise man, lived by the tenet that we should always leave a room or a situation just a little happier than we originally found it.

How different our world would be if we all did just that!

October 26

> ## "Ah, but a man's reach should exceed his grasp, or what's a heaven for?"
>
> *Robert Browning*

There is so much more to life than what we can actually see, hear, and touch. It seems that sensual awareness is only the starting point for appreciating the "all of it all." Developing the ability to appreciate what exists beyond the material realm allows us to plumb the depths of reality. This ability can enhance our practice of law, when for example, listening mindfully to a client's story, we are able to intuit the importance of the things that the client does not say. Similarly, in our homes, sensing our child's lack of enthusiasm in pursuing previously enjoyed activities, we can explore the reason for the current malaise.

The spiritual realm contains many intangible components that are not subject to the normal apprehension of our sensual powers. While, for example, we may feel love for another, and participate in loving acts with others, we cannot see, touch, or hold love as we could with a physical commodity. Love is a "fruit of the spirit" that, along with joy, peace, kindness, and other similar spiritual attributes, maintains a primary residence within the spiritual realm.

On rare occasions, hearing a particularly beautiful piece of music, witnessing the birth of a child, or sitting quietly with a dying friend, we seem transcended, as the soul reverently rises in response to the incredible magnetism of invisible forces. A starlit night, a raging storm, a glorious sunset—each can reawaken a deep inner knowing that the majesty of life is so much greater than what we merely see or hear.

As we reverently behold these glimpses of the eternal, we might recall that millions before us, in every place and every time, have likewise contemplated the mystical, and, like us, have sought fulfillment in the invisible, the eternal, and the sacred.

October 27

> ## "A moment's insight is sometimes worth a lifetime's experience."
>
> *Oliver Wendell Holmes, Jr.*

Twelve-step recovery wisdom holds that nothing, absolutely nothing, pays off like restraint of pen and tongue. (Many people would add email in the needed restraint categories.) Who among us has not sent the "shoot from the hip" response, quickly wishing we could shoot ourselves for having done so? The fact of the matter is that nothing good comes of heated emotional debate, whether we are dealing with family, employers, colleagues, clients, court officials, opposing lawyers, or others.

When disturbed by the words or behavior of others, we should not allow ourselves to be seduced by the desire to immediately retaliate or prove others wrong. In the passionate heat of the moment, we risk much greater harm to ourselves and to our cause by escalating the growing hostility. Rather, we should train ourselves to pause and reflect on a properly worded response, which will neither constitute acquiescence to the objectionable situation, nor fan the flames of negativity. Very often, we can respond by saying that we must further consider the matter before responding. If practicable, we should apply the "twenty-four-hour rule," whereby we take emotionally charged matters "under advisement" for a full day before determining the correct response.

Hard-won experience confirms that a temperate response, *saying what we mean but meaning what we say*, will advance our cause more than any heated exchange regarding the matter. Irrespective of the final outcome, by exercising appropriate restraint, we will have conducted ourselves with the integrity and professionalism befitting a lawyer of stature.

October 28

> ## "Beware how you take away hope from any human being."
>
> *Oliver Wendell Holmes, Jr.*

The manner in which we relate to our clients is, first and foremost, a matter of great spiritual concern. By virtue of our training and abilities, we are charged with caring for the material and spiritual well-being of those who seek our guidance. Often at their most vulnerable, our clients frequently approach us when fear has reached extreme levels, when chaos has replaced any semblance of order, and when hopes for the retrieval of any past notions of normalcy are growing more dim by the moment.

If, within the urgency of such settings, we believe we are merely called to explain, for example, the elements of a cause of action, we should *think again*. We actually stand on sacred ground during such intimate moments of dealing with a hurting client, and whether we act in such a manner as to consecrate the hallowed space, or to irreverently diminish it, determines who we are as lawyers, and who we are as human beings.

Our response to the client in need reflects the exact measure of the strength of our characters, and the depth of our souls.

October 29

> "My job was to be eliminated, and soon I would be unemployed. My mood darkened to match the night outside…. Twenty-five years later I still do not know where the words came from, but I recall writing them down on a paper napkin: 'Without fear there could be no courage. Without courage there would be no hope. And without hope, life would not be worth living.'"
>
> *Lyman Randall*

No matter how mindfully and authentically we attempt to live our lives, harsh winds are sure to blow at certain times. Death, illness, divorce, financial turmoil, and troubles with children and other relationships thread their way through the human condition. When they strike our hearts, as fear begins to erode our confidence, we question whether we have what it takes to meet the threatening conditions. Where, we ask, is the courage and bravado we have so often demonstrated when acting on our clients' behalf? Are we now to discover that, when our most important treasures are endangered, we are not courageous at all?

Courage and fear are not *either/or* occurrences. Rather, they seem to inhabit a somewhat symbiotic sphere, where the words *both/and* are more appropriately descriptive. Few authentic tales of heroic exploits omit a discussion of the forged partnership that combined the fear *and* courage that characterize the true hero's journey.

The title of Susan Jeffer's book, *Feel the Fear and Do It Anyway*, speaks volumes. *Courage is not the absence of fear*. Courage is accepting the existence of our sometimes overwhelming fear, yet digging deeper within than we have ever before, clawing away, if necessary, to uncover new levels of strength, and then doing the next right thing, notwithstanding our terror.

A lifetime of good practice is not upended by the strongest pelting storm of terror. If we journey deep within, we will find what we need to persevere, even during the most turbulent times.

> ## "The only way to keep your health is to eat what you don't want, drink what you don't like, and do what you'd rather not."
>
> *Mark Twain*

The growth of a human being is measured by reference to at least four separate dimensions: physical, mental, emotional, and spiritual. Lawyers, by training and professional endeavor, most often advance in their mental acuity, frequently reaching remarkable cerebral heights. However, the other dimensions of the "whole" person—physical, emotional, and spiritual—frequently occupy a diminished position for the intellectuals who populate the noble profession.

The physical well-being of the lawyer often ranks last on the self-care spectrum. Amiram Elwork, a psychologist who specializes in working with the legal profession, and author of *Stress Management for Lawyers, How to Increase Personal and Professional Satisfaction in the Law*, has contributed greatly to the cause. His book contains simple, common-sense suggestions for maintaining health and vitality, while keeping the particular challenges of the lawyer at the forefront.

A neglected body will eventually make its case known to us in no uncertain terms. When proper nutrition, exercise, rest, and joyful movement are consistently set aside in favor of rushed, reactive activity, unhealthy meals on the run, and unrelenting stress, the organism will experience decreasing performance ability and will eventually exhibit disease.

The usual "affirmative defense" asserted against the physical self-care suggestion is the ubiquitous "not enough time" retort. Yet, if we are sincerely seeking personal and professional growth, we might alternatively reformulate the issue, asking ourselves whether we can justify *not* taking regular periods to recharge and revitalize the "machine" that houses our being.

True humility embraces an appreciation of our incredible abilities and talents, together with an appreciation and respect for our finite limits. When viewed through this lens, appropriate attention to our physicality can become one more spoke in the wheel of our personal development. The benefits of such a course of action are legion, and, by including physical self-care in our regular regime, we will increase our commitment to fully live "*our one wild, and precious life.*"

> "The only promises we are truly
> required to keep are those
> we make to ourselves."
>
> *Lou Kircher*

Will we be accountable at the end of life with the rendering of deeds and choices critical to the well-being of self and others? In many great traditions and renderings of the afterlife, we are called to account for our behavior, great and small, while here on earth. Whether we take stock in such notions of an afterlife, a frequent review of our character is a necessary and healthy psychological requirement for a life well-lived.

How, then, do we currently measure up? Do we like who we have become? Are there attitudes and behaviors we need to change? Do we need to be frightened, like Christopher Marley, as we perceive the errant nature of our ways? Perhaps we are pleased with our life choices, our treatment of others, our investment in our profession, and our personal and familial contribution to those things we deem important and life-sustaining.

Perhaps we have yet to achieve our greatest work, and believe that our greatest contribution lies ahead of us. As professionals, and as individuals, each of us must ultimately measure up to the realization of the ideals that we select for ourselves, and that we are uniquely able to fulfill.

November 1

"...and I say to myself,
what a wonderful world..."

Thiele Weiss

When life gets tough, as it sometimes does for all of us, time spent in quiet reflection can provide appropriate perspective, balance, and relief. Inner reflection, viewed through the eyes of gratitude, is a very effective tonic for restoring equilibrium. Gratitude shines light on the current blessings of our life and illumines the contours of the purposeful plan that has characterized our prior life's journey.

Albert Einstein maintained that the most important question we can ask ourselves is whether we believe that the world is friendly or not. While Einstein maintained that he did not believe in a personal God, he wrote: "If something is in me which can be called religious then it is the unbounded admiration for the structure of the world so far as our science can reveal it." When we consider some of the absolute marvels that modern science has revealed, for example, that the sun, an ordinary star, contains more than 99 percent of the total mass of our solar system, or that the planet Saturn incredibly houses more than 50 moons, 15 of which were recently discovered, all of us, whether believers, agnostics, or atheists, can find a common starting point from which gratitude, awe, and "unbounded admiration" for life itself can emanate.

Whether such sentiments and awe initially derive from contemplation of the sacred, nature, life's blessings, science, or any other source, our mindful attention to the majesty and bounty of all creation, which continues to unfold, uninterrupted, and unaided by human hands, can be a continuing source of perspective and balance for each of us.

November 2

> "I finally came to the realization that I am the only person who can control how I practice law. By not allowing myself to be bogged down emotionally with out-of-control court rules, brutish behavior by some members of the bar and bench, unappreciative clients and societal stigmas, I am free to focus on the things I can accomplish in this noble profession."
>
> *David A. Larson*

It seems to be the natural order of things that each generation seeks to pave a better life for their offspring. Many lawyers have immigrant parents or grandparents who worked long and hard so that we might have more choices in deciding how to live our lives.

Today, many current and upcoming members of the legal profession have choices that are beyond the wildest dreams of our predecessors. However, many of us deny ourselves the full measure of choices available, electing to remain within self-constructed prisons of soul-crushing work, stress, and burnout. As our depression mounts, we despair of ever finding satisfaction in the legal profession.

When we are challenged to explain why we continue in such despairing conditions, the answer is almost always the same: *"I can't afford to give it up; even if I could, I don't know of any other areas that interest me."*

These are very sad words from anyone, and particularly from society's favored sons and daughters. Such defaulting on ourselves, on our noble profession, and on life itself, is not an acceptable option. To whom much has been given, much is required. We are charged by no less than the forces of life itself to take responsibility for creating ourselves, and for consciously choosing a life that we value and enjoy.

Fear is the greatest barrier of all to our personal growth and the free exercise of choice. Fear that we won't get what we want, or that we will lose something we already have. Fear of failure, fear of others' opinions, fear of harm, and innumerable other fears, keep us imprisoned.

There is a solution. Spirituality is the path that leads away from fear and toward freedom. While we may freely choose the components of the spiritual path that we will follow, we *must* seek and find a spiritual path, if we wish to exit the darkness.

November 3

> "Mama exhorted her children at every opportunity to 'jump at the sun.' We might not land on the sun, but at least we would get off the ground."

Zora Neale Hurston

To be mindful entails expanding our consciousness toward a state of heightened awareness. This Buddhist concept, while spiritual in origin, has found a new place in our thinking. The expression "to be mindful of something" connotes a cognitive valuing, created through ongoing attention and mental focus.

Social scientists' research reveals that an individual can, through sustained and persistent mindfulness practices, attain greatly expanded understanding, awareness, and clarity that had previously been beyond the individual's psychic reach. The fact is that most people barely scratch the surface of the brain's thinking, problem-solving, and learning capacities, and scientists speculate that the average person rarely uses greater than 7 percent of the brain's potential.

Human beings are structurally capable of radically elevating their thinking, processing, and learning capacities, to previously unexplored heights. Therefore, we should all be encouraged to push through every personal limit, and, who knows, as we reach for the stars, we may end up discovering our own new planets and galaxies.

November 4

> "The ones who count are those persons who—
> though they may be of little renown—respond to and are
> responsible for the continuation of the living spirit."
>
> *Martin Buber*

Many courtrooms throughout the country prominently display the national motto of the United States: "In God We Trust." The words often appear to bespeak a profound mockery when viewed amid the goings-on of the courtroom participants. Nonetheless, the motto can serve as a potent reminder of the more pressing question that we should each seek to answer: *In whom, or in what, do I trust?*

An important part of knowing ourselves includes an honest assessment of who and what we deem trustworthy. What persons, groups, deities, principles, things, and institutions do we consider worthy of our allegiance, trust, service, and defense? For whom or for what will we suspend disbelief, no matter how difficult the circumstances?

Do we forthrightly claim the right to select and name those people and things we deem trustworthy, or are we content to blindly adopt the handed-down religion, political party, attitudes, beliefs, likes and dislikes of our ancestors? Does the prevailing cultural norm determine trustworthiness for us, or are our selections more authentically based on personal reflection, experience, and inner guidance? Are we willing to set aside certain allegiances when they no longer parallel our current understandings, and let go of rituals that no longer serve us, or do we insist on clinging to them like a child with a beloved security blanket? Can our circles of trust be sufficiently permeable to allow appropriate ingress and egress, or must we fearfully maintain the barriers of a closed universe?

Spiritual maturity partakes of both a gentle holding on, and a gentle letting go, as we traverse our path to wholeness. We can trust this flow if we are willing to hold ourselves accountable for identifying and naming that which enhances our wholeness, and that which does not.

November 5

> "Really big people are, above everything else,
> courteous, considerate and generous—
> not just to some people in some circumstances—
> but to everyone, all the time."
>
> *Thomas J. Watson, Sr.*

The legal profession has long been proud of its unique heritage of multifaceted professional courtesy. Legends abound concerning the fierce court adversaries who, by day, zealously advocate for the conflicting interests of their clients, only to meet later in the evening for a cordial and leisurely dinner.

Inherent in these tales is the clear recognition that a mature professional respects and supports the passion with which a legal colleague rightfully pursues client goals, even if those goals run counter to one's own. Our entire legal system rests on the proposition that, having accepted a client's representation, every valid legal claim must be zealously pursued on the client's behalf.

In current times, however, professional courtesy is often discarded and replaced by war-like tactics. Justice Sandra Day O'Connor, in her book, *The Majesty of the Rule of Law*, discusses the numerous and disturbing ways in which the profession likens litigation and client representation to engaging in war. Says Justice O'Connor: "…incivility disserves the client because it wastes time and energy—time that is billed at hundreds of dollars an hour and energy that is better spent working on the client's case than working over the opponent. It is hardly the case that the least contentious lawyer always loses. It is enough for the ideas and positions of the parties to clash. It is wasteful and self-defeating for the lawyers to do so as well."

November 6

> "The important thing is this:
> To be able at any moment to sacrifice what
> we are for what we could become."
>
> *Charles Dubois*

Humility is a frequently misunderstood term, particularly among legal professionals, who, public opinion holds, are much more familiar with humility's opposite, hubris.

The word humility derives from the root, *humus*, meaning earth. A humble person may be seen as "being down to earth" or "having one's feet on the ground." In my own experience, humble lawyers are not particularly common, but when they are encountered, it is a joy to behold. A particularly beloved professor of mine, a scholar beyond compare, incorporated intelligence, humility, and an overall strength of character that provided an unparalleled model of professionalism. After the passage of many decades, I am still influenced by his power of example in humbly aiming toward excellence.

Humility has much to do with our perception of ourselves—who we are currently, and who we could become, with increased personal development. Honesty is a hallmark of humility, for without an honest assessment of where we are now and where we are going, we cannot correctly set the compass to steer our growth.

A further aspect of humility involves our willingness to honestly discuss our characters with another, for in so doing, we announce to ourselves and to the universe that we will no longer harbor the fearful paralysis that supports the sturdy infrastructure of self-deception.

Humility in lawyering does not mean softness or passivity; rather, it favors assertiveness over arrogance, and teachability over an assumed infallibility. When we are humble, we become teachable, and when we are teachable, there is no limit to the heights we can reach in our lawyering.

November 7

> ## "One who knows how to show and to accept kindness will be a friend better than any possession."
>
> *Sophocles*

It is my experience from counseling couples in therapy that kindness, or the lack thereof, is the most important indicator of long-term marital happiness.

At different stages of life, and for different reasons, physical attractiveness, athleticism, economic status, intelligence, and humor are the valued commodities that elevate social status and desirability. Yet, a broader perspective and consciousness reveal that kindness is the primary value that consistently buoys the treacherous journey through the rough patches of life. Kindness is what we want to wake up to, and come home to. Kindness tells us where we want to be, and who we want to be near.

Kindness toward self and others is an attitude that can be intentionally cultivated and lovingly conveyed in very simple and practical ways. As always, reflection, attention, and action are the necessary prerequisites to developing this enchanting and life-enhancing quality.

November 8

> "Each time I follow my deepest desires, fear is there wringing her hands, cautioning with her litany of what-ifs. I do not try to counter with reasonable arguments about acceptable risks.... I simply move in the direction I have chosen to go, taking care to do the things I know will help me keep the fear at a level that allows me to continue to feel it and yet still keep moving."

Oriah

I knew that I was meant to leave my well-paying legal job long before I actually departed. As my spiritual practice deepened, the small voice within began calling for attention, like a child who will not be silenced, whispering, "Come, you have visited long enough in this world of commerce and responsibility. You have learned your lessons well, but now, come, dwell in the land of your soul."

At first, I did not know what a soul-dwelling was, but my growing discontent foretold that changes were in order. The former pleasures and challenges of my work had begun to be dreaded as soul-crushing hurdles to be overcome. I was restless, irritable, and discontent. Entering the second half of my earthly existence, my soul would no longer tolerate complete allegiance to the cultural norm of making a living rather than making a life. And souls are difficult things to manage.

As I let myself dream of new ventures, a thousand forms of fearful projections arrayed themselves on the path before me. Internal queries demanded: "Who are you to think you can leave a prestigious job, just to follow some dream you can't even define?" "You owe it to your family to stay where you are—what if our money runs out?" "This is the work you know how to do, stick with it." "Do you know what some people would give to have a job like this one?" The litany of "what-ifs" served up by friends compounded my terror. Yet, as I haltingly journeyed in the direction of an unarticulated goal, my dissatisfaction and soulful longings were transmuted into a form of energy that fueled the journey through the desert and brought me through to the other side.

November 9

> "How do geese know when to fly to the sun? Who tells them the seasons? How do we, humans, know when it is time to move on? As with the migrant birds, so surely with us, there is a voice within if only we would listen to it, that tells us certainly when to go forth into the unknown."
>
> *Elisabeth Kubler-Ross*

I set forth my current understanding of death.

Dying is like giving birth to one's soul. We labor upon our deathbed in short, gasping breaths, much like the labor process that precedes the birth of a child. Within the dying process, we often attempt to stave off the inevitable, yet we see forward, across the great divide, into the world that is to come. What lies in wait across the abyss is our ultimate destination, and, with it, the hope that we might be born again to the eternal life of the soul. We pray, hoping to keep any pain and fear at bay. We ask for strength and support from loved ones, on both sides of the divide, hoping they will act as guides as we journey from this corporeal plane of existence, and eventually arrive at a place of eternal abode.

As we journey toward the final crossing, we take comfort in a faith and belief that transcends this earthly experience. Our bodies give over to a force greater than life itself, with the hoped for fruition of rebirthing in a higher realm.

With hope for things unknown and unseen, death is viewed, through a glass dimly, as giving birth to one's soul.

November 10

> ## "If we can really understand the problem, the answer will come out of it, because the answer is not separate from the problem."
>
> *Jiddu Krishnamurti*

The nature of law practice is generally "open-ended," in that cases or projects may remain open for extended periods of time. Any matter of significance often requires bursts of concentrated activity, intermingled with short periods of attention to incidental questions and collateral issues. Thus, the professional satisfaction that accompanies complete closure of a matter is not the norm of the lawyer's workday. Additionally, the legal questions we consider each day seldom have a specific "yes" or "no" answer; rather, in our *res judicata* jurisprudence, our tentative conclusions are often dependent upon analogy, extrapolation, and, eventually, our educated projection of what the court "should decide."

The fact that legal prognostication is much more art than science, and so often lacks complete closure, carries an inherent tension, in that neither our analyses nor our cases are regularly set aside with finality and certainty. Lawyering as art rather than science thus creates an unsettling and uncertain environment for both the lawyer and the client.

The lawyer's continuing challenge to attract and retain clients, who increasingly scrutinize how the lawyer's time is spent and billed, is also a stressful one. Additional tension within the attorney-client relationship can arise in those instances where the client expects the lawyer to act as a "hired gun," subject to the client's minute directions and demanded outcomes.

While all work situations have dark sides, lawyering comes fully loaded with its unique set of frustrations, delays, and conflicts, of which the above are examples. If we are to successfully navigate legal waters with a degree of grace and equanimity, we are well-advised to examine and name the specific causes of dis-ease that occur within our workday. Identifying the exact source of the tension within a given situation often suggests the nature of the corrective action needed.

November 11

> "Modern mystics form a kind of spiritual underground in the world today, seeking to transform everything. We are everywhere, as mystics have always been everywhere; we come from every religion...and some of us relate to no religion at all.... The mystic has been called to an inner journey..."
>
> *Marianne Williamson*

Organizational psychologist Marsha Sinetar's spiritual classic, *Ordinary People as Monks and Mystics*, presents the stories of ordinary people who have designed a lifestyle geared toward wholeness and self-actualization. The author states her premise clearly: ordinary, everyday people can become whole, if they are willing to take the sometimes arduous work of "merging their inner truths with the demands of everyday living."

While the author highlights the importance of solitary time and spiritual practice, she maintains that becoming an everyday "monk" depends much more on our heartfelt response to an inner call. Sinetar makes clear that the term "monk" does not refer to a particular gender, status, or occupation; rather, the nurse, the laborer, the unemployed, and the lawyer are equally welcomed. The distinguishing feature of the "everyday monk" is a decision to emotionally and, to varying extents, physically, detach from the known, the familiar, and the comfortable, to embark on an uncharted inner journey.

According to Sinetar, the course of journeying most often results in a reinterpretation of one's way of being in the world. An examination and, perhaps, re-sculpting, of everything we had previously held close—our relationships to others, beliefs and values, work, marriage, the Sacred—are all fertile terrain for exploration and reinterpretation by the "everyday monk."

As lawyers, we have already been "called" to work within a profession dedicated to ministering to others and to the common good. Even if we have long lost sight of, or never claimed, our "ministry," it is never too late to reinterpret our work as meaningful service to others.

> ## "The truth does not change according to our ability to stomach it."
>
> *Joseph Campbell*

Although we may be skilled at counseling our clients in their decision-making processes, we often exhibit far less acuity in dealing with the problematic aspects of our own lives. It has been rightly stated that most lawyers spend more time planning their annual vacations than they do assessing the state of their professional and personal lives.

While the very bread and butter of our professional lives involves the ability to issue-spot and problem-solve, our fear often compromises our exercise of these skills when personal matters are at stake. In the personal arena, fear that we will not get what we want, or that we will lose what we have, often limits our ability to objectively see, accept, and work toward correcting those life situations that cause us pain and discomfort. Fear can also fuel our denial of the existence or gravity of a situation, and can foster our childlike hopes that a problem will eventually disappear of its own accord.

If we follow the practices outlined in this book, especially allowing ourselves "quiet time" each morning, we will begin to become aware of those situations that truly require our current attention. Is my child too neglectful of his studies? Is my boss overstepping all appropriate boundaries with incessant and unrealistic demands? Do I need to speak to my wife about her drinking? Do I need to stop making excuses about being overweight and overstressed, and begin taking action to address these matters?

Our inner wisdom can separate the wheat from the chaff and present us with the "real deal" if only we take the time, and summon the courage, to go within. We need not be overly fearful of what we will find—the looking does not create the situation, *since the situation already exists*. An honest and open acknowledgment of the true facts of our lives is always the first step toward ascertaining the appropriate response.

November 13

> ## "If the only prayer we ever say is 'thank you,' that will be enough."
>
> *Meister Eckart*

Sometimes, as we perceive the near ending of a dark emotional time, we can also experience a deep and profound gratitude for life's graciousness. A health crisis is averted, an adult child finds self-direction, a marital relationship is reinvigorated, a new job restores our creativity and purpose—at these times, life begins to take on new meaning, and we feel alive again.

Relieved of deep emotional pain and turmoil, our hearts seem poised to storm the heavens with gratitude. Our spoken and unspoken terrors have been resolved, and our lives are once again restored to "ordinary time." Never has "ordinary" felt so awe-inspiring! Near spiritual death, we have been restored so completely, so deeply, so sacredly, and so lovingly, that even the poet's words do little justice to the awe and trembling within.

"Amazing grace, how sweet the sound…," begins one of the most beloved songs of all times. The author, John Newton, was the self-proclaimed "wretch" who once was lost, and then was found. Newton was the captain of his own slave-trade ship in the late eighteenth century. When a particularly violent storm arose during a trading voyage, Newton, overtaken by abject terror, called upon the Divine Power that he had long ago forsaken. Miraculously surviving the storm, Newton was inspired by radical gratitude to compose the hymn *Amazing Grace*. As his life continued to be totally transformed, Newton became a devoted minister and an active abolitionist.

While our own stories of "turnaround" may not be so dramatic, many of us can identify the personal "lost-found-reborn" patterns that have characterized our prior times. Our resultant gratitude, when given a full and free expression in our attitudes and actions, can, like Newton's contributions, be a most powerful legacy for a needy world.

November 14

> "May your work never weary you. May it release within you wellsprings of refreshment, inspiration and excitement."
>
> *John O'Donohue*

It is always gratifying to witness people who engage in their work with passion and excitement. Many of us have been fortunate enough to encounter teachers, health professionals, co-workers, and others who exude an almost childlike enthusiasm when doing or discussing their work. In my own experience, I often find that people who work with their hands, who see a project through from beginning to end, are often very enthused about their work. Vermont woodcrafters are some of the most "alive" human beings one can encounter!

For such people, work is never a wearying event. As Kahlil Gibran tells us, such work is love made visible. This love is a wellspring of all that is good and creative and exciting, and generates additional energy through the creation process. Like the child at play who builds a fort, or creates a schoolroom, the work is play, and the play is energy-producing and invigorating.

The creative practice of law can release within and about us an excitement that nourishes our very souls while generating a similar response in others. George Eliot encapsulated this understanding as follows: "Blessed is the influence of one true loving human soul on another."

As enthusiastic practitioners, we can raise the quality of service offered by every lawyer we encounter, since the creative state is the natural state, and our exuberance makes us an attractive power of example to others. Few lawyers would choose to identify themselves as trudging through a meaningless haze of robotic motions, just waiting to "call it a day." No, the person who arrived for the first day of law school, joyously hoping to create a better legal system and a better world, would never want to settle for being a mere cog in the slowly turning legal wheel!

As people of renewed personal and spiritual growth, we can reignite our personal and professional dreams, and we can, with persistent action, reach our goals one day at a time. Then, as the poet promises, our work can be "...*a wellspring of refreshment, inspiration and excitement...*" for ourselves and others.

November 15

> "After all, it is those who have a deep and real inner life who are best able to deal with the irritating details of outer life."
>
> *Marcel Proust*

There is a story from ancient days that has become a staple of Twelve-Step recovery wisdom regarding acceptance. As the story goes, an old Sufi asks a friend, whose tent is planted next to a group of whirling dervishes, how he can possibly be at peace or get anything done while the whirling dervishes carry on their "over the top" activities. "Very simple," replies the friend, "I just let them whirl."

This short and direct response holds profound wisdom. The acknowledgment that we cannot change other people, and that we can change only ourselves, allows us to detach from the futile and frustrating "bombardment" of problems with self-will. Our life energy is then restored to its proper productive capacity, where before, our energy was being sapped by misdirected attempts to control others, with all its attendant frustration, resentment, and anger.

As lawyers, we are trained to advocate, to change, and to transform. Whereas before there was an unaddressed wrong, the skilled working of our craft can result in a just measure of redress. These lawyerly skills are priceless when applied in the appropriate forum and in the appropriate manner.

While our professional service and skill may result in such changes, not even the force of law can change people who are not ready for change. We may be able to secure the release of a felon, but we cannot transform a criminal mentality. We may negotiate a fair settlement, but we cannot transform the resentment that the parties continue to carry.

In each of these, and every other situation, we do well to acknowledge our own limitations regarding who and what we can change, and proceed accordingly. By allowing the "whirling dervishes to whirl" in those situations we cannot change, we can properly channel our life energy to further advance those things that are within our control.

> "Civilization can only revive when there shall come into being in a number of individuals a new tone of mind, independent of the prevalent one among the crowds, and in opposition to it..."
>
> *Albert Schweitzer*

According to Anthony Kronman, former dean of Yale Law School, the revered status of the "lawyer-statesman" of earlier generations was explained more by reference to the developed character of these lawyers rather than their level of legal expertise. Judgment, not mere legal knowledge, was the treasured coin of the realm.

Kronman details the demise of the lawyer-statesman model as a result of three factors: 1) the dominant movements within legal academia, which devalued the lawyer-statesman type as a "quaint antique," and promoted individual faculty scholarship over engaged teaching and mentoring of students, 2) the explosive growth of law firms as mega-commercial enterprises, with the resulting dissatisfaction of the lawyers therein, and 3) the bureaucratization of courts, which, Kronman maintains, has resulted in "...the transformation of the ancient art of judging into a species of office management whose main virtue is efficiency rather than wisdom."

While Kronman's analysis lifts up many a professional deficiency that is in need of correction, there are many positive developments that signal a rising tide within a demoralized profession. In particular, the attention commanded by various analyses of the law school experience, and its deleterious effects on professional formation, coupled with energized professional reform movements, signal a brighter future for a beleaguered profession.

Most importantly, however, the individual practitioner's potentially reinvigorated quest to reclaim those aspects of the noble profession that accounted for yesteryear's vigor and meaning, are the most hopeful signs of the re-emergence of today's "lawyer-statespersons."

> ## "A man who has committed a mistake and doesn't correct it, is committing another mistake."
>
> *Confucius*

At times, the press of life's responsibilities overwhelms us, and, like unwinding impossibly tangled strands of Christmas lights, we might dive in, not knowing which part to tackle first, and only make things worse. Paralyzed by fear, we become unable to efficiently attend to any substantial portion of our work.

If such disorder persists, we begin to fail in the little things first—we don't follow up with our clients on a timely basis, we fail to calendar important matters, and we lose contact with the nuances of interpersonal relationships within the office.

Despite some pointed criticisms, we may not comprehend the gravity of our declining situation until some very public and difficult consequences are encountered—we may be fired, or we may mishandle a trial due to an obvious lack of preparation and attention.

If we are to remedy our difficulties prior to the onset of these serious consequences, we need to create the time and space to sort through our problems. We should immediately re-engage the spiritual practices that previously brought awareness, clarity, and a sense of perspective. If possible, we should connect with a reliable confidant, with whom we can discuss the deteriorating situation, and strategize our corrective actions.

The first steps are always the hardest, but, one day at a time, one matter at a time, we can begin to unravel our tangled situations. We must summon the courage and strength to directly face our circumstances, understanding that further delay will increase the negative consequences.

Feel the fear and do it anyway!

November 18

> "Never work just for money or power.
> That won't save your soul or build a decent
> family or help you sleep at night."
>
> *Marian Wright Edelman*

It comes as no surprise to find that law students and lawyers generally aim to work for the most prestigious and highest-paying employers. While few of us wish to deprecate the financial and other benefits associated with our practice of law, we should, at a minimum, select our employers intentionally and thoughtfully.

The childhood adage, *"Show me your friends and I'll show you who you are,"* also holds true in the workplace. While we are researching the compensation structure and working conditions of a potential employer, we should also be diligent in researching the potential employer's "character." If a potential employer is known to "cut corners" in the professional arena, we should appreciate that, as employees, we may become witting or unwitting participants. Since our goal is to practice law as persons of full integrity, we should shy away from association with such employers. The legal and business world already contains sufficient challenges without adding the slippery slope of ethical shortcuts.

As in selecting a life partner, we should select our employers with much care and discernment. The ethical culture and character of the employer should be a primary concern. While, fortunately, the dramatic and excruciatingly painful facts of filed grievances, criminal action, and disbarment are known by relatively few lawyers, the daily soul-torture of working for an ethically challenged employer should be avoided at all costs.

November 19

"Initiative is doing the right things without being told."

Elbert Hubbard

Despite some very negative reports on the current state of legal education, several innovative schools have long been at work in implementing or planning major innovations in legal education. *The Complete Lawyer,* a periodical for lawyers seeking to enhance their professional lives, recently compiled a report on educational initiatives, including those summarized below, which have been undertaken by several law schools.

Mercer University has long been engaged in developing the "whole lawyer," offering many opportunities for law students to further develop their values, self-awareness, and emotional skills, together with the traditional cognitive analysis.

University of Dayton Law School offers a *"Lawyer as Problem Solver"* program as an integral part of the law school's "whole person" approach to education. The initiative also involves externships for every student, clinical opportunities, and a *pro bono* commitment to community programs.

Stanford Law School has focused on making the last two law school years more practical by designing initiatives that translate classroom learning into an actual client context. The school has developed courses that encourage students to *think like clients*, as well as lawyers, and has enhanced its clinical programs for more hands-on practice. Importantly, the design also incorporates a "values initiative" that provides models for public service.

Santa Clara University School of Law has implemented a leadership skills course, which incorporates well-established concepts from business school programs and elsewhere.

In addition, the American Association of Law Schools recently approved a new subcommittee, *Maintaining Balance in Law School*, which provides a crucial forum for academia's leadership to strategize and improve methods for enhancing the law school experience.

These and other developments favorably portend that the more than 100-year-old law school protocols will be updated far beyond the "thinking like a lawyer" model.

> "Your outlook upon life, your estimate of yourself, your estimate of your value, are largely colored by your environment. Your whole career will be modified, shaped, molded by your surroundings, by the character of the people with whom you come in contact every day."
>
> *Orison Swett Marden*

If relationships in our work setting become connected with a dissonant experience, such as a conflict focusing on a value we consider elemental, the work setting itself often takes on the phobic qualities of the unresolved conflict. We no longer enter that work environment with an open mind and heart; instead, we enter like a well-defended knight in a suit of armor. Over time, we daily weigh and measure the price of entering the dreaded venue, recalling the pros, the cons, and the sheer necessity of entering the forum of discontent.

Unless we take the necessary actions to resolve the underlying conflicts, our work environment will become toxic. If left unattended too long, we may eventually succumb to psychosomatic symptoms, elevated levels of anxiety, and ultimately, depression and despair.

With this awareness, however, also comes the realization that we are no longer helpless children, trapped in a dysfunctional maze. We can, with the help of the spiritual practices discussed here, make the necessary changes in our selves and in our environment, so that we can enjoy the work lives that we have chosen to pursue.

November 21

> "The deepest vocational question is not
> 'What ought I to do with my life?'
> It is the more elementary and demanding
> 'Who am I?' 'What is my nature?'"
>
> *Parker Palmer*

Practice taking positions that deeply reflect who you are and what you stand for. The older you are, the clearer it becomes how few of us can stand up for what we believe in, and how few of us can even clearly articulate what we believe in. If you were to create your own Ten Commandments to govern your life, what would they be? Can you imagine living your life in accordance with a set of guidelines that you made up for yourself? Can you see yourself living your values and practicing law effectively? If you can, you will be a successful and happy lawyer.

November 22

> "They sat with him on the ground seven days
> and seven nights, and no one spoke a word to him,
> for they saw that his suffering was very great."
>
> *Job 2:13*

Silent presence is one of the most difficult spiritual practices to develop, yet it is one of the most reassuring and generous gifts that one human being can give to another.

When a beloved uncle, and later, a beloved brother-in-law, each was dying over a period of several months, I silently committed to return to them and their grieving spouses some of the love and delight that they had shared with me during their lifetimes. Since I have no medical training, my quiet presence was the only sacramental gift I had to offer. As time passed, there were no more medical reassurances to be truthfully given, no more "interesting" conversations to orchestrate, no more overly exuberant greetings and exchanges to be had, as both my dear ones came to know that their time was at hand. My job was to sit quietly, to journey with them to the last, and to quietly witness their courageous moving toward the dark night.

Since our lawyering often involves sadness, mystery, and sometimes even devastation, we do well to pause, to reflect, and to discern those situations when the best gift we have to give our clients is our respectful silence. Thus, when a mother receives the news that her beloved child is to be incarcerated, or when the court decides that a devoted father will be barred from seeing his children, these are not the moments for hurried talk of appeals, or legalistic analyses of who did what wrong. These are times for reverent and silent co-journeying, as a fellow broken-hearted human being stands on the precipice of unbearable grief.

Silent, compassionate journeying with the saddened of heart is one of the most profound and sacred aspects of our professional calling. Lawyers cannot fix everything that is broken, yet, compassionate journeying with our clients and their loved ones can provide a sense of reassurance that is priceless beyond measure.

November 23

> "There is a principle which is a bar against
> all information, which is proof against all arguments and
> which cannot fail to keep a man in everlasting ignorance—
> that principle is contempt prior to investigation."
>
> *Herbert Spencer*

It seems to be paradoxical, that when we seek something for ourselves, whether it be peace, security, generosity, or understanding, it comes to us when we begin to give it away. This "priming the pump" phenomenon, like any other paradox, does not play well in our rational minds, yet the experience of so many proves that it works, often when nothing else seems to. The spiritual program, *A Course in Miracles*, poses the following directive: *"Whatever you perceive as lacking in the world is what you are required to give to the world. The giver and the receiver are one, so by assisting and giving to others, we are healed."*

It seems that, for a spiritual practice to be effective, it is not necessary that we understand or agree with the seeming contradictions contained in it. Rather, as with most things spiritual, it is only necessary that we make a decision to move beyond our intellectual comfort zones, and be willing to "try on" the suggested practice to ascertain whether it works for us.

Analytical lawyers are especially quick to question the efficacy of the "softer" spiritual practices such as prayer, meditation, and mindfulness practice. Yet, almost all who try these practices for a reasonable period of time, and with an open mind, experience transformative effects that they never anticipated.

Unlike the formula-driven material world, where, if we do X, we will receive Y, the spiritual world rewards the "beginner's mind," the childlike approach, where no expectations exist, and an attitude of openness prevails. Untold personal rewards can be attained if we are willing to remain open to the wisdom of the ages, suspending our own "contempt prior to investigation," and experimenting with these practices that have worked so well for countless others.

November 24

> **"Don't ever confuse the two, your life and your work, that's what I have to say. The second is only part. You cannot be really first-rate at your work if your work is all you are."**
>
> *Anna Quindlen*

While many lawyers are known to be slavish in keeping their "to do" lists, we might also consider developing an equally important list, our "to be" list. The "to be" list might contain those attitude and behavior changes that we might want to achieve in our professional lives.

For example, do we wish to become a more compassionate supervisor, a more enthusiastic contributor, or a person who consciously honors the integrity of every person encountered in our office? Do we want to specifically seek out those work projects that are the most consonant with our talents, or to speak more authentically when dealing with supervisors? Perhaps we intend to establish boundaries for our work time, maybe establishing a "firm" quitting time, absent a true emergency. Or maybe we finally want to actually *schedule,* not just think about scheduling, *pro bono,* mentoring, or training activities.

As lawyers, we generally have the latitude to be more than cogs in the wheel of a giant machine. Most of us experience great diversity in the matters we handle, and have great autonomy regarding the manner and order in which our work is created. Few of us could be said to be required to produce a daily quota of "piece work," to be laid out for inspection at day's end.

While some matters certainly have to be attended to as a core requirement of a legal position, with appropriate planning, one or more aspirational entries on our "to be" list can be accommodated on most work days. So, for example, one of the busiest and most successful trial lawyers I know regularly finds the time to teach a trial techniques class at his *alma mater.*

The ever-present hue and cry, "I don't have the time," might more honestly be stated, "I don't have the time to do anything that I choose not to do first."

November 25

> "Here are some of my favorite prayers:
> Help. Please. Don't. Show me. Guide me. Change me.
> Are you there? Why'd you do that? Oh. Thank you."
>
> *Melody Beattie*

Melody Beattie's books, which incorporate the principles of Twelve-Step recovery programs, have helped many people to recover from alcoholism, drug addiction, and other addictive behaviors. The crucial Eleventh Step of these programs is: "*Sought through prayer and meditation to increase our conscious contact with God, as we understood Him, praying only for knowledge of His will for us and the power to carry that out.*"

The manner in which we establish and maintain a conscious contact with the God of our understanding is as unique to each of us as are our fingerprints. Some of us have a simple friendship with our creator, such that we can mimic the informal exchange quoted above. Others of us are more formal.

Many of us can describe a time in our lives in which our conscious contact with God, or creation, or all humanity, was so intense, so heightened, so clear, that we momentarily became one with all of eternity. Parker Palmer, a noted spiritual writer, tells an illustrative story that was reported in *The New York Times* the day after the collapse of the Twin Towers.

"*On the morning of the attacks, a policeman tried to help an investment banker who had fled the Twin Towers and appeared to be in shock. 'I'm not in shock,' the banker replied…'I've never been more cognizant in my life.'*"

While the exact meaning of the banker's words are known only to him, Palmer conjectures that the banker meant something like: "Never have I thought more deeply, felt more profoundly, or been more fully aware of who I am, of what I love, of the suffering and joy around me. Never have I seen the world and my place in it more clearly than I do right now."

Amid the deadly chaos, this survivor was on "high alert," not just to the dangers of terrorism, but to himself, to others, and to the giver of life itself. According to Palmer, "…the normal tunnel vision [of the survivors] had failed, and they suddenly found themselves living with eyes wide open."

Conscious contact with a higher power can run the gamut from Melody Beattie's simple but heartfelt prayers, to the profound and intense experience of the investment banker on that day that will live in infamy. Our time and attention are the only prerequisites.

"The only thing that interferes with my learning is my education."

Albert Einstein

Do we ever hearken back to the memories of our law school days?

While we may sometimes bemoan the poor fit between our academic preparation and the life we have led as lawyers, do we also remember the excitement, the absolute bliss of being introduced to the inner sanctum of legal learning, and a dramatically new way of thinking? Do we remember those talks in the cafeteria, when the dawning of our new intellectual capacities began to break through? When we could actually understand a court's rationale and distinguish one holding from another?

For Einstein, the love of learning and the pursuit of answers to life's age-old riddles drove him to formulate the greatest advances in physics that mortals had yet achieved. The story is told, that, in his youth, Einstein was part of a string quartet, but he had trouble keeping time with his instrument. Who is to say whether, later in life, Einstein's theory of relativity was not, in some measure, influenced by his inability to keep time in his music?

How do we attend to, and keep pace with, our own continued learning? Do we read only the trade sheets that pertain to our finite piece of the legal landscape, or do we keep aware of the larger trends affecting society generally, and its effect on the development of law? What nonlegal learning do we involve ourselves with? Are we teachable, or have we drawn impermeable boundaries around our own form of "subject-matter jurisdiction," allowing in only that knowledge that pertains to matters with which we are familiar, and already have attained some competency? Or, like the inquisitive children we once were, do we seek greater information and facility in every matter we encounter or wonder about?

The desire to learn is innate, and it is intrinsically reinforcing. Thus, we do not have to teach children how to learn, they do it instinctively. As professionals and leaders, we do well to keep our minds open to the novel, the interesting, the profound, and the just plain fun, as we continue our journey of personal and professional growth.

November 27

> "Compare the serene and simple splendor of a
> rose in bloom with the tensions and restlessness
> of your life. The rose has a gift that you lack:
> It is perfectly content to be itself."
>
> *Anthony DeMello*

It often seems that in the course of our professional engagements, a substantial portion of our "lawyer's persona" requires extreme self-assurance, posturing, and appearing unflappable. It is no wonder that we lawyers may eventually begin to "buy into" the adopted persona, preferring its attractive appearance over our actual vulnerable states. I recall that in my early days of lawyering, for example, when giving advice on a legal issue, I was often reluctant to ask my clients probing questions about their business or operations, fearing I would look less "powerful" or less "in control" if I did not somehow intuit these facts.

If we continuously project a heroic, superpower image to the world, we risk losing touch with the reality of our vulnerable and imperfect selves. As a consequence, we may unrealistically demand of ourselves an inappropriate invincibility, whether operating within the contours of the courtroom, or within our own living rooms.

The antidote to the perils of perceived invincibility is the ability to remain teachable—to be honest, open, and willing to accept who we currently are, what we know and what we don't know, and who we might become, if we continue on our road of personal growth. We can "live the questions" in a positive way, as Rainer Maria Rilke advised, and, in so doing, we can combine our own inner knowing with the insights, wisdom, and powers of example offered by others.

Above all, we must always remember that bravado and supposed self-assurance are never substitutes for strength of character.

> "The habit of ignoring our present moments in favor of others yet to come leads directly to a pervasive lack of awareness of the web of life in which we are embedded.... [Mindfulness is] an attempt to appreciate the deep mystery of being alive and to acknowledge being vitally connected to all that exists."
>
> *Jon Kabat Zinn*

Many law schools and law firms across the nation are becoming familiar with the beneficial effects of mindfulness meditation and its application to the practice of law. Mindfulness is a way of paying attention, moment to moment, to whatever is going on in the mind and body, without judgment. By cultivating such mindfulness through meditation and other practices, the law student and lawyer are able to bring a more relaxed, open, and creative perspective into their work.

Professor Leonard Riskin has been a pioneer in merging mindfulness and the law. Beginning in 1999, he began training mediators and law students in mindfulness practice. Later, his seminal article, *"The Contemplative Lawyer: on the Potential Contributions of Mindfulness Meditation to Law Students, Lawyers and Their Clients,"* was published in the Harvard Negotiation Law Review, and the profession began to take note of the potential and actual good effects of this practice in the everyday life of the lawyer. Riskin's work has had a domino effect, and, today, mindfulness meditation is being utilized by many law schools and firms.

Many books, articles, web sites and retreats are readily available to help us understand and learn the simple (but not easy) process of mindfulness meditation.

November 29

> "Be still and know that I am God.
> Be still and know.
> Be still.
> Be."

One of the greatest rewards that results from the persistent commitment to "suiting up, showing up, and doing the next right thing," is that we finally feel comfortable in our own skin. And this comfort can prevail whether we are safely ensconced in our own homes, presenting a crucial argument on our client's behalf, having a difficult conversation with an employee, or engaging in any other activity. When we assume total responsibility for returning to our own inner center, honoring our personally held values and beliefs, and acting accordingly, the rain and winds that temporarily assail our exterior being will dissipate in due course. It has been well said that serenity is not shelter *from* the storm, it is peace *within* the storm.

Our level of comfort and serenity is directly proportional to our current spiritual conditioning. If we have been consistent in following our personally selected practices, we will experience a progressively greater liberation from the vulnerability that so often accompanies frenetic rushing from one crisis to the next.

November 30

> "It doesn't interest me where or what or with whom you
> have studied, I want to know what sustains you,
> from the inside, when all else falls away."
>
> *Oriah*

Petty annoyances, hurtful gossip, the proverbial broken shoelaces—are one thing. The true shaking of our foundations—issues of health, loss of loved ones, betrayal, major emotional shakedowns, and economic devastation—are another. All of these situations, both great and small, repeatedly challenge us to open our hearts to life, and to accept the fact that there is only one solution to our pain and angst: greater spiritual growth.

However, if we wait until the moment of crisis to determine what spiritual practices will sustain us in our terror, we act like the litigator who fails to anticipate the opponent's defense until the moment of trial. The practices that we develop during gentler, softer times are the practices which will sustain us during times of great upheaval and turmoil.

The spiritual author Oriah advises, in her book, *The Invitation*: "What sustains us when all else falls away are the things that make waiting and staying open to life possible. I have been lucky enough to find three such things in my life—my practices of prayer and meditation, writing and spending time close to nature. These activities enrich my life when I have hope and faith, and they give me a way to bear the waiting. What makes them practices is that I do them regularly, whether I feel like it or not."

If we are to find sustenance during the soul-crushing times, we must do what good lawyers counsel their clients to do: *plan ahead*. The time of crisis is not the time to experiment to find what brings us spiritual sustenance. *Now* is the time to name and claim those practices that, like a warm blanket, provide succor and shelter within even the worst of storms.

> "Every blade of grass has its angel
> that bends over it and whispers,
> 'Grow, grow.'"
>
> *The Talmud*

Albert Einstein said that the most important question that an individual must ponder and answer is: "Is the universe a friendly place?"

Certainly there are people, places, and things that attack us, that cause us to lose our balance, that put us on the defensive, that make us feel powerless and small. Yet, as an aching tooth demands our 100 percent attention, even amid many delights, so too will the charged negative exchange, the "personhood-bruising" encounter, and the family member who persists in drawing us into the vortex of his or her depression.

Negativity is most compelling and memorable. Many of us can recall, with astonishing precision, the self-righteous interviewer who diminished our accomplishments, the law professor who embarrassingly critiqued our answer in class, and the senior partner who had disparaging comments about our well-prepared memorandum.

But what of the proper remembrance to be accorded the supporters, the parents or the parent surrogates, and the "angels," that the Talmud references? Those people who individually and collectively conveyed to us: *"Yes, yes, I tell you, you can and you will do it!"* Recollection of perhaps long-forgotten, but preciously invigorating memories of the helpers, the comforters, and the supporters creates fertile ground for energizing our gratitude and for disengaging from that which is inhospitable in our lives.

The great teacher and scholar Rabbi Abraham Herschel taught that much of what the Bible demands can be summed up in one word: *Remember*. Remembrance restores to its proper space the beneficence and blessing in our lives, helping us to tune into those special people who, by the sheer graciousness of their being in the world, cause us to respond, *Yes, Mr. Einstein, the universe is a friendly place.*

> **"If your success is not on your own terms,
> if it looks good to the world but does not feel
> good in your heart, it is not success at all."**
>
> *Anna Quindlen*

It almost seems absurd to suggest that lawyers maintain a list of their accomplishments for any given day. But is it, really? Why do we so casually cast aside the many successful endeavors of the day, choosing instead to remonstrate concerning the tasks left undone or handled less than perfectly? How can we ever confidently assert that "*We are enough, we have enough, and we do enough,*" if we refuse to honestly acknowledge our many hard-won victories, including those of the daily variety.

Max Ehrmann's *Desiderata* rightly urges us to "*…honor our accomplishments as well as our goals.*" In a lighter vein, author Julia Cameron suggests that we maintain a "Ta Da" list of the items we not only completed, but completed in accordance with our own unique capabilities and creativity.

Celebration, mental or otherwise, is a rightful aspect of our professional lives. Celebration as an intentional recognition of our personal and professional accomplishment and growth, is a healthy and enriching ritual that gives witness to the progress that we first imagined, and then attained. While it is not unusual to salute someone's tenure with a firm, is not the quality of a person's intentional professional growth so much more a matter of recognition than merely showing up at the office for a given number of years?

While we do not need corporate recognition of our growth and development, we do require our own periodic assessment of our progress. An honest recognition of where we were, where we currently are, and where we could be, if further intended changes were accomplished, is motivationally important for our continued progress, and for obtaining a clearer perception of ourselves.

December 3

> "I shall tell you a great secret, my friend.
> Do not wait for the last judgment, it takes place every day."
>
> *Albert Camus*

We probably all have friends or acquaintances who are dealing with health issues, sometimes very serious ones. In discussing these situations, whether or not the actual words are spoken, an underlying theme often seems to rise up: *"Will we ever fulfill our abiding dreams?"*

Life gives us no exact timetable for our personal ending, yet we know that we all have an expiration date. Whether we will leave this earth on the 7:00 a.m. train, or the 11:30 p.m. train, is unknown. As in mathematical equations, the timing is the variable, while the leaving itself is the constant.

Does it make any sense at all for us to await hearing the doctor's advice "to get our affairs in order," before doing that which we always knew we had to do? The time is now. *This* is the time to name who and what we value, and to take every action necessary to assure that we stand in right alignment with valued persons and endeavors. Deathbed regrets and reconciliations are better than nothing, but not very much better.

A life well-lived contains many experiences and expressions of love, pride, loyalty, and delight. Neglected or bruised relationships with partners, children, friends, and other significant persons need to be amended now, if we are to *live and die* peacefully and fulfilled.

We are called to participate in the "very life of life" on a daily, hourly, and minute-to-minute basis. Our goal is not merely to avoid a restless death; our goal is to achieve a meaningful life, thereafter bequeathing a legacy of nobility and excellence. The time is NOW.

> "Always leave enough time in your life to do
> something that makes you happy, satisfied, even joyous.
> That has more of an effect on economic well-being
> than any other single factor."
>
> *Paul Hawken*

Stress is any adaptation to one's environment. Stress is neither good nor bad. Some positive events, such as one's wedding, are experienced as stressful. Stress allows us to muster the necessary arsenal of motivation to meet the task at hand. Stress is perceived differently by different people in the same situation. It is helpful to identify the healthy level of arousal, "stress," that motivates us to do the good work before us.

Sometimes in lawyering, as with all professions, there is a part of our jobs that we find daunting and personally challenging. If we have the good fortune to be able to delegate these tasks to others, and adopt a team approach to problem-solving, we reduce our negative evaluation of our lawyering, because even the "stressful" part of our job is not "too stressful." However, not all of us are in a position to delegate away the unpleasant or personally challenging portions of our work. Identify the correct motivational tactic in approaching challenging work. Sometimes extreme arousal is required to overcome the anxiety, restlessness, and avoidance associated with the underbelly of the beast. Do what is necessary. All professions have a quota of blood, sweat, and tears. See stress as a friend.

Strain, on the other hand, which is any intense, uncontrollable, unpredictable, and repeated stressor, will wear us down over time, like a wave pounds and breaks stone into sand. Strain is associated with high-volume work, long hours, unsolvable problems, and personality conflicts at the office. Strain, if left unchecked, will lead to burnout, escape behaviors (addictions), elevated levels of anxiety, and ultimately depression. Strain, not stress, is the long-term enemy of the lawyer.

> "I count him braver who overcomes his desires than him who conquers his enemies; for the hardest victory is the victory over self."
>
> *Aristotle*

When in a dark night's passing we are brought face-to-face with the lure of temptation's gravitational pull, we may be distracted into believing that a short-term fix can solve a complicated issue. Whether its name be alcohol, food, sex, quick money, drugs, an affair, or a new purchase, we often succumb to the call to numb the pain of the present moment. The inevitable consequence: the same problem we sought to run from will rise the next morning to greet us, having become ever more multilayered and complex by our cowardly attempts at escape.

We are not perfect, and we will always be challenged by certain character deficiencies. Yet, we do not need to sap the joy from life's pleasurable moments by overbearing exactitude, if those moments portend no harm to ourselves or others. Rather, our job is to maturely weigh the expected consequences of our actions and to determine whether the price we might pay for temporary solace is an acceptable one.

December 6

> ## "Not a day passes over the earth, but men and women of no note do great deeds, speak great words, and suffer noble sorrows."
>
> *Charles Reade*

Bob Hope always ended his shows, including those he performed in war zones, with his signature song, *"Thanks for the Memories."* How many of us, sitting comfortably in our living rooms, viewed the hopeful young faces of so many soldiers, enjoying, for a mere hour or two, reminders of home and normalcy, before returning to their sometimes treacherous duties?

Today, a Library of Congress permanent exhibit provides poignant reminders of Bob Hope's contributions to his country, including many letters of thanks he had received from Armed Forces personnel. One letter, written by a pilot while a POW in Hanoi, thanked Hope for his work on behalf of the POWs. The letter was written on the back of a candy wrapper. The pilot was later released, after six and one-half years of imprisonment.

If ever there was a person who combined his talents with the world's needs, it was Bob Hope. His fifty-year commitment to public service has made him one of America's most honored and esteemed heroes.

We encounter, but do not always recognize, many heroes on our life's journey. Some, like Bob Hope, receive appropriate fame, but most are honored, if at all, quietly, deep within the awakened and grateful heart. There are innumerable neighbors, doctors, police, firefighters, co-workers, ministers, rabbis, mentors, teachers, bosses, bus drivers, church members, authors, artistic performers, and others—some even complete strangers—who have greatly enriched our individual lives. So often, they remain "unsung" by us, as we busily race around, much too harried to recall the undeserved benevolence of so many. Yet, right now, in this place, and in this moment, we can stop and say simply, *thanks for the memories.*

This universe is a good, benevolent home—flawed in many ways, yet incredibly perfect in others. Its occupants include both heroes and rogues, with the former greatly outnumbering the latter. Let us, this day, summon our remembrance of heroes past, silently pledging to emulate their courage and dedication to making this universe a better place.

December 7

> "Some luck lies in not getting what you thought you wanted but getting what you have, which once you have got it you may be smart enough to see is what you would have wanted had you known."
>
> *Garrison Keillor*

Is it fairness that determines who we are, and how far we get in life? Or does fate mete out circumstance in less than an impartial manner?

In attempting to apply logic to the equation of life, we might like to believe that hard work always pays off, that good vanquishes evil, that truth and justice eventually prevail, and that, ultimately, success comes to the most deserving.

Reality, unfortunately, dictates a somewhat less perfectly balanced life equation. Luck, timing, social status, age, social positioning, and various and sundry intangibles, ultimately combine with the logic-based formula to produce a less-than-precise probability equation.

Our job is to see life as it is, to play the cards we've been dealt, and to do the best we can with what we've got. In finding and accepting our uniquely sculpted selves, we can contribute our personal best to the ultimate mystery that is life.

December 8

> ## "Each honest calling, each walk of life, has its own aristocracy based on excellence of performance."
>
> *James Bryant Conant*

On the eve of a momentous professional performance, we experience the unease of suspense, the midnight jitters, as we anxiously anticipate our presentation. Striving to effectively interweave critical details with our overarching thesis, we continuously rework our mental outline until the wee hours of the morning.

Each significant performance requires a concise unity of knowledge, preparation, and mental rehearsal. We seek to gain mastery over two areas: 1) the substantive, procedural, and practical aspects of the subject matter involved, methodically derived and artistically choreographed, and, 2) the inner workings of our mind, our ultimate computer, that determines all levels of possibility, as we take our place at the podium.

Before the actual event, we should assure that we look our best and feel confident, paying extra attention to detail in our morning routine. We need to eat right, and, if it is our wont, to engage in a personal ritual, as is so often done by athletes and other celebrities. Is there a pair of shoes or a new suit worn only on such occasions? A small object, a reminder from a loved one, that keeps us centered in stressful times? Is there an internal process, such as a mantra we repeat, or prayers we recite, to ease the tension?

Whatever our personalized regimen and ritual of preparation, we all arrive at our center stage moment, never feeling quite prepared for the task. For each time we deliver a speech, or cross-examine a witness, or otherwise engage an audience, it is a unique experience, with potential mystery ominously lurking in the corridors, the courtroom, and the judge's chambers. Consequently, the final element of preparation is remembering the need for flexibility—the capacity to truly listen, and then switch gears on a moment's notice.

Having so prepared ourselves, there is no occurrence that will constitute our "undoing," for, in this moment, we are, in fact, much more than enough.

> # "To consider persons and events and situations only in the light of their effect upon oneself is to live on the doorstep of hell."
>
> *Thomas Merton*

It is sometimes difficult to deal with unexpected interruptions when we have thoughtfully planned our busy day. Yet, it is a fact of life that the authentic needs of others do not necessarily present only when it is convenient for us.

It is very possible that the interruption carries a message or opportunity that is necessary for our own growth. Perhaps we need to be reminded of our interconnectedness, or our need for human contact, as we sit near swallowed-up by our sophisticated office technology.

The unexpected does not have to be a source of frustration if we remember our authentic mission of service. Our own needs to bring projects to completion, or to cross matters off our "to do" list, can be postponed, if, by so doing, we can bring guidance and comfort to a colleague or client who is in distress.

Theologian Dietrich Bonhoeffer discussed the concept of "divine interruption" as follows:

"We must be ready to allow ourselves to be interrupted by God. God will be continually crossing our paths and canceling our plans…sending us people with claims and petitions…. It is a strange fact that even ministers frequently consider their work so important and urgent that they will allow nothing to disturb them. They think they are doing God a service in this, but actually they are disdaining God's 'crooked yet straight path.'"

So many of us have experienced the severe alienation of the workplace, where management and colleagues just do not have the time for us, and treat us as a bother when we seek needed assistance. Let us seek to take the initiative in making ourselves available to hurting and confused others, as we would wish them to do for us, when we are in need.

> "Work has more to do with the heart than we have been led to believe during the machine-like worldview of the last three hundred years. We are best motivated for work not by being pushed into it or by outside compensation, but by inner desire."
>
> *Matthew Fox*

Souls are difficult to manage. For a while, you can manipulate them, fool them, cajole them, bribe them—but the soul always complains when it has had enough. When our work becomes too difficult, or too boring from a soul perspective, its intrinsic value diminishes, and the soul becomes discontented. Matthew Fox writes that true work, meaningful work, "…comes from the inside out…the expression of our soul, our inner being. It is unique to the individual, it is creative. Work is an expression of the Spirit at work in the world through us. Work is that which puts us in touch with others, not so much at the level of interaction, but at the level of service."

If our soul is not at home in our work environment, if there is not a common meeting point for our inner and outer lives, we will eventually experience a serious depletion of our resources and energy. Conversely, when we are engaged in that work for which we were uniquely created, our work is an effortless expression of who we are. According to author Parker Palmer, when we are living our authentic calling to work, at its deepest level, there is an inner understanding that communicates: "This is something I can't not do, for reasons I'm unable to explain to anyone else and don't fully understand myself, but that are nonetheless compelling.'"

Our challenge is to find and foster those ideals, values, and projects in the workplace that enliven our souls and facilitate wholeness, creativity, teamwork, and fulfillment. We no longer have to limit ourselves to operating within the expectations defined by the norms of the marketplace. The time has come for us to redefine, at least for ourselves and like-minded others, what constitutes good and meaningful lawyering that is consonant with the soul's requirements.

December 11

> ## "A man paints with his brain and not with his hands."
>
> *Michelangelo*

To accompany us along our life's journey, our psyches are equipped with the unique adaptation capacity of the modern-day brain. The open-ended problem-solving capability of the evolved brain allows us to deal with uncertainty, ambiguity, inconsistency, imperfections, contradictions, and compromise.

As lawyers, we are often called upon to make straight the winding and crooked roads of life, including the innumerable legal problems encountered thereon, for ourselves, for our clients, and for society at large. Legal calls, moral judgment calls, "political" calls, and common-sense calls, are often harbored between the lines of the brief memorandum that summarizes a new office matter.

As conscientious lawyers, we do not rest easy. Most of our day, and much of our evening, is spent restlessly grappling with the issues, details, and unanswered questions concerning our cases. Innumerable analyses, hypotheses, strategies, alternative constructions, and anticipatory worst-case scenarios, work their way through the private laboratories of our minds, before ever passing through the filters of our legal system.

The mental martial arts employed with each significant client matter leave us wiser and more professionally adroit. And, should we take the time to contemplate the incredible acuity with which our brains handle such complexities, we are also left awed and humbled.

December 12

> ## "Earth provides enough to satisfy every man's need, but not every man's greed."
>
> *Mahatma Gandhi*

While working on Wall Street for many years, I came to understand the conventional wisdom that dictates that, in the epicenter of finance, being greedy is acceptable, but "being a pig" is a damnable occurrence. While such an "ethical standard" might prove somewhat workable for a financial trader struggling to stay alive within the capitalistic feeding frenzy, it hardly suffices as any form of guidance in the lawyer's pursuit of financial integrity.

The ubiquitous and ever-irritating "lawyer jokes" often center on the perceived greed of lawyers. In reviewing our own professional standing, it is always appropriate to evaluate whether we are exacting a fair wage for our services. While the just laborer is worthy of his or her wages, our clients should not be held accountable for maintaining our high lifestyle, or keeping up with the law firm down the hall, or repaying the loans that financed our legal educations.

Justice in billing is achieved when a client pays a fair and reasonably competitive price for professionally delivered and competent services. Mindfulness in billing might also include intangible components, such as the client's ability to pay. A lawyer's billing should not necessarily equate to the "what the market will bear" standard that is more appropriately reserved for the more ordinary marketing of goods and services.

Justice Sandra Day O'Connor, in describing an envisioned standard of legal professionalism, writes:

"The one distinguishing feature of any profession is that unlike other occupations...membership in a profession entails an ethical obligation to temper one's selfish pursuit of economic success [even though that obligation cannot] be enforced either by legal fiat or through the discipline of the market. Professionalism refers to those goals, values and attitudes which exemplify the nobler aspects of the practice of law that enhance the public image of lawyers and the legal profession."

> "We are lonesome animals. We spend all our life trying to be less lonesome. One of our ancient methods is to tell a story begging the listener to say—and to feel— 'Yes, that's the way it is, or at least that's the way I feel it. You're not as alone as you thought.'"
>
> *John Steinbeck*

When we tell our story, and put into the universe our own personal "infomercial," we permanently alter the reality of who we are, and who others might become in the telling, for the story has a life of its own. A good story will be retold over and over again, allowing the memory of an event or a character to live on for a long time, perhaps perpetually. New life is breathed into our recalled identity by the recounting of the tale.

We are somebody remarkable, and we must be known far and wide as such, by letting our stories also journey the circles of life that we navigate. If we have wonderful thoughts and gifts and talents, but fail to speak of them openly and share them with others, we deprive humanity of the richness that we were created to bring to this world. The Bible tells us that, as the light of the world, we are called to let that light shine before others. The world is not enriched by our remaining small. As Nelson Mandela advises, "There is no passion to be found playing small—in settling for a life that is less than the one you are capable of living."

December 14

> "Be careful what you water your dreams with. Water them with worry and fear and you will produce weeds that choke the life from your dreams. Water them with optimism and solutions and you will cultivate success."
>
> *Lao Tzu*

Just as lawyers carefully parse the elements of a cause of action, so too, the components that block creativity can be specifically enumerated. Julia Cameron, author of *The Artist's Way*, the invaluable guide to unblocking our innate creativity, advises that these blocks include: fear, limiting beliefs about ourselves, false and disparaging notions about "artists" generally, self-sabotage, jealousy, guilt, addictions, and other inhibiting forces. Through a series of exercises, Cameron's twelve-week creativity program allows the seeker to replace these blocks with artistic confidence and productivity.

While intentionally acting to enhance our own creativity, we should suspend judgment and practicality during the problem-solving process. We can honor the creative process itself, and all of its by-products, by making space for all proposed solutions, no matter how unusual. We can allow time to let the problem "cook on simmer," perhaps turning our attention to an unrelated activity during the simmering process. Self-criticism should be firmly dealt with by an expedient return to open-minded receptiveness.

Ultimately, if we can playfully, and not fearfully, engage in these behaviors, creative solutions will eventually assume their own place at center stage.

December 15

"Where there is no vision, the people perish."

Proverbs 29:18

The materialistic society in which we live daily entices us to relinquish our true identities as deserving and worthy citizens of the universe. We are bombarded with reductionist messages: *"You are what you earn," "The one with the most toys wins,"* and *"Power, prestige, and possessions are the only keys to happiness."* This never-ending seduction is a concerted plan of identity theft at depth. It is a spiritual fraud to contend that we can be "okay" only if we are the highest wage-earners, the greatest power-brokers, or the most hedonistic paradise-dwellers.

Unfortunately for lawyers, this competitive campaign begins early in their training, when it becomes clear, well before the completion of the first year of law school, that the main contenders in the game are those with the highest GPAs and the most invitations to participate on journals. Well-established law school lore further maintains that prestigious jobs await only the top 10 percent, while all others will wither in the pit of mediocrity.

Although this is an absurd ideology, ask any 1L who the class "winners" are. If they are honest, most will report the "heroic" tales of the top 10 percent of the class. While most law students entered the hallowed halls with dreams of meaningful work, service, and making a difference, increasingly studies confirm that these intrinsic motivators are often cast aside in favor of the material, extrinsic goals of rankings, jobs, and journal positions, within the first year of law school. These extrinsic motivators become more entrenched as time goes on, and accompany the young lawyer into professional practice.

The profession, the academy, practicing lawyers, and law students themselves, must take responsibility for correcting this unacceptable value substitution. Fortunately, emerging leaders, including hundreds of law school deans, professors, and others, have undertaken reforming initiatives in their own classrooms, and through participation in the *Humanizing Law School* movement. These leaders are gaining an effective voice within professional circles as they provide alternative perspectives with which to view professional identity formation, training, value development, and legal practice.

Many of these knowledgeable proponents are unwavering in their conclusion that the near-total substitution of material goals for spiritual goals, which begins early in law school and carries throughout one's legal career, is one of the primary reasons for attorney dissatisfaction.

> "The world's spiritual traditions have all given the same advice for finding answers for life's big questions: Look inside. The answers can't be given, they must be drawn from within."
>
> *Matthew Fox*

The quality of our day is directly proportional to the quality of our spiritual condition. Spending time taking care of ourselves, physically, mentally, and spiritually, particularly in the early morning, sets the tone for the upcoming day. If we allow time for the restoration of the body, mind, and spirit, then we are ready to give the best that we have to our work, to our loved ones, and to the other important aspects of our lives.

Just as our bodies need good nourishment, sleep, and exercise, so the spirit yearns for connection with nature, contact with a higher power, and communion with all things uniquely refreshing to our soul. A spirit deprived of such refreshment will cause as many, or more, problems than a body which is malnourished.

Conversely, the care and feeding of the soul on a daily basis will reap immeasurable benefits. A mere twenty minutes spent in reflection, prayer, meditation, journaling, or other sustaining practices, will add many hours of productivity, creativity and enjoyment to our days.

December 17

> "In spite of illness, in spite even of the archenemy sorrow, one can remain alive long past the usual date of disintegration if one is unafraid of change, insatiable in intellectual curiosity, interested in big things, and happy in small ways."
>
> *Edith Wharton*

How can we set our inner compass so that living the second half of life can be happy, satisfying, and meaningful?

Like any other matter that we mindfully consider, we are called upon to make choices concerning our attitudes toward the aging process. As our bones ache upon awakening, when the memories of our children's births fade, when we look in the mirror and do not always recognize ourselves, we are challenged, yet again, to enter our transformative triangle of awareness, acceptance, and action, to determine how best to navigate life's new terrain.

This transition period is not devoid of great and uncharted challenge, since our culture has, at least until recently, worshipped only the young. This attitude may be changing as the population is rapidly aging. By 2030, the number of Americans aged 65 and older will more than double to 71 million older Americans, comprising roughly 20 percent of the U.S. population.

The ABA estimates that 40 percent of lawyers practicing today will leave the full-time practice of law within ten years. In recognition of this fact, the ABA recently commissioned its *Second Season of Service Initiative* to provide information and tools to the affected attorneys.

Thus far, the Second Season Commission has examined law firm retirement practices, identified best practices for lawyers moving out of full-time practice, determined how firms might use the skills of retiring lawyers, and studied *pro bono* and community service practices. The Commission's research reveals that more than half of the 2,000 law firms surveyed require lawyers to retire by a certain age, usually between 60 and 75. The research also reveals that many firms continue to depend on their transitioning lawyers, as mentors for younger lawyers or to generate new business.

Life transitioning, life productivity, and quality of life are evolving matters for our aging society. How do we envision our continued role as we energetically and elegantly move toward and through our older years?

> "People are like stained-glass windows.
> They sparkle and shine when the sun is out,
> but when the darkness sets in, their true beauty is
> revealed only if there is a light from within."
>
> *Elisabeth Kubler-Ross*

When circumstances do not favor our preferred view of reality, and we are forced to contend with circumstances not of our own choosing, how do we handle this dilemma?

The mark of a person's character is shown in greater measure by his or her reaction to adversity, than in performance under favorable conditions. If we can reach beyond the boundaries of self-interest, and recall our connection with a cause greater than our limited selves, we can overcome great adversity, while also acting as leaders and models for others.

Those who are new to the practice of law, along with many who are struggling, need encouraging examples of leadership in crisis and strength in adversity. If we have appropriately nurtured our own character, we are poised to provide such guidance to those we encounter through the noble practice of law.

December 19

"When ambition ends, happiness begins."

Thomas Merton

Martin Seligman, author of *Positive Psychology: The Science of Happiness and Virtue*, discusses the application of positive psychology principles in addressing "why lawyers are unhappy." Seligman believes that much of the unhappiness in the legal profession is caused by: a) lawyer "pessimism," b) low decision latitude (pertaining to the number of choices one has, or one *believes* one has), and c) the "zero-sum game" nature of the lawyer's job.

Seligman believes that there are readily available antidotes to the first two issues, including: 1) teaching lawyers the tools of "flexible optimism" (a "disputing technique" in which lawyers learn to marshal evidence against their fearful thoughts), 2) tailoring the workday to assume greater personal control over the day's activities, and 3) strengthening professional relationships through mentoring, shared decision making, and other collegial activities.

According to Seligman, however, there is much greater difficulty in addressing the zero-sum game mentality of lawyers, where, for every gain by one side, there is a counterbalancing loss by the other. The adversary system of American jurisprudence has long been viewed as a zero-sum game, and lawyers are trained to be aggressive in order to "win." Yet, research confirms that, to the extent a job consists of zero-sum situations, the negative emotions of sadness, anxiety, and anger prevail in the workplace. Conversely, positive-sum situations, where there are gains on both sides, generally lead to more overall positive outcomes.

Seligman suggests that the legal profession should try to substitute alternatives that seek to soften competition with cooperation; for example, by preferencing mediation over litigation in appropriate situations. Seligman believes that cooperation within the adversary process is neither a new nor overly idealistic goal. He concludes: "The prospect of a profession that better understands itself is not utopian. Our purpose has been to show that positive psychology offers techniques that can be fitted into existing programs. We suggest that by decreasing pessimism, increasing decision latitude, and leavening zero-sum games with a cooperative dimension, the practice of law can become healthier and no less profitable."

> "Try many things. When you find what
> you love, do that. Then figure out
> how to make a living doing it."
>
> *Matthew Fox*

Despite many contrary assertions, money is *not* the root of all evil. Money is merely a form of solidified energy.

The authors of the intriguingly titled book, *Your Money or Your Life*, explain that since we "pay" for money with our time, we express the meaning and purpose of our life by how we allocate our life's energy. Through the use of actuarial tables, the authors estimate that a 40-year-old person has approximately 329,601 hours (thirty-seven years) of life energy left before death. After deducting for sleep and other necessary maintenance time, there are approximately 164,800 hours of "useable" life energy left to allocate to self, family, relationships, profession, recreation, and so on. The authors assert that the chosen allocations determine whether individuals will use their time to "make a life," or solely to "make a living."

It seems paradoxical, but money is often one of the primary barriers to a sense of abundance, a sense of having enough. Abundance is a state of mind, not a number on a bank statement. Those who seek money as a means of achieving personal security will forever live within the grasp of the "big empty" within. The inner yearning for wholeness cannot be filled with non-satisfying substances such as money. Conversely, those who allow money to flow in and out of their lives, in the natural course of exchanging love and service, will experience the abundance and psychological freedom of always "having enough."

December 21

> "I don't know what your destiny will be, but one thing
> I do know: the only ones among you who will be really
> happy are those who have sought and found how to serve."
>
> *Albert Schweitzer*

As we mature, life seems to consist of a continuing letting go of things—youth, innocence, freedom, friends, loved ones, dreams, jobs, playfulness, and, finally, the ultimate letting go, our own death. In the well-matured person, time also provides for a letting go of extreme self-centeredness, acquisitiveness, neediness, prestige, and control. These attributes are frequently supplanted by gentler and more peaceful characteristics, such as compassion and tolerance.

A maturing lawyer's life will generally reflect greater tranquility if the letting-go process is allowed to unfold in accordance with its own natural timing, and if service to others is a substantial component of the lawyer's daily life.

M. Diane Vogt, a lawyer and legal consultant, describes the five stages in every lawyer's career: 1) the newly minted lawyer; 2) the early years (when the lawyer is searching for a specialty); 3) the middle years (often marked by marriage and beginning a family); 4) the "long distance run"; and 5) retirement and slowing down. Interestingly, Vogt's analysis indicates that, from the middle years on, although legal salaries generally increase considerably, lawyers are less satisfied in their work than during prior periods, when they made much less.

Many lawyers greatly fear the final stage of their careers, yet, as in so many other areas, society is slowly coming to appreciate the value of its most learned and experienced constituents. In recognition of the fact that 40 percent of the lawyers practicing today will leave the full-time practice of law within ten years, the ABA has inaugurated the Commission on the Second Season of Service to provide needed tools for practitioners making this transition, while, at the same time, ensuring that society benefits from their knowledge and expertise.

Incredibly, the ABA estimates that based upon just 50 hours a year per retiring attorney, this population would represent a potential *two million-plus volunteer hours* annually.

Could not the marshalling of this incredible potentiality portend greatly transformative events for the profession and society as a whole?

> "We are what we repeatedly do.
> Excellence, then, is not an act, but a habit."

Aristotle

How do we find our way when no light shines in the dark, when no hope appears before us, and when our way seems blocked by the stubborn hand of fate?

These are the days that challenge our resolve to meet despair with courage, to persevere in a cause that is deeply under siege, and, in the most basic terms, to continue to suit up, show up, and do the next right thing. Yet, show up we must, for ours is a noble cause, and a journey worth pursuing. To yield now to weakness, doubt, and uncertainty would do untold damage to our heroic, yet vulnerable, souls, and to our fellow citizens in need.

While, as lawyers, we are neither superhuman nor above frailty, we have consciously chosen a professional path that demands that we act with full integrity when fulfilling our responsibilities. Thus, when days of challenge unfold, we must go forth resolutely with recommitment to pursue all that is demanded by the law, our profession, our hurting world, and our watching souls.

December 23

> ## "The outer conditions of a person's life will always be found to reflect their inner beliefs."
>
> *James Allen*

What do we hold as true beyond the shadow of a doubt? Do we believe that people are good, or do we believe that they are born with the innate potential to be good, provided the right life circumstances are encountered? Do marriages last a lifetime through love eternal, or are human bonds frail and held together more by attachment, belief systems, and social conventions? Does the law bring us within the sphere of justice and higher principles, or is it a mere signal, pointing the way toward justice and truth, but not serving as the road itself?

Where we take our stand on these and other important issues alters who we are as people. Many seek to find and live a life based on truth, but, as all genuine seekers will attest, the truth is often hard to assimilate, especially when it affects our assessment of ourselves and our treasured beliefs.

We should continue studying our attitudes and actions in thorough self-reckonings, assessing where we stand and why on the signature issues of life, for these beliefs, like the roots of a tree, direct the growth and shape of our lives.

December 24

> "To the extent you see the legal profession as a calling, the practice of law is about hunger. The hunger for resolution; for healing the lives of individuals, organizations and communities; for enabling society to function harmoniously and productively; and, ultimately, for justice."
>
> *Steven Keeva*

When we are truly at peace with ourselves, without the intruding angst of impending deadlines, personal deficiencies, or other innumerable "I-centered" matters, we find there is an innate joy and playfulness within us that naturally seeks wholeness, unity, and connection with all of creation. The purest calling to the legal profession is found in the deep yearning and thirst within that seeks completion through the creation of meaningful work and service to others. This calling can be playfully realized as we seek to "connect the dots" for others, utilizing every fiber of wisdom, experience, and imagination that dwells within us.

Working through complex legal problems, and their accompanying complex human involvement, is our craft, and a job well done can certainly be at least as satisfying to behold as the woodcarver's finely hewn table. There is a natural creative force within us all, "the force that drives the green fuse through the flower," as Dylan Thomas phrased it, that seeks unity and wholeness, and, most importantly, expression.

The creative and compelling urge to expand the circle of those who have sought and found justice, and who have become healed in the process, is the essence of pure lawyering, the "green fuse" of the noble profession. Whatever we call this force—be it God, or energy, or source—we need only know that it is available in abundant supply to give vitality, creativity, guidance, and meaning to our work.

Creativity is not allotted solely to painters, composers, and designers; it is as much the attribute of the self-actualizing lawyer as it is the playground of the artist.

> "Every blade in the field,
> Every leaf in the forest,
> Lays down its life in its season,
> As beautifully as it was taken up."

Henry David Thoreau

The older we get, the more we realize the true complexity of our life's tasks. Painted across the backdrop of one finite life, we are called to find meaning and purpose, live by a code of professional and personal ethics, lead lives that are productive and satisfying, and, ultimately, to arrive at a place of wisdom, learning, and contentment.

Having progressed well in our tasks, we now find that our accumulated accomplishments are situated atop a precipice of diminishment and loss, as mortality begins to peek its head from around one too many corners. We come to appreciate how our human journey parallels nature's fruit, as first it comes to bloom, then abundantly ripens, only to fall from the tree, spreading its seed for future generations.

And so the cycle of life repeats, generation unto generation. Yet, we need not be concerned with our ultimate fate if we follow the direction of the Sanskrit poem "to look to this day, the very life of life." Author Leo Buscaglia reports that the ancient Egyptians believed that, upon death, they would be asked two questions, and their answers would determine whether they could continue their journey in the afterlife. The first question was, "Did you bring joy?" The second was, "Did you find joy?"

December 26

> "Do your work, then step back
> The only path to serenity....
> He who clings to his work
> Will create nothing that endures."
>
> *Tao Te Ching*

Like life itself, the path of lawyering is strewn with rocks and potholes, together with newly paved freeways and beautiful vistas. Each nook and cranny of lawyering opens us up to the possibility of the sublime and the ridiculous, potentially exhibiting every possible ambiguity. While our profession, rightly practiced, can sometimes allow for the exhilaration of victory, it is just as likely to broker an encounter with the "torn-to-pieces-hood" described by the philosopher William James. The good, the bad, and the ugly often share the center stage of lawyering.

An effective mechanism for maintaining balance is, as Scripture advises, to wear life like a loose garment, and not to take anything *too* seriously. "*All the world's a stage*," said Shakespeare, and no group can better attest to the drama of life than those who are so often called upon to clean up the messes created by the world's many actors! While our calling as lawyers is to sow as much clarity and peace and "right relationship" as possible, as always, we are responsible only for the footwork, and not for the outcomes.

The world around us continuously changes, for good or ill, person by person, situation by situation. We stand tall, we contribute our best, but we also remember to let go once we have done that. Our evolving awareness reveals that our lawyering requires that we aim for all that is pure and excellent and noble, and then, having completed our work, we leave the situation alone, believing, as *Desiderata* states, "*...that the universe is unfolding just the way it should.*"

> "To me success means effectiveness in
> the world, that I am able to carry
> my ideas and values into the world—
> that I am able to change it in positive ways."
>
> *Maxine Hong Kingston*

"Self-transcendence" sits regally atop Abraham Maslow's pyramid of needs. Maslow advocated the cultivation of "peak experiences" as a way of attaining personal growth, integration, and fulfillment. Peak experiences are unifying and ego-transcending events that bring a sense of purpose and integration.

While talk of self-transcendence may appear overly lofty in a world of pressured deadlines, overbooked calendars, and demanding clients, it does emphasize the need for lawyers to view their work within the larger context of their lives. When viewed in the "crisis of the hour" mode, our days may seem like an endless progression of agitated clients, unreasonable judges, and uncooperative colleagues. However, when viewed in the "noble warrior" mode, our daily rounds can be seen as skilled efforts to achieve the best possible results for our clients, no matter what the cost to our egos. When we answer to a higher calling with a heightened sense of purpose, personal affronts are often deflected by the sheer power of our positive energy.

If we are to consistently maintain such a positive force, however, we are well-advised to take frequent notice of the details of our past, present, and anticipated professional experiences. Great wisdom teaches that if we can imagine an outcome, we can achieve that outcome. However, it also teaches that infrequent, casual attention to our goals will not carry us to the self-transcendent heights atop Maslow's pyramid.

December 28

> "And it is there, in that moment when it seems impossible, when we think we have nothing more to draw upon, that something else can enter, if we surrender to the tasks life demands of us. In this place, there is no more trying. There is only being and doing what needs to be done...."
>
> *Oriah*

We are so much more than we think we are. Yet, when weary, bruised, and feeling betrayed by life, we may despairingly believe that our good-luck streak is over, the sun will never shine as brightly as it did before, and all that we previously treasured has turned to ashes.

If severe enough, this "mini-death" may trigger some or all of the five stages of grief detailed in the writings of psychiatrist Elisabeth Kubler-Ross. The Kubler-Ross model describes in five discrete stages (denial, anger, bargaining, depression, and acceptance), the process by which people deal with death and tragedy. Scholarly research confirms the personal experience of many, that, after working our way to the acceptance phase—where, as Oriah says, "there is no more trying"—we ultimately know, deep in our souls, that *not only is it going to be okay, it is okay now.*

Especially for highly result-oriented attorneys, the idea of acceptance or surrender, or "giving up the good fight" often smacks of cowardice and defeat. Yet spiritual maturity requires that we reach some type of fundamental accord with the principles enunciated in Reinhold Niebuhr's *Serenity Prayer*, wherein one seeks "*the serenity to accept the things I cannot change, the courage to change the things I can, and the wisdom to know the difference.*"

If, notwithstanding our fear and discouragement, we can remain on the spiritual path of awareness, acceptance, and action, we *will* pass through life's storms and we *will* once again find the peace and serenity that comfort our souls. Nothing lasts forever, neither good nor bad, joyous or sad, easy or hard. When life's storms hit, we will survive them if we stand strong, if we keep engaged in the spiritual practices that give us strength, and if we just don't quit five minutes before the miracle!

> "Every profession requires prophets.... Prophetic work contributes to the growth of justice and compassion in the world; it contributes to social transformation, not for its own sake, but for the sake of increasing justice."
>
> *Matthew Fox*

Theologian and author Matthew Fox maintains that all work worthy of being called spiritual, and worthy of being called human, is in some way prophetic work. A prophet, by definition, attempts to arouse the masses from the sleepy state induced by a non-questioning compliance with the status quo. The prophet critiques the cultural norm, and recalls what we used to be like, what we dreamed of becoming, and, irritatingly, the prophet measures how little progress we have made in reaching that goal! Is it any wonder that prophets have had such a hard time of it throughout history?

The legal profession could use an exaltation of its own prophets to reestablish the desired formula for the noble practice of law. What lies at the heart of the prophetic voice is the capacity to bring a vision of a better, more service-oriented legal profession within our grasp.

Almost all new law students begin their studies in an enthusiastic fashion. Although they are often keenly aware of the profession's ills, they assume the mantle of lawyering with a fervent desire to practice law in the manner of the masters—with courage, leadership, and a sincere desire to change the world for the better. Yet, the institutional status quo is so formidable, that, within a very short time, many of these students are transformed from prophetic carriers of the noble tradition into competitive aspirants in the game of "what's in it for me" lawyering.

Nonetheless, courageous and prophetic legal voices continue to emerge, voicing unpleasant truths about the current state of our profession, our legal norms, and our training processes. These prophets seek to stir us from our lethargic complacency into needed corrective action. We are wise to listen to the impassioned prophets who so care about revitalizing their beloved profession that they are willing to risk misunderstanding, ridicule, and personal affronts in order to do so.

> "Choose well.
> Your choice is brief,
> and yet endless."
>
> *Goethe*

Our short studies now come to a close. While we have been dealing with topics that are serious, a lightheartedness begins to emerge as we continue scraping away at the darkness that has previously kept us down. As we practice self-reflection and summon the courage needed to face ourselves and the actions required to become persons of full integrity, a path begins to emerge, where before there was none. The secrets and behaviors we have regretted and concealed, seem to dissolve, or at least lighten, when exposed to the light. That which we previously saw as distressing or humiliating about ourselves, comes to be seen as yet another manifestation of the imperfect human condition.

Lawyers are generally a good lot. Most entered the profession with a sincere desire to somehow make the world a better place. And they have done that. But not always in an ideal fashion. The profession has its warts, as the media gleefully details. Nonetheless, we live and dwell and have our beings within sacred ground, where hopes for fairness, justice, and the preservation of personal freedoms, have long found expression. And we have each played a part in those accomplishments.

Today, the state of our world and our profession is such that, as never before, lawyers of excellence are needed to help make right the many crooked paths that the world's citizens travel. The hurting world needs *us*. And we need to give the world the best we have: our excellence, our skill, our integrity, our nobility. Let us delay no longer. Let's go for it!!!

December 31

Index

Quotations

About the Authors

F. Gregory Coffey is a clinical psychologist who has more than twenty-five years' experience in therapeutic practice, including acting as a life coach for many attorneys.

Maureen C. Kessler spent 30 years as a practicing securities attorney in New York City, later becoming an ordained minister.

Create a Career Plan Built Around You!

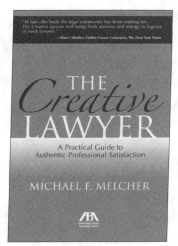

"At last—the book the legal community has been waiting for... *The Creative Lawyer* will bring fresh answers and energy to legions of stuck lawyers."
—Marci Alboher, Online Career Columnist, The New York Times

The Creative Lawyer:
A Practical Guide to Authentic Professional Satisfaction

By Michael Melcher

The Creative Lawyer is a self-help book for lawyers. It is a practical, fun, inspirational guide to building and maintaining a life that is personally and professionally satisfying. Lawyers are the highest-paid professionals in America, yet have the lowest job satisfaction of any profession. The problem is, most lawyers don't understand how to make themselves happy. *The Creative Lawyer* shows lawyers how to design an optimal career and life.

The book includes exercises for helping the reader examine his or her personal values, and then compare these values to the actual requirements of legal jobs. This information is then used to create a personal fulfillment plan, with specific action steps to be taken both inside and outside the job. By the end of the book, the reader will have a different attitude toward the possibilities of life and career, will have fully evaluated his or her experiences, interests and ambitions, and will have created a plan for life and career that corresponds to who he or she actually is.

> "The Creative Lawyer *is a smart, practical, and often inspirational guide for any lawyer seeking to build both a better business and a richer life.*"
>
> —Daniel H. Pink, author of *A Whole New Mind*

2005 6 x 9 192 pages Paper Product code: 1610160
Regular price: $39.95 ABA Member price: $34.95

Order on our Web site at **www.ababooks.org**
Or call toll-free **1-800- 285-2221**